Arabs, Oil

and History

Arabs, Oil

and History

The Story of the Middle East

BY

KERMIT ROOSEVELT

KENNIKAT PRESS/Port Washington, N.Y.

This book is dedicated to Polly, who has contributed even more than she can realize.

It is also dedicated to my friends in all parts of the Middle East, with affection and hope for success in their labors to build better societies. I have written with the conviction that understanding between the Middle East and America is vital to both. Each has much to offer, and to learn. For that there must be understanding and frankness. There are critical words in this book, and I make no apology for them. Words spoken truthfully between friends are, or should be, the best proof of friendship, even though for a time they may be hard to take.

February, 1949   K. R.
Washington, D. C.

Contents

PART ONE

Land and People

⚉ I ⚉

Traffic at the Crossroads

IN CAIRO there is a famous hotel called Shepheard's. Nothing is quite what it used to be in this world, and Shepheard's is no exception. But it still puts up quite a front. Every way you look there is a white-robed servant in a red tarboosh. Iron-lunged, rapacious, persistent dragomen hover at the entrance ready to pounce when you set foot outside; bothersome though they are, they do serve to keep away the beggars, pickpockets, purveyors of post cards and aphrodisiacs. In the early morning the bray of donkeys wakens you, and if you look out the window you may see camels being led past on their way to be butchered —a sight which will, quite properly, cause you to eye with some caution the steaks you are later served.

There is still a shabby grandeur to Shepheard's lobby and rooms, an authentic kick to the drinks served at the Long Bar. And this saying is still current:

"If you sit on the terrace at Shepheard's, sooner or later everyone you have ever known will pass by in front of you."

It is rather like what is supposed to happen to a drowning man— your whole life flashes before your eyes as you go down for the third time. I have never gone down for the third time, and perhaps I just haven't sat on Shepheard's terrace long enough to see *everyone* I have known go by. But one afternoon in May of 1947 I kept track of those I did see, and it makes an interesting list.

A French general, on his unhappy way out to Indo-China by air, who had stopped off in Cairo to see old friends. We had last met in Washington at a cocktail party for Field Marshal Dill.

An archeologist, who had been doing intelligence work when I knew

3

him during the war. He claimed he had left that field entirely and had gone back to his digging. But neither I nor anyone else who knew of that interruption in a life otherwise centered on the past, would ever feel sure of that.

An American oil man, on leave from Saudi Arabia's western port of Jidda. He was going to be picked up by his company's plane in Cairo, and would be in New York within two days.

A newspaper friend, who had never been in the area before but had come, a month earlier, to write a critical story about how Congressional investigating committees were wasting the taxpayer's money in pointless tours of Athens, Istanbul and Cairo. He had stayed behind, he told me, because he suddenly realized that the Middle East is important to us, and became scared about its future. "I still know those congressmen are fools," he told me cheerfully. "They musta come here by mistake." He was leaving for Palestine in a few days, to balance the pieces he'd been writing about Arab nationalism by a story on Jewish nationalism.

Then there was an Arab leader from Palestine, who had just returned from the UN Special Assembly meeting, breathing out defiance and breathing in despair.

Also, a smooth, white-suited man, fresh from London, telling in his clipped British accent how awful the shortages there were. I remembered him as one of the best bridge players I've ever been lectured by. He is young, almost too quick in his perceptions, desperately anxious (but unable) to trust the British government. Although his mother was half-English, he regards himself as wholly Arab. Other Arabs are not so sure.

This was not the whole of the day's bag. There was an assorted lot— tourists, soldiers, newspapermen, diplomats, businessmen—an airline official from our Midwest, a Greek ex-cabinet minister, an NBC reporter whose quick and bawdy tongue was a byword in the East—by no means everyone I've ever known, but enough of them, and enough variety, to give point to the old saying. And, of course, point to being in Cairo myself.

A good way for me to begin this book might be to describe how I first came to Cairo, and why I returned. My first coming was simple enough. I was assigned there, during the war, originally with the State Department and later with the army, doing special intelligence work.

In both assignments I was required to do much traveling and to be in frequent contact with local people. I was particularly lucky in this, for most Americans there on war duty had little chance to see anything outside their office or base area, and the people they met were largely, like themselves, foreigners in a strange land. Our army medicos, who must bear a large part of the blame for the isolationist views of the average American soldier, did their best to scare us out of any contact whatsoever with local life.

Thus most of us who spent a part of our war there loathed the Middle East. The occupation of soldiering, even when a theater has become inactive, does not seem conducive to a friendly interest in foreign parts. And to an American, the Middle East is very foreign indeed, more so than any other part of the world except the rest of Asia. The heat, the dirt, the lack of modern plumbing (to which we attach supreme, perhaps unreasonable importance), the fact that not only the language but the alphabet and numbers are strange—all combined to make us feel uncomfortable and far from home.

Most of us got no chance to know and like the people. Most of us got no chance to see the area as a whole, to see its place in the world. I was one of the lucky ones, who got the breaks. Even so, when I left the Middle East in 1944, I wasn't thinking of anything but my next assignment, Italy.

When I next returned, in the spring of 1947, it was not the government's choice but my own. My wife and I had decided to spend five or six months in the Middle East to learn all we could about it and to gather material for some writing.

This struck many of our friends—those we have not yet encountered on Shepheard's terrace—as a crazy idea. Why the Middle East? they asked. If it had been Russia, or China, or eastern Europe, they could have understood. But who was interested in that particular dreary part of the world? The only answer I could give which satisfied them was, "The Russians are so interested in it that if we don't look pretty quickly, we won't see it—because it will be behind the Iron Curtain." Would that be bad? Yes, they supposed it would.

In many countries the attraction of the Middle East—from the point of view of world trade, world politics or world strategy—is well understood. An interest in it is nothing to be ashamed of. But in the United

States, unless you are one of those harmless eccentrics who likes to look at pyramids, an explanation is required. A man with such an interest who is neither an Egyptologist or a Zionist, I have discovered, automatically falls under suspicion.

One may, of course, be a missionary—but even they have come to be regarded in some quarters as distinctly sinister figures. Or, it is widely conceded, the American foreign service has a legitimate concern in the area. Foreign service officers who have been stationed there are, however, doubly or trebly suspect: First, they are in the foreign service which, to those whose acquaintance with it is second-hand, is well known to be a reactionary body of men who wear striped pants. Second, as Americans who have lived in the Middle East and who, annoyingly, have much the same views as other Americans who have also lived there, they must have come under the influence of the sinister British—actually Americans and British in the Middle East get along rather badly, on the average—the sinister missionaries, or the sinister oil men.

The last represent a final group of Americans who may be expected to take an interest in these barren lands. Oil is a subject which, the reader is hereby warned, will be raised from time to time in the course of this book. For various reasons it is a subject which strikes many Americans as dirty if not downright obscene. It is embarrassing to discuss it, especially in connection with our foreign policy. One friend, seeking to explain this illogical attitude, suggested that subconsciously we may regard this black slimy stuff which comes out of the ground as an excretion of the body earth. This may be mildly far fetched. The early record of the oil companies in Central America and the Teapot Dome scandal seem more likely explanations of the disrepute in which the industry is popularly held. Certainly the explanation is not the record of present American oil company operations in the Middle East, for these have been enlightened, humane and of tremendous value to Americans and Arabs as well.

However that may be, if you are not a missionary or a foreign service officer, you must necessarily, by process of elimination, be connected with oil. Or so it seems.

Why couldn't you be a historian? That's what I had been before the war dropped me in Cairo—a historian with a yen for travel and the occupational disease of historians, the disease that makes you feel incomplete unless you have a book in front of your face. This combination had made me aware, first, of the strategic significance of the area through all history. Second, it made me acquainted with the incredibly rich travel literature (much of it in English) about the Middle East. Looking back in 1947 on my wartime experiences in the Middle East, I discovered that they had given real meaning to what was formerly an abstract appreciation. I remembered I had found the land and people stimulating, full of challenging differences, encouraging and discouraging similarities.

And I had learned for the first time of the unique role which the United States, through individual citizens, had played and was still playing in the area. This had created for us a national asset of incalculable value—but one which we seemed to be tossing away without a second thought.

As most Middle Easterners see it, there have been two main relationships between them and the West. One is an imperial relationship, through which Western powers (including Russia as "Western") have sought political domination and economic exploitation. This relationship the Arabs, Turks, and Iranians reject with all their power.

But there is another relationship with the West which they have welcomed—one that is based on common interests, to be advanced without unfair advantage to either side. This is represented chiefly by educational bodies such as the American universities of Cairo and Beirut; by technical missions working in the fields of agriculture, public health, sanitation, engineering and the like; and by business undertakings in which the motivation is reasonable profit for both parties, rather than political or economic domination by one.

The United States, alone among the major powers, has entered the Middle East only in this second relationship. Despite Russian propaganda, and despite the bitterness engendered by the issue of political Zionism, that fact is still pretty widely recognized. On the whole, it is reflected in a different attitude toward us as distinct from other Westerners. That is our great national asset in the crossroads of the world.

It is one that we can ill afford to lose. For the Middle East is sure to be even more important in the immediate future than it has been in the past.

First because it is bound to become a main theater in the struggle between humanism and totalitarianism, between democracy and Communism.

Second because its one economic richness, oil, is essential to the saving of European society by the restoration of its economy.

And third because the Middle East may offer the most promising ground for Occident and Orient to meet and understand each other. If one world is to become a reality, there must be not only Russians and Americans in it; there must be 250 million Moslems, 250 million Hindus, 450 million Buddhists and Confucianists, together with Shintoists, Taoists, Zoroastrians, and others. If we're going to understand one another, we'll have to start trying on all fronts; perhaps the most immediately important is the Middle East.

⚰ II ⚰

What Makes the Middle East?

BEFORE going any further, let us settle the question, what *is* the Middle East? The phrase has been used in various ways, to include everything from Morocco to Ethiopia, Turkestan and India. For the purposes of military strategists, Greece is often included. In this book, however, the more limited definition is used, embracing Turkey, Iran and Afghanistan, and the Arab League countries—Egypt, Lebanon, Syria, Iraq, Transjordan, Saudi Arabia and Yemen—together with disputed Palestine, and the sheikhdoms, principalities and various political oddities of the Persian Gulf and southern Arabian peninsula.

There are two important geographic facts about the Middle East. First, its location; second, its terrain and climate. Both have deeply affected the life of its inhabitants.

The importance of the location is obvious the moment you look at a map. The countries comprising the Middle East form, in effect, the hub of three continents—Europe, Asia and Africa. Communications between those continents, in the present air age no less than in the age of caravans and caravels, must pass within sight of the Sphinx, the Mount of Olives, or the Street Called Straight. It is no coincidence that the great world conquerors of history have fought in and over the Middle East. The armies of Cyrus, Alexander, Caesar, Tamerlane, Napoleon and Hitler have battled across its deserts and relaxed gratefully in its oases. Any power that has hoped to extend its domination over continents has learned that domination of the Middle East is an essential step. And any power trying to resist continental expansion by another has learned in turn that the Middle East must be protected at all cost.

This was given most dramatic recognition during the last war. After the heroic but costly evacuation of Dunkirk and the fall of France, Britain was left to face—alone and almost without equipment save for her navy and the RAF—victorious Nazi armies poised for invasion across a narrow strip of water. At that perilous moment, the British had just one fully equipped armored division. Naturally, you would think, that division would be held in Britain to withstand the expected assault.

But no. Churchill and his chiefs of staff had a broader vision. They realized that, in spite of surface appearance, the place where there was greatest danger of losing the war was in the Middle East. And so this one strong division was loaded aboard ship and sent to Egypt, where it helped stave off Rommel's attempt to drive through from Libya to the Suez Canal and beyond to the Persian Gulf. Military historians agree that this was one of the most crucial single decisions of the war, one of the decisions that mark the line between victory and defeat.

Since the defeat of Germany it has become apparent that the Middle East is as crucial in the cold war with Russia as it was in the shooting war with the Axis. Soviet Russia, like czarist Russia, has sought to expand southward and westward, to reach the Mediterranean and the Persian Gulf. In Greece, in Turkey and in Iran it has exerted pressure to that end. Only the most determined opposition by Britain and the United States has held their wartime ally in check, but the danger is by no means over.

In the past, the inhabitants of the Middle East have suffered far more than they have gained as a result of their lands' strategic location. They have been fought over, held in subjection, by a series of "great" powers. From just one conquest alone—that of the Mongols in the thirteenth and fourteenth centuries—the Persians and Arabs have suffered and continue to suffer almost incalculable losses. That conquest led to one of the first deliberate employments of scorched-earth tactics on a large scale. For Tamerlane, wishing to make sure that no enemy could retrace his own line of march to attack him, deliberately set out to create a desert as his defense. In addition to his mass slaughters, he systematically destroyed the irrigation systems of Persia and Mesopotamia (now Iran and Iraq), and the waste lands created then have not been substantially reclaimed to this day.

In general, if conquerors could not hold, they destroyed. Except for comparatively brief periods of glory, the peoples of the Middle East have lived either in slavery or poverty when they were not living in both. To this the geographical *location*, as well as the geographical *features*, of their homes contributed. There is a possibility now that one of these at least may work to their advantage.

That possibility depends upon us. The argument runs as follows: Admit that if an aggressive power should become dominant in the area, whether by conquest in time of war or by infiltration and revolution in time of peace, the security of a far wider zone would be threatened. Admit that this would be against American and British national interests. The Anglo-Saxon powers, then, can oppose such a hazard by taking direct action to block Russian expansion, as we have already attempted in Iran, Turkey and Greece. We are learning, however, that such action taken by itself is an expensive and never-ending operation.

There is an additional possibility. We can back up such direct action, where it is indeed required, by bolstering the political stability and the social and economic advancement of Middle East peoples. We can recognize that while Communism thrives on violence and chaos, it can be beaten by security and progress. We can realize ourselves—and lead the peoples there to realize—that the best weapon against Communist infiltration and revolutionary tactics, the best defense of our security and theirs, is a joint effort to improve their lot.

If we and they can agree on that, the vicious cycle of war, conquest, exploitation and degradation, and renewed war, might at last be broken.

The physical features of the land have had an effect upon its inhabitants at least equal to its strategic location. You must begin with the land and the climate. They force their attention on you in the Middle East; obviously they have played a great part in forming the character and aspirations of the people who inhabit this "hot spot" of the earth.

In technical language, the Middle East is part of the great steppe-and-desert belt which stretches from the Atlantic coast of Africa through the steppes and deserts of central Asia to the Bering Sea. The climate is chiefly "low latitude desert" or "low latitude steppe"—continuously hot with little or no rain, less than ten inches yearly. But in the Mediterranean coastal areas of Palestine, Lebanon, Syria and Turkey the climate is quite similar to that of Southern California, with hot summers, mild winters, and fair rainfall chiefly during the winter. There is excellent skiing in the Lebanon mountains, and winter in Teheran is not, even by New England standards, "mild."

The soil over most of the Middle East is, to continue (very briefly) the technical description, desert soil, the vegetation largely desert shrub and desert waste. The agriculture of the area, save for the valleys of three great rivers, is described as "nomadic herding." Along the Nile, Tigris and Euphrates rivers the map shows "intensive tillage"; Lebanon and Palestine have a Mediterranean-type agriculture, growing a profusion of fruits. And there are black patches on the map in southern Arabia and Iran indicating absolutely no agriculture whatsoever.

The greatest contrast is in population density. In the Nile valley, this runs to five hundred or more inhabitants per square mile, which is close to the world high. But most of Egypt has less than one inhabitant per square mile. So does most of Saudi Arabia, Transjordan, and a large part of Iraq. Sections averaging more than five people to the square mile are few and small. Yet the congestion in town and city— the congestion wherever there is water—is so great that in spite of the barren stretches several of the countries are more densely populated than the United States. Syria, Lebanon and Yemen for instance average just a bit higher than the U.S. Palestine, a poor bare little country, has three times the population per square mile that the United States has. The sparsely populated lands of Saudi Arabia and Transjordan are, in spite of their deserts, more thickly settled than Wyoming or Idaho. Population figures emphasize the fact that where water can be provided, the land is incredibly rich. But the maps showing soil and vegetation emphasize the even greater fact—the domination of the desert, which cannot be concealed even in the most fertile oasis.

Inevitably, inescapably, it is the desert that strikes the newcomer first and hardest. After a while you come to accept it, as the inhabitants do to a far greater extent of course, without particular thought. But in the beginning it preys on you. Wherever you are—Cairo, Damascus, or Baghdad—the desert is just outside your window, just around the corner, if it is not actually underfoot, in your shoes, or in your eyes and nose.

The desert has different names. West of the Nile it is the Sahara, east of it the Arabian Desert, including the Sinai Desert. In Arabia proper, it is the Nefud Desert and the Rub al Khali or "Empty Quarter." Between Damascus, Amman and Baghdad, it is the Syrian Desert, in Iran the Dasht-i-Kavir and Dasht-i-Lut. It may even appear in different guises—bright waves of sand stretch to infinity, and you might be in the Sinai or Sahara, or it may be dark and dour, as in Jebel el Druze. It may even, momentarily, be green after the rare rains. In the Negeb, the Beduin grow sparse crops of barley, and most of the desert is not, strictly speaking, barren. The skies open once a year or so, and amazingly the sand and rocks are specked with green—except in the Empty Quarter, or the Iranian wastes, where there is almost no life at all, whether vegetable or animal.

But whatever its name or surface appearance, it is always desert—infinite, empty, a reminder of the smallness of man and the certainty of death. Even the cities remind the traveler of the endless struggle of humanity against the unfriendly elements. As Professor Haas writes: "They are islands in an ocean of barrenness, and their existence is due to the toil of man constantly occupied in enlarging the fertile area by irrigation and in defending his conquests against the evil powers of desert and steppes, burning sun, sand and wind."[*] Perhaps this is what gives them such compelling charm for some, what makes the names Isfahan, Palmyra, Medina, Shiraz, Jerash and a host of others so magic on the tongue—that and the contrast of green in dusty, dingy yellow-brown, of life in the vastness of death.

The land and climate have a more direct effect upon most foreigners than an uneasy or romantic awareness of the desert. This effect is variously described as "Gyppy" or Teheran tummy, Baghdad belly, or by other less polite names. Each newcomer is plied with advice on how to avoid or minimize this inconvenient, and extremely uncomfortable, complaint. One school of thought, numbering many Britons among its adherents, blames the whole business upon intestinal chills and holds that flannel worn next to the stomach is the sovereign remedy.

Others claim that specific foods—in general any uncooked fruits or vegetables, particularly apricots, melons and lettuce—must be avoided. According to most doctors, this is a sound idea anyhow; unsanitary methods of fertilizing crops persist in many parts of the Middle East,

[*] *Iran*, by William S. Haas, Columbia University Press, 1946.

and there is danger of catching dysentery, bacillary or the even nastier amoebic variety, from eating uncooked fruits or vegetables. Other health hints for the area: be very careful of the water you drink, and avoid all raw milk products from which you might pick up the widely prevalent undulant fever.

There is another school of thought, however, which argues that you cannot possibly avoid the local bugs so it is better to accustom yourself to them. Followers of this theory point out that at home you would eat plenty of fruits and salads. Not to do so abroad is to court ill-health. Therefore, at a party in Cairo, one is likely to see most of the visiting foreigners refusing lettuce and fresh strawberries, while a small but enthusiastic group consume both with aggressive, even boastful avidity.

The U.S. Army was of the extreme abstaining view. From the medical briefings we got, you might have thought we were entering a death trap. Everything was to be regarded as polluted if not maliciously poisoned. Nothing must pass our lips except good GI issue, preferably from a can opened before our very eyes.

If the army doctors could have found some way of preventing us from breathing the local air, I'm sure they would have done so—and then their campaign to avoid diarrhea and dysentery might have had more success. It seems likely that climate and the effort of adjusting to its unfamiliar strains, together with the heavily laden air of a large city like Cairo, is at least as much to blame as the food for ordinary digestive upsets. The heat alone may account for many cases. If you don't think that can be a shock to the system, try walking down Rashid Street in Baghdad at three o'clock on a summer afternoon. The official weather report will give a temperature, perhaps, of 124 degrees, but that is taken in a specially shaded and ventilated site out at the airport; in the glare and dust of Rashid Street you will be willing to swear it is more than 140. To go into it from an air-conditioned embassy (where the temperature is a cool 95 degrees) is like walking into a blast furnace.

In any case, neither the army system nor any other I know of assures the visitor that his internal organs will continue to function smoothly. My own work during the war involved regular and irregular contacts with local people of all degrees; it seemed to me that politeness and efficiency required me to eat what they gave me. So after a few cautious weeks I ignored the dietary regulations except so far as milk, and where possible water, were concerned.

Whatever its traumatic effect upon our nervous systems, the army's lurid picture of the perils of living in the Middle East was bound to affect, in one way or another, our attitude toward the land and the people. For some it added zest to life. Others reacted unconsciously in the manner brilliantly described by Edmond Taylor* while writing of the next station down the line—India. The army medicos, as Taylor points out, were not taking a new line. Their warnings followed the traditional white man's approach. "This nightmare of lurking menace, this fear, purely bacteriological at the beginning but gradually answering an unconscious sexual connotation of contagion through contact with the native, strongly colors the inter-cultural attitude of all Westerners toward the East and is probably an important ingredient in the almost pathological hatred of the East which so many Westerners, especially germ-conscious Americans, develop when they are forced to live there."

Personally the whole business reminded me of an earlier experience, years before, when a schoolmate and I went to hunt jaguars in Mato Grosso, Brazil. We took with us a book about Mato Grosso picturesquely entitled *Green Hell*, which gave a lurid picture of the perils to be encountered there. Death, according to the author, was at your elbow every second. When we got bored with the quiet camp life between hunts we used to read excerpts aloud, laughing ruefully and unable to avoid the feeling that, somehow, we had been cheated. If it was the drama of palpable peril we were seeking, we could have found it better on Broadway and Forty-second Street than in the orderly structure of jungle life in Brazil. (It should be pointed out, in fairness to Broadway, that in Mato Grosso we were south of the worst fever belt. As a hazard I'd take the errant taxicab in preference to the jungle fevers any day.)

In any case, the Middle East came as no shock to me. My father was not only an inveterate traveler himself but was in the shipping business, which made traveling easy for us children and often cheaper than staying at home. So dirt and germs were nothing new. Some of the smaller South American ports, for instance, can hold their own in any league

* *Richer by Asia*, chapter 3, "The Art of Awareness," Houghton Mifflin, 1947.

on those scores. And after ten days on third, or "hard," class Russian trains, the insect world has little new to offer. For what it may be worth to international relations, I offer my observation that the Communist and the Beduin louse—encountered in Sarokka or Riyadh—the Russian and the Middle East bedbug—found in Kharkov, Amman, or Tel Aviv —are sisters under and on the skin.

Because of these sordid acquaintances in my past, I was not as concerned as were many of my fellow Americans by the terrifying pictures painted by our medicos. Those who reacted as I did found themselves in a special category. They ignored "danger," and if some of their comrades thought them rash fools, others were admiring. They appeared to have a special immunity and therefore, perhaps, a special intimacy. Who knows? Perhaps it was not history but digestion which has been most important in maintaining my interest in the Middle East.

Certainly those who could and did eat the food felt closer to the people. It is a cheap, painless and beneficial experience which I wish could be more widely shared. Intimacy is a good thing, even if it is sometimes an illusive intimacy. Obviously it is well, and profitable, to *want* to know people better, to *try* to surmount the barriers which block understanding even if you don't always succeed. Particularly to be surmounted are the barriers which block the very desire to know people better.

One of the most important of these, as far as Americans are concerned, is plumbing. Plumbing is an excellent thing; in its place, I am very fond of it and like most people who have become used to it I miss it very much when it isn't there. (I have, incidentally, a somewhat stiff leg which makes the standard old-fashioned Middle Eastern bathroom fixture—which is simply a hole in the floor—a special problem for me.) Plumbing's place, however, is not in politics, or as a bar to friendly relations between peoples. Yet we seem to judge a people by their plumbing. That was an important factor in the reaction of our GI's to the different countries of Europe. German plumbing fixtures are more like the American than are British, Italian or French. It appears that some of our boys were not averse to drawing the conclusion that the German people are more like us as well.

Surely that is not a sound basis for judgment. We should not, of course, go to the other extreme and delight, as some tourists do, in picturesque filth. Abstractly, cleanliness of itself may be no better than good clean dirt; it may be ridiculous to say that "cleanliness is next to Godliness"; but health is certainly better than disease. A healthy man, in general, makes a better citizen and a better human being than a diseased one. But a man who takes a bath once a day may be no better, and no healthier, than a man who bathes but rarely.

✿ III ✿

The Desert

BY AND large the elements—sun, water, wind and sand—exert
their control over human lives and destinies more openly and
often more brutally in the Middle East than in the more highly developed countries of the Occident. In western Europe and North
America city dwellers, at least, are well insulated against nature. Flood
or drought occasionally break through the defenses; a ball game may
get rained out; in the relatively few moments the city-dweller spends
outdoors, he must adjust his clothing to the seasons. But that is vastly
different from the impact of the elements upon the Beduin of the Nejd,
the *fellahin* of the Nile delta, or the city Arab of Damascus. Even the
visitor finds that nature makes herself felt in his life far more than
at home.

Nearness to nature here involves nearness to death, which in turn
sharpens the sense of living, gives an immediacy to life and, at the same
time, tends to make individual life cheap. In the Western world, war
does that, but war is not, in theory, our constant state. We consider it
an abnormal condition, an interruption of life's proper schedule.

In the Middle East (as in other vast areas of the world) war *is* life's
proper schedule. Not necessarily war between men, although in the
vanishing tribal societies this was true, and, to a lesser extent, it was
and is true of those countries struggling for independence from foreign
rule. It is surely true of Palestine. But there also is a constant war, in-
volving frequent and severe casualties, against the elements. Death by
starvation, thirst or epidemic disease is an ever-present companion to
life—and a man is affected by the company he keeps. It is essential to

bear this in mind when trying to understand the mentalities and values of Middle Eastern people.

There is no doubt that a sense of the nearness of death, together with the time for contemplation without undue distraction, leads men to intense speculation about forces outside themselves. Desert lands are particularly conducive to thoughts of eternity, and they are free of those artificial distractions which assist man's natural desire to avoid looking eternity in the face. Your physical self is very small in the great stretches of stone and sand. It is hardly surprising that the three great monotheistic religions of the world were born in these deserts. Egypt, Palestine, Syria, Mesopotamia, Arabia, Persia—these have always been lands of mystics and ascetics. Among them are Ikhnaton, the Pharaoh who was one of history's first prominent believers that God is One; Isaiah and the other great prophets of Israel; John the Baptist, Jesus of Nazareth and Paul; Marcion and the Gnostics; Antony and Pachomius, the great early exponents of, respectively, eremitic and coenobitic monachism (the fact that the word "hermit" comes from "eremite," the Greek for "desert-dweller," is a reminder itself); Mohammed; the Sufis, or Moslem mystics, such as the renowned female ascetic, Rabi'a of Basra, the Persian Bayezid, and Jalal-ud-din Rami; and later day prophets and reformers, of whom the Wahhabi sect offer a good example.

The traditions and the interest, and the conditions which created them, are still prevalent, although of course movies, the radio, and the increasing urbanization of life are bound to weaken their hold. But I have heard, I think, proportionately more talk among Arabs than among Americans of the larger mysteries—the nature of the soul, the meaning of infinity, the relationship between God and Fate and Man. It may be argued that this is a subconscious attempt by Arabs to escape from the complexities and decisions forced upon us by modern "civilization," and I am sure that in many cases the charge would be substantially true—as it has been throughout history. (Men turn to theology from many different kinds of compulsions.) But there are many more instances where it obviously does not apply.

I remember in the summer of 1947, when I visited King ibn Saud at Riyadh, his interpreter was a young Arab from Hejaz (the western part of Saudi Arabia) named Abdul Aziz Mu'ammar. Abdul Aziz had studied in Cairo and Beirut, in Egyptian, French Jesuit and American nondenominational colleges. He speaks excellent English and French and has in addition, I believe, a good reading knowledge of German. Among his duties is that of preparing three times a day a summary of world news for the king. These reports, based on careful monitoring of news broadcasts from the main capitals of Europe, Asia and America, keep ibn Saud remarkably well informed on world affairs.

Abdul Aziz is not trying to escape the complications of modern life. He puts in a good working day helping to bring his isolated country up to date. But in his rare leisure moments he studies—philosophy. His ambition, if he can ever be spared for long enough from his strictly practical contributions of the present, is to come to this country and take his Ph.D. in philosophy at one of the great American universities of which he has heard so much. He would like to write his doctoral dissertation upon Immanuel Kant, and has already begun work on it.

Although the desert is inescapable in the Middle East, the desert is not all. And when people say there is no lovelier place in the world, you want to remember that they are not necessarily talking of desert. We are inclined to think there is something a little odd about a man who loves the desert (perhaps he takes religion more seriously than is fashionable). But there is nothing strange to our eyes in a man who raves of the beauty of Capri, the Adriatic, or springtime in the Rocky Mountains.

The Middle East has its share of similarly lovely places and perhaps their loveliness is enhanced by contrast with the waste lands. Young goats and donkeys frolic by the edge of a delta canal, the snow-capped mountains of Lebanon rise, red-brown and white, above the sweep of green and yellow Bakaa fields; Cairo's normally vivid colors run riot when the blue jacarandas and the passionate red blossoms of the flamboyant trees are in flower; peach, apricot, plum and cherry trees are incredibly delicate over the flash of white water, against the hard-ribbed mountains of the Elburz in Iran's late spring; scarlet poppies and pink oleanders brighten the green streaking stream beds of Transjordan.

The desert, particularly at dawn or dusk, has beauties too, harsh but compelling. And these have compelled many who come from softer lands. One cannot avoid the feeling that some of the most spectacular foreign lovers of Arabia have been drawn to the desert by a sort of

masochistic force within them. The same sort of compulsions which may
be discerned, for instance, in T. S. Eliot's *The Waste Land,* suggest
themselves most clearly in the letters of Lawrence. In other cases the explanation may be less complicated—simply a desire to replace the confusions and conflicts of urban civilization with the simpler forms of
primitive agricultural or nomadic life.

The Middle East has been one of the last refuges for the Occidental
romantic who has at one time or another found similar comfort in the
noble Indian, the Esquimaux, or the simple natives of Malaya, the Gold
Coast, or the South Sea Islands. But the Middle East, like the rest of
the world, is becoming less and less suitable as a sanctuary.

I remember George Wadsworth, then our ambassador to Iraq, saying
of Jerusalem and its surroundings that they should be made into "a
spiritual Yellowstone Park." But even the attempt to preserve that last
sanctuary seems to have failed.

Although religious or political sanctuary has vanished, although
even the desert offers no safe haven for the romantic escapist, there is
still the refuge most important to the local people—refuge from the
desert itself. The beauty spots already mentioned are more than just
beautiful. They are extremely fertile. For centuries the Middle Eastern
countries have been known for their rich foods and spices, and for the
lavish hospitality with which these have been dispensed. As a child I
remember being fascinated by a passage from the story "The Porter and
the Three Ladies of Baghdad" in *The Book of the Thousand Nights
and a Night.* It describes the shopping tour for which the first lady hires
the Porter. First, from a Nazarene, she bought for one gold piece what
she required of "strained wine clear as olive oil." Her next stop was the
fruiterer's shop where she got "Shami apples and Osmani quinces and
Omani peaches, and cucumbers of Nile growth, and Egyptian limes
and Sultani oranges and citrons; besides Aleppine jasmine, scented
myrtle berries, Damascene nenuphars, flowers of privet and camomile,
blood-red anemones, violets, and pomegranate-bloom, eglantine and
narcissus. . . ."* At the butcher's she purchased, rather prosaically, ten
pounds of mutton, which the butcher wrapped for her in a banana leaf.
Then she stopped at a grocer's for dry fruits, pistachio-kernels, Tihamah

---

* Burton's translation. To clear up some of the archaic names: Shami equals Syrian,
Osmani Turkish (Ottoman); Omani refers to eastern Arabia (the Oman). A nenuphar
is a water lily.

raisins and shelled almonds. Next to the confectioner's where "she bought an earthen platter, and piled it with all kinds of sweetmeats in his shop, open-worked tarts and fritters scented with musk and 'soap-cakes,' and lemon-loaves and melon-preserves, and 'Zaynab's combs,' and 'ladies' fingers,' and 'Kazi's tit-bits' and goodies of every description." At a perfumer's she acquired "ten sorts of waters, rose scented with musk, orange-flower, water-lily, willow-flower, violet and five others; and she also bought two loaves of sugar, a bottle for perfume-spraying, a lump of male incense, aloe-wood, ambergris and musk, with candles of Alexandria wax." Her shopping concluded with a stop at the greengrocer's where she purchased "pickled safflower and olives, in brine and oil; with tarragon and cream-cheese and hard Syrian cheese." Aside from the final attractions, on which the storyteller later dwells, it must have been a wonderful feast!

Baghdad now is not as rich a city, comparatively, as it was a thousand years ago, and people do not eat every day now in the style suggested by the shopping of the lady, any more than they did then. When you are entertained in a private home in Baghdad, Damascus or Shiraz, or any place where the traditional cooking and hospitality are still practiced, you do indeed eat surpassingly well. But, as ibn Saud remarked as we sat over a groaning banquet board, the Arabs do not eat like that all the time. "We are a poor country," the king reminded me, "and much of our food has to be imported. It is only when we have the pleasure of entertaining a guest that there is a feast like this."

It is hard not to feel guilty when you think of that, even as the food melts in your mouth.

The fertility of the Middle East is as much a part of the picture as its barrenness. Much of the land *could* be made to blossom. The margin between fertility and desolation is, as it always has been, narrow—and very precise. It is a matter of water.

In most parts of the Middle East, as in a few places in America, life has to be planned entirely around water—its absence and its rare presence. Occasionally there is a strange, and very transient, embarrassment of riches, as in the incident reported by St. John Philby from Arabia. The story still lives, though it is a generation old. Wadi Dawasir, back in 1917, actually experienced a flood. "As the roaring tide, originating in a great cloudburst in the upper reaches of Wadi

Tathlith, approached the oasis, the people ran to the governor with the alarming news. He laughed in their faces, saying: 'Bring me a coffee-cup and I will drink the flood!' But the waters rolled down, filling the valley for days. . . . Much damage was done, but the Wadi would prosper for years from its unwonted wetting."*

Men of course have tried to control and retain the waters of the desert with better means than coffee cups. The underground irrigation and storage system of Persia and Mesopotamia, destroyed by Tamerlane, was one of the most remarkable engineering feats of the age. Governments and private groups are now engaged in hopeful projects employing the most modern techniques; but these have gone slowly in the face not only of physical difficulties but shortage of finances and qualified personnel. For centuries, life in the Middle East has been so close to the margin that resources must be carefully husbanded. What a man can expend in trying to overcome bad soil or drought is strictly limited by what he, and his small group—tribe or village—have to devote to the whole task of keeping themselves alive.

Consciousness of this gives bitter color to Arab reactions to the sight of big landowners installing fabulously expensive irrigation devices, or, more particularly, to the practices of Zionist agricultural developments in Palestine. If you press him hard enough, an Arab will admit that they are admirable. But, he will say, they are not farming. Or he will call them "political" or "propaganda farming." And he will point out that according to their own figures the Jewish Agency's agricultural program has always operated at a loss and that, even so, with all the money poured into it, it has been able to produce only a third of the food requirements of the Jews in Palestine. Many of its farms, of course, are profitable. But others are not and never will be. They are made possible only by the expenditure of vast sums.

In the summer of 1947 I visited, for example, one of the Jewish settlements in the Negeb. Beduin have been growing an average of one annual crop of barley in this region (near Beersheba) for generations, but further development did not seem to them possible or rewarding in terms of their resources.

Now the Negeb enjoys, if it is lucky, one rain a year. This usually resembles a flash flood; the water pours down the dry wadis until it

* H. St. J. B. Philby, *Arabian Days*, Robert Hale, Ltd., London, 1948.

disappears underground, and comparatively little benefit of it remains aside from replenished wells. The Zionists reasoned, quite rightly, that by building traps and dams and reservoirs, it would be possible to hold this yearly rain and apportion it for irrigation until the next rain comes around.

At the particular settlement I visited, they had succeeded in keeping a couple of hundred acres of land in pretty regular production (though nothing could save it if the rainfall were to skip a year, as it does every so often). To do this they had spent 250 thousand Palestinian pounds or one million American dollars. To eat a carrot or a melon produced off that land is like eating solid twenty-two carat gold; Arabs say severely that no human being can afford such a diet—even if his money does come from abroad. The only justification for spending such sums for food is in time of war, to maintain an army in the field. It remains to be seen if a national existence can be solidly established on such a basis.

This is one illustration of the way in which climate and soil, making life hard, have also made it more contentious. Oases and wells have been *causi bellae* since men have valued them. And the Zionists are not the first to find a land which appears to resist their will as stubbornly as its inhabitants.

✵ IV ✵

Buried Treasure

BESIDES its location and its surface attributes of climate and terrain, there is another very important way in which land can affect the people on it. That is by its content, by what lies under the surface. The soil of the Middle East is, on the whole, fertile where water can be provided. In its depths may be found some gold, a little coal, a smattering of other mineral resources. But the great richness is oil. And the richness is such that Middle East oil is not of local only but of world concern. One qualified geologist has estimated that, if enough equipment and transport were supplied, the area could supply by itself the entire world with petroleum for an indefinite time. Looking to the more immediate future, the plans of the European Recovery Program count upon Middle East fields to supply 80 per cent of the oil needs of Marshall Plan countries between 1948 and 1951. Any serious stoppage in the flow of Middle East oil has immediate repercussions upon the political as well as the economic balance of the world. Oil *is* important in the winning of the peace.

Since that is so, Middle East oil is of major and legitimate interest to foreign offices and State departments everywhere. You can't change that fact by saying it isn't so, any more than you can make the sun go away by blinking at it.

Of the First World War, it was said that the Allies floated to victory on an ocean of oil. That is even more true of the Second World War, in which American mass production far from the scenes of battle played an even more decisive role. Without oil in huge quantities that production would have been impossible, and what was produced could not in any case have been transported to the fronts for use against the enemy. If war should come again in this generation, the necessity for oil will not be less, and the biggest "ocean" is in the Middle East.

To take a more hopeful view, if we can win through to peace this same oil holds out tremendous promise. It can provide not only Europe but the East as well with the cheap fuel needed by modern industry. India and China, for example, could also be enabled to skip the cumbersome and wasteful phase of large-scale rail transport—whose main present advantage is in saving oil—and move straight to reliance upon road and air. Faraway lands could grow richer and healthier because of the treasure buried at the crossroads.

That is a hope for the future. The present does not promise it. So far, in fact, comparatively few people have had reasons, even in the Middle East itself, to bless the discovery of this oil. Undoubtedly many Arabs share the view of the young Iraqi who said to me bitterly, "If only Allah had not seen fit to drench our lands in oil, maybe the British, the Russians, the French and even the Zionists would leave us alone and let us live in peace and freedom!" It was clear that in this respect at least the young man was not convinced that "Allah knows best."

The Saudi Arabians, on the other hand, find oil the most indisputable proof of Allah's bounty and good will. The American oil companies with which they deal have not interfered in local politics, do not show any signs of imperialist ambitions. The dollars they pay are very welcome indeed; so is their assistance in other matters—road and railroad building, antimalarial compaigns, widespread vaccinations against smallpox, the creation of schools and hospitals. The Saudi Arab will of course feel differently if his country becomes a battleground for the great powers because of its oil. But so far the development of his oil suggests to him, and to his neighbors, the surprising and very hopeful possibility that it may prove profitable to him as well as to a bunch of unbelieving foreigners.

As in other highly technical fields, laymen are at the mercy of the "experts" so far as their information on oil production is concerned. If there is one thing experts can be counted on to do, it is to disagree. If they see eye to eye on present facts, they can differ violently on what the future will bring. So it is with oil. Most will agree that, in this country, we have taken the cream from the top of the bottle, that from now on oil operations here will be more expensive and less rewarding.

Some experts contend that we should concentrate all our energies, our steel, our equipment, capital and skilled personnel on the development of fields within our own borders. This would, they agree, be less rewarding financially, and also less satisfactory to the consumer who would have to pay far more for his gasoline and other petroleum products than he does now. But, they assert, unless we push ahead now, we may find ourselves dangerously short in case of war. Then it would be hard to catch up lost ground, particularly since the huge tonnage of steel needed could be obtained only in competition with military requirements.

Other experts argue, on the contrary, that world petroleum consumption makes development of Middle East reserves a necessity. If American companies do not participate, and if the American public and government do not help to make their participation possible, other nations and other companies will go ahead without us. The United States, they argue, cannot afford to be left out of the picture. All our national interests, at home and abroad, politically, economically and militarily, demand our participation.

Those who disagree on policy are nonetheless in agreement on what the present situation is. Middle East oil production has been growing at a fantastic rate, and it is, comparatively speaking, still in its infancy.

Oil exploration began, so far as the Middle East is concerned, in Southwest Iran, where oil was discovered in 1908. This oil became so important to the British that by 1913 the British government acquired a controlling interest in the Anglo-Iranian Oil Company. The biggest producing field in Iraq, the Kirkuk field, was discovered in 1927. Production of oil in Bahrein began in 1932 and it was not until 1938 that oil was discovered in Saudi Arabia in commercial quantities.

"When you talk about oil out here," a driller at Dhahran remarked, "remember that we've barely begun to look for oil properly. Even so, proven reserves—oil that we *know* is in fields already explored— proven reserves are at least equal to those of the entire Western hemisphere. Take the U.S., which is considered to be rich in oil. Operations began almost one hundred years ago, and have been very active indeed. The oil taken and the reserves discovered in those hundred years run to about 30 billion barrels. Here in the Middle East, in barely more than a generation of exploration, we've uncovered reserves of 32 billion barrels. We're as sure as can be that further exploration will find many times that total.

"Nowhere in the world have oil men found any region with anything like the size of these oil pools. The average well here produces more and faster than the average anywhere else. And in exploratory drilling we've had an amazing rate of successes."

He went on to tell me that in 1936 the total Middle East oil production amounted to 265,000 barrels per day. That total is now exceeded by Saudi Arabian fields alone, which were not then even in production. As of the middle of 1948, the Saudi Arabian fields were producing 410,000 barrels of oil per day and the Middle East as a whole was producing 1,057,000. Provided political disturbances do not make it impossible, the output is expected to double within the next few years.

So far as present explorations show, the oil region of most importance in the Middle East is in and around the great basin occupied by the Tigris and Euphrates rivers and the Persian Gulf. Although oil has been produced in Egypt for many years it has not been discovered in important quantities except in the Egyptian Negeb, bordering on Palestine, where recent tests are most promising. Tests are continuing in Egypt and are also underway in Syria, Lebanon, Palestine and Transjordan as well as in the sheikhdoms of the southeastern and southern Arabian coast. But so far, the countries with important production have been Iran, Iraq and Saudi Arabia. The small island of Bahrein, however, has been producing significant quantities of oil for many years and the sheikhdom of Kuwait, where fields have only recently been put into production, is already producing more oil than Iraq.

Those are the countries owning the oil. Perhaps it is not proper to describe them as the producers of the oil, for the Middle Eastern countries have neither the knowledge nor the technical experience nor the capital necessary to exploit their own good fortune. Actual production is in the hands of foreign companies owned chiefly by British, American, French and Dutch.

The petroleum attaché in one of our embassies explained this complicated setup for me. "In Iran, the Anglo-Iranian Oil Company (AIOC) holds the concession for the south and the Russians have so far failed to secure the concession for the north. The British government owns 56 per cent of the stock in AIOC.

"Three companies with identical ownership hold the concessions in Iraq. For practical purposes you can speak simply of IPC, for Iraq Petroleum Company Ltd. has the Kirkuk area where all the production so far has been. One individual, C. S. Gulbenkian, owns 5 per cent of the three companies, which must make him one of the richest men in the world. He's an Armenian, now of British citizenship, who used to be a 'runner' for the old Ottoman Bank and was instrumental in getting the original concession from the Turks when they ruled Iraq before the First World War. Someday," said the attaché reflectively, "I'm going to figure out some excuse for an official call on the old man. He lives in Lisbon now, and I imagine he does himself quite well.

"The remaining 95 per cent is divided equally between British, French, Dutch and American interests. The American companies involved are Socony Vacuum and Standard of New Jersey. They also own a part interest, together with the Texas Company and Standard of California, in the wholly American concessions in Saudi Arabia and Bahrein. But they are not the only American companies active in the area. The concession in Kuwait is held by a company half British, half American. The American half-interest is owned by the Gulf Exploration Company. The American Independent Oil Company, of which Ralph K. Davies is president, has recently obtained a half-interest in the so-called Kuwait Neutral Zone."

In addition to the complicated pattern of concessions, there is the equally difficult, more controversial issue of pipe lines. Even though the world importance of Middle East oil is now recognized, that oil cannot be fully utilized. Production is held back because it would not be possible to move the oil produced. Obviously there would be no gain from producing additional hundreds of thousands of barrels daily if all that could be done with that oil was to leave it lying around the deserts of Iraq or Arabia. To be useful it must get into the hands of the consumers, and since there are comparatively few consumers in the Middle East, that means a long haul. Tankers can do the job, though they are relatively inefficient and expensive. The route from the Kirkuk fields, for example, to the big Mediterranean markets is ten times longer by water, around the tip of the Arabian peninsula, than it is overland as far as Haifa and then by sea. Smaller but still substantial differences exist for Abqaiq and many other Middle Eastern fields. Also tankers are in short supply. From purely technical and economic views, it is far better to move the oil by pipe line.

The first Middle East-Mediterranean pipe line, from the Kirkuk field to the sea, was completed in 1934. The Iraq Petroleum Company now has two pipe lines, one reaching the Mediterranean at Tripoli and the other at Haifa. Three major pipe-line projects are in various stages of completion. The IPC is constructing two sixteen-inch pipe lines from the Kirkuk field running alongside their two present twelve-inch lines. If all goes according to schedule, the new line to Haifa will be completed in 1949 and the one to Tripoli in 1951. The Trans-Arabian Pipe Line Company is continuing its plans, in the face of obstacles at home and abroad, for the construction of a thirty to thirty-one inch pipe line from the Saudi Arabian fields to the Lebanese coast. Finally there is a proposal to build a thirty-four-inch line from Iran to the Mediterranean. This would be jointly owned by Anglo-Iranian Oil Company, on the one hand, and Socony Vacuum and Standard Oil of New Jersey on the other. The latter of course have no interest in the Iranian concession but have agreed to take large quantities of Iranian crude oil when and if the project is completed. It is also proposed that Kuwait production be tied into this line. There is talk of an additional pipe line from Kuwait to the Mediterranean to be built by the Gulf Oil Company and Shell.

Although in time of peace and political stability the proposed pipe lines are obviously worth while, such time is not yet upon us. Until it is, the expenditure of money, steel and energy on the lines will be a gamble—a gamble we may not be allowed to make even if we want to. At this writing, Trans-Arabian is actually laying pipe; but the Syrian government has not yet granted permission for its line to pass through Syrian territory, as the company's plans require. Conditions are equally unpropitious in Palestine and Egypt. A pipe line which is stopped short of a Mediterranean port is no good to Aramco or IPC. Moreover, there is as a further drawback: the fear that if war should come with the Soviet Union, the pipe lines might be useless, or worse than useless if they should fall intact into Russian hands.

Another bottleneck halting full use of Middle East oil is in refining capacity. The refineries of the region are by no means adequate. The largest plant is at Abadan, and can cope with 500,000 barrels a day.

The next largest is at Bahrein, with a capacity of almost 150,000 barrels daily. The Aramco refinery at Ras Tanura, which was built for an estimated capacity of fifty thousand, is actually running over 115,000 barrels a day. The refinery at Haifa can handle ninety thousand per day, but it is held by the Israelis and therefore for the time being cannot get Middle Eastern oil. (Apparently some shipments from Rumania have been received.) Refining capacity thus is far short even of present output.

Although the United States Navy has been taking a large part of the output of the Ras Tanura refinery, the importance of the Middle East oil fields to the United States is not primarily one of direct supply of American requirements. Rather, use of Middle East oil is expected to prevent drains upon the diminishing reserves of the Western hemisphere. At one time much was made of the point that in the event of war with the Soviet Union the United States would not be able to rely upon oil from Arabian fields. That is, of course, quite true and no responsible governmental or oil company official has ever claimed otherwise. Military authorities differ on the possibility of Anglo-American forces being able to hold any given part of the Middle East against possible Russian assault, but even the most optimistic military man would never suggest relying upon Middle East oil in case of war. The real significance for the United States, however, is the fact that the Middle East area should be able to take over the burden of supplying Eastern hemisphere requirements which have previously had to be met from this hemisphere. In 1938, for instance, oil was moving from West to East at a rate of close to 700,000 barrels per day. The United States was importing 170,000 barrels per day and exporting 447,000. At that time the Middle East was exporting only 237,000. By 1949 world consumption had increased by half again what it was in 1938. Consumption in the United States alone was up more than 75 per cent. (We became net importers of oil for the first time since 1925.) Although world consumption had risen so heavily, Eastern Hemisphere consumption, due to shortages, was up only by 5 per cent. The Western Hemisphere was still exporting oil to Europe at the rate of 583,000 barrels per day. Although Middle East production had risen to 830,000 barrels per day, the Middle East could export only at a rate of 286,000 per day due to inadequate facilities. As soon as those facilities can be increased, the

Western Hemisphere should be relieved of much of its present burden.

Middle East oil has proved, and should in future prove most advantageous to other parts of the world. Of equal importance is the present and prospective benefit to the Middle Eastern countries who have found an unexpected source of wealth in their barren lands. The Middle East is not highly industrialized, nor is it likely to become so, due to sparse population and scarcity of essential raw materials. The Middle East countries themselves, therefore, could never use more than a small fraction of the oil reserves within their territories. The proceeds from sale of this oil, however, can be and are already being used for the development of the countries and the improvement of living conditions, of education and of public health. (See, for examples, the chapter on Saudi Arabia.)

The direct payment to governments in the form of royalties or other payments for oil produced in 1948 was approximately as follows: Iran received 33 million dollars, Iraq seven and a quarter million dollars, Saudi Arabia 28 million, Bahrein a million and a half, Kuwait four and three quarters million. In addition, the governments in many instances received cash rental payments on undeveloped portions of their country held under concession. Iraq, for example, gets more than three and a quarter million dollars annually from the Mosul and Basra concessions. The national economies and individual citizens benefit also from large local expenditures by the oil companies for wages, supplies and so forth. Anglo-Iranian in Iran pays wages in excess of four million dollars each month. Aramco in Saudi Arabia pays about a million and a half monthly. It is important to recognize that these payments create serious economic and fiscal problems as well as bringing prosperity which would otherwise not exist. Some of these problems will be discussed in more detail in later chapters.

It would, of course, be foolish to assume that all, or even, in some cases, a major part of the revenues resulting from oil have been spent to public advantage. Much of the profit has gone directly into the pockets of a few individuals. Human nature in general and conditions in the Middle East in particular being what they are, this was obviously inevitable. However, already the people *have* benefited. The job is to see that they benefit more. Oil, which has made the Middle East strategically more important than ever, offers to the Middle Eastern peoples a unique chance for self-improvement. To take advantage of this chance, they will need help and understanding from outside. Above all they will need peace. Aside from other considerations, there is a good chance that many of the best fields in the area would not survive another war. According to geologists, they are of a type most easily destroyed.

Most Middle East oil comes from very thick formations of porous limestone. As *The New York Times* reported: "With enormous heads of water on the sides of each structure pushing the oil up and gas at the apex pushing the oil down, a few well-placed wells in time could drain an entire field despite its size. The pressure on these wells ranges up to 8,000 pounds a square inch at great depths and extreme care must be used lest one get out of control and drain the entire structure." That calls for caution in peace. But what about war? How could the wells be made useless to an enemy? To blow up one well means the loss of the whole field. Bombing of the wells would be disastrous.

Left to themselves the Arabs and the Persians might choose to preserve rather than destroy their fields. But the decision is not likely to remain in their hands. Like everything else in the Middle East, the future of oil may turn to either extreme, well-being or absolute destitution.

⁜ V ⁜

Germs, Arabs and Etiquette

IN SPITE of the misunderstandings which seem to have arisen over oil in the Middle East, it is easier to understand oil, and any of the problems arising out of the land, than it is to understand the people and the problems arising from them. Most of us think, for example, of the Arabs in peculiarly unrealistic ways—as fascinating but sinister Rudolph Valentinos dashing over the sand dunes on spirited steeds; as rather mangy types who live off the water secreted in the humps of a camel and who are always silently folding their tents and as silently stealing away; as hawk-eyed, hawk-nosed individuals dressed in sheets who go crazy at the sight of an unveiled woman.

Or else we call them "wogs" and dismiss them from our minds as inferior beings, somewhat higher than the lower forms of animal life but definitely subhuman. That is not a conscious attitude—which makes it, subtly, all the more insulting.

Even when our intentions are good, our ignorance of the people often makes our efforts to win their friendship totally worthless. I remember, for example, a trip I took to Jidda, the main western seaport of Saudi Arabia, in the spring of 1944. A shipment of riyals (the silver coin of Saudi Arabia, worth about 30 cents) was being sent down as part of the wartime economic assistance provided by our government. The U.S. Army headquarters in Cairo decided that we should make an "occasion" of this delivery, though it was not the first, and build up some good will. So a mission was assembled, consisting of one colonel commanding, a couple of majors, a public relations captain, an OWI man, two lieutenants one of whom could speak a bit of Arabic, two enlisted

34

men photographers, and the necessary crew to fly them down. I had other business in Jidda, and went along for the ride.

The colonel was an old ordnance man, and may have been a good one, for all I know. His qualifications for this assignment were obscure from the beginning; they became no clearer in the course of the mission.

One of the majors was a pleasant fellow who had a vague civilian connection with oil and was mildly interested in Egyptology. (We stopped to view the temples of Karnak on the way back.)

The other was a medical officer, who played an active leading role from the moment we boarded the plane—when he gave us an unusually dramatic medical briefing; upon our return, he had us gargle some relatively harmless little pills before going back to our Cairo quarters. There was one brief interruption in his reign, when the substantive business of the mission was supposedly under discussion. At that point the PRO took over briefly.

The Arabic-speaking lieutenant had been in North Africa, and was under the unfortunate delusion that all Arabs are like the street vendors of Casablanca, and that if you talked loudly enough and slapped their back hard enough, they would be very pleased and flattered. (Most Arabs are noli-me-tangetarians—they don't like to be pawed by strangers.)

Next to the medical officer, the camera men were the most active members of the expedition. They took, I should estimate, six hundred pictures in the day and a half. Most of them were excellent; a few were relevant to our task. The colonel, it is to be feared, had ambitions for a spread in *Life*.

When we arrived at the Jidda airfield, the American minister, Jimmy Moose, met us in some puzzlement. He had only learned that we were coming a few hours earlier, and neither he nor the Saudi Arab government knew what the precise purpose of our trip was. The top officials of the government were in the interior conferring with ibn Saud, but the Finance minister had rushed back to receive us. Now Mr. Moose, politely, wished to know WHY?

The colonel consulted the PRO, while the medical major distributed emergency medical kits and mosquito nettings. We had come, Mr. Moose was informed, to deliver the riyals.

Jimmy Moose looked puzzled. The ship had arrived the previous evening, and early that morning the riyals had been unloaded and taken to the bank. There had been, he admitted, grinning, some slight difficult about delivery. A heavy guard of MPs armed with tommy guns had brought the sacks of riyals. At the dock a couple of unarmed Arabs drove up in a truck, loaded the bags in it—one broke open; passers-by helped pick up the coins and put them back—and casually started to drive off. The officer commanding the MP detachment didn't think that was proper procedure at all. It took some time to persuade him: Punishment for theft is drastic in Saudi Arabia—for the first offense you lose your hand, for the second your head. So there is little stealing; no one, as Jimmy Moose remarked, would think of taking from the king.

But that was all settled now. The MP officer had been soothed. The delivery had taken place.

The PRO objected. The delivery *couldn't* have taken place. Not without pictures and speeches. That was what we had come for.

At this point Moose might have delivered the first lesson of the expedition. Arabs have been receiving subsidies for years and ours was, after all, a pretty small one (several hundred thousand dollars), best passed over in discreet silence. Moreover, if we'd wanted to make an occasion of it, to send a motley assortment of junior officers and photographers, topped by a colonel, was no way to do so. Finally, one didn't visit Saudi Arabia except by invitation from the King; it was very rude to cable as we had, a few hours ahead, simply announcing our arrival. All of this information was available in Cairo for the asking. No one had asked.

Our next move was to the Ministry of Finance where Sheikh Abdullah Suleiman, the minister, received us most politely. We had coffee, the bitter Beduin brew, and conversation was desultory. Finally Sheikh Abdullah asked what he could do for us. There was much embarrassed shuffling around, Moose kept glumly silent, and finally the colonel, at the urging of the PRO, said we had come to get some pictures of the ceremony.

Sheikh Abdullah looked bewildered. What ceremony did we have in mind? He was immediately deluged with suggestions, most of which, I fondly hoped, were beyond the grasp of the interpreter. He must, for instance, have wondered what "cheesecake" had to do with riyals.

The least extravagant of the proposals was to photograph the minister with a stream of riyals pouring through his hands or, like a magician at a children's party (or a galli galli man), plucking them from behind his ears.

The minister protested that the riyals had already been delivered; before he could be photographed with them he would have to get the explicit permission of his king. He looked very unhappy. Mr. Moose, who had been exercising a stoic self-control which any desert ascetic would have had to admire, intervened at last. A compromise was reached. The Finance minister was photographed receiving a piece of paper—actually a letter from a photographer's wife—from the colonel and the American minister. No silver was in view; that was covered in a separate picture, for which several MPs were produced, complete with Tommy guns. Several sacks of riyals were removed from the vault, and the most finely equipped Nubian guards were photographed receiving these from the MPs. The ceremony was, at last, enjoyed by all.

In my report on the mission, I wrote: "At one point I believe the Finance minister was more than a little suspicious, but by the time proceedings were over, I think he simply regarded us as pixilated."

Courtesy dictated that the American visitors should be entertained at a banquet, so the entire party, now swelled to include the crew of our plane and two officers from the transport which had brought the riyals, was invited to return to the Ministry at 7:30. The Arabs present were the minister and his son, an English-speaking deputy-minister of Transportation, and two interpreters. They were outnumbered and outshouted.

A great effort had been made to produce a good show. The banquet table was impressive with silver platters, fine linen and much cutlery. A gigantic feast had been prepared. Most of our party accepted the lack of cocktails without undue grumbling when Moose pointed out that it was contrary to our host's religion to serve intoxicating beverages. But the reception accorded the food left much to be desired. It was what the Arabs regard as a European-style banquet, and began with freshly-pressed tomato juice. I would not have blamed our medico for discreetly indicating that it might be as well not to drink this. In fact I would have left mine, but the minute it appeared the hall was filled with shouts.

"Hey, doc! Is it OK to drink this stuff?"

"Don't you touch it!" yelled back the doctor.

The interpreters, responding to the questioning glance of our host, translated. I looked at Moose and, following his example, drank the juice with a flourish and expressions of joy. Inwardly I was filled with gloomy foreboding not only for my digestive future, once the bugs had had time to operate, but more immediately for the rest of the meal which, I feared, might be uncomfortable in ways other than purely gastronomical. The bugs, it turned out, were kind to me; but aside from that the next few hours exceeded my most dismal expectations. The appearance of every course was greeted with more shouts.

"Give us the word, doc! Safe to eat this stuff?"

And usually, the doc said no. A few of us grew bloated while the rest hungered and the Arabs sat with faces politely blank. The Arabs are very hospitable people. They are also proud. This demonstration was not easy for them to take. It was made no easier by a remark drawn forth by the colonel, who was laboring valiantly to fill the silences between "Hey docs!" He asked the captain of the MP detachment what kind of a trip he'd had, and the captain said it was fine. The food was especially fine; they'd had pork chops almost every day!

Now pork, to a Moslem, is unclean, actively filthy. It was as if an American host entertaining foreigners had seen them refuse his steak, potatoes and salad as unclean and had then heard one say to another, "Oh, we had a fine meal on the way over. We dined on horse manure."

Aside from the conversations about food, the other main feature of the meal was the activity of the photographers. They wandered around shooting off flash bulbs and taking candid camera shots, to the evident bewilderment and distress of the Finance minister. Various members of the party took turns sitting next to him while their picture was taken, thus discombobulating the service of a meal that was already wildly indecorous—not at all in conformity with the grave courtesy of traditional Arab hospitality. This, remember, was a "good will" mission.

I concluded my report: "On the whole it is just as well that almost everyone important was in Riyadh (the king's capital in the interior).

Our prestige is clearly strong enough to survive an occasional descent of this sort, but I can see no satisfactory reason why it should be subjected to such a strain." Unfortunately, this was not the first or the last time in which amateur meddling in Middle Eastern affairs has damaged United States prestige.

On the other hand, it is only fair to recall that our prestige has been high largely because of the activities of "amateurs," or at least of private American citizens. They were amateurs, however, only in the sense that they were not professional diplomats, politicians, or government representatives. In knowledge of the people and the land, they were anything but amateur.

✵ VI ✵

Nationalists—and Nomads

OBVIOUSLY generalizations about the peoples of the Middle East—Arabs, Turks, Persians, Kurds, Armenians, Jews, and a host of others—are just as difficult, just as likely to be misleading, as generalizations about any other peoples. One might think that generalization becomes easier and safer as the group about which it is made diminishes in size. Of the Samaritans, for instance, who number less than three hundred, certain observations may be made with confidence—and the number of exceptions cannot be great. On the other hand, is it easier to make generalizations about the 600,000 Jews of Palestine than about the 30 or 40 million Arabs who are their neighbors? I think it is harder. What significant generalization will apply to a Sephardic Jew coming to Palestine from Spain by way of Turkey, an orthodox rabbi from Poland, an agnostic from Austria, as well as to Jews from Iraq and Yemen? Anything that is true of them all is likely—at this early stage in the history of Israel—to be true of all men. Certain Israeli national characteristics may be expected to appear, may even be already discernible. But it is at least as easy, if not easier, to generalize about Yemenite Jews and Arabs, Kurds and Armenians, as it is to suggest meaningful similarities between Yemenite Jews and their fellow Israelites from Europe. And anyone who still thinks there is any such thing as a "Jewish race" should go to Tel Aviv. In this all-Jewish city you see more racial types than, I believe, in any city of comparable size in the world!

Similar complexities rise to plague you everywhere you turn. For example, what does the Cairene have in common with the Bedu of the Egyptian desert, or the fellah of Upper Egypt? Or, for that matter, what do a Sudanese *suffragi*, a Greek banker, a Copt tax collector, an Armenian watch repairer and a Syrian pasha who made his fortune in cotton, have in common, though all are citizens of Cairo?

Recognizing the difficulties, and the qualifications which must hedge any generalizations about numbers of people, the effort to generalize must still be made as a preliminary step to understanding. The first stage is that of formulating some over-all statements. The next is recognition of the tremendous number of exceptions and contradictions. Then, if you are optimistic enough to feel the task is possible and persistent enough to make it possible, you may find that in spite of all differences there are a few basic and significant similarities which really do prevail. You may agree with Edmond Taylor who, after studying the Indians, concluded that there would be hope for him as long as he remained bewildered. If he ever "discovered the truth" about India, he would be good for nothing save for getting into arguments with friends who had discovered some contrary truth! But there is a difference between discovering *the* truth, and discovering *some* truths which seem to offer a reasonable guide to understanding and action.

Aside from physical geography, common economic pressures and other accompaniments of propinquity, there are a number of forces which operate on peoples to give them "regional" characteristics. Some of these may work both as unifying and as divisive factors. That is, they may make certain elements of the area's population aware of what they have in common chiefly in terms of contrast with other groups. Nationalism is an obvious example.

Nationalism, one of the great products and exports of the European Renaissance, has proven to be pretty murderous in any context. Its birth in Europe was a bloody one. The explosive Balkans, adopting it with enthusiasm, have shown what willing hands and tempers can do with it. But some observers, watching its development in the Orient, have warned in gloomy tones that the world hasn't seen anything yet. They fear that Orientals—reacting to Western imperialism and following the example given by the Japanese, the Moslems and Hindus in India, and the violent new nationalism of Zionism against the equally violent, almost equally new nationalism of the Arabs—may combine such nationalism with rabid xenophobia, a mixture which promises no good to the rest of us.

At first, nationalism in the Middle East exerted a generally unifying force, because it was directed against people who were outsiders. Not just outside of a particular group, but from outside a geographical area. The desire to throw these outsiders back out has been at times common, uniting (aside from the small but influential number who were bought, converted or subverted by the outsider) Arab, Turk, Kurd; Sunni, Shiite, Druze, Maronite, Greek Orthodox, Syriac, Copt and Jew. Now the strongest single political force for unity among the Arabs of all the countries is nationalism—called into hot fierce being by what Arabs conceive to be the latest and most dangerous threat from "outside," from Zionist nationalism. What divides Palestine draws together the neighbors of Palestine—even though a few titular leaders such as Abdullah may try to act otherwise.

Certain generalizations, unhappy ones, can be made about this drawing together. It is a drawing together for destructive rather than constructive ends. The common goal is the rooting out of Zionism rather than the building of a new or the improving of an old social order. It would be entirely untrue to say that there are, among these peoples united in a task of extirpation, no elements anxious to work together for progress and improvement. But it is true that the effect of the Palestine conflict upon Arabs so far has been to set back progressive forces everywhere among them. The shaky and reactionary governments, badly frightened by the defeats they have suffered, have seized the occasion to impose strict censorship (especially on news of their defeats) and to suppress all opposition. This has happened even in the countries where most progress had been made. Lebanon, for instance, now has a stricter censorship than she had under the French, when Lebanese patriots had raged against it.

Thus in most of the Middle East the people who have gained strength from recent developments have been the reactionaries and, as will be explained later, the Communists. This has not been true in Israel, nor is it the fault of Zionism though it is the result of the struggle arising out of Zionism. It is, to some extent, the fault of those United Nations countries who refused to recognize the presence of any justice in the Arab case. This refusal, which inevitably led to violence and an atmosphere favorable to extremists, may have been due in large part to the belief that there were no progressive elements in the Arab world. It ignores, and endangers, the existence of a group known, in the words of Freya Stark's dedication to *The Arab Island*, as "the Young Effendis."

For there have been progressive elements in Arab life of recent generations. One of the most striking features of the twentieth-century Middle East has been the appearance of groups working, some of them vigorously and unselfishly, for the improvement of public health and education, and the elevation of political morality, in what are still comparatively backward and corrupt lands. These groups have organized along national lines in many cases, but they have also reached across political boundaries to join forces in specific programs. Recently the national governments have given formal expression and assistance to collaborative efforts in health, agricultural and broad economic programs. The Young Effendis, sober crusaders in education, government and medicine, are no phenomenon peculiar to any one state. They or their counterparts are to be found from Istanbul to Aden, from Cairo to Teheran.

They are, or could be, the nascent middle class in countries which have known no such thing. Perhaps, the fundamental weakness of the Middle East is that it has, practically, no Middle Class—no bourgeois, educated, professional or white-collar or substantial "middle-man" class. This is both an explanation of its inability to resist Zionism and of its deep-rooted fear of Zionism. The efficiency of modern society depends upon a middle-class—so Arab society has failed so far against the challenge of Palestine. And Zionism is a middle-class movement— with the energy, ability and desire to take over the job of being the middle class for the whole area, which they would thereby rule. The Arabs, who would like to rule themselves, resent and fear the growth of such a group, though many fail to diagnose their resentment and fear for what it is.

Many Young Effendis, however, do reach the correct diagnosis. They know that throughout Arab history there has been, except for a comparatively small urban artisan class, only the aristocracy—the sheikhly families in the tribes and the wealthy merchants in the towns—and the poor, the Bedu and the peasant. Many Arabs divided the world simply into two classes, free men and slaves. The Young Effendis have seen the gap and tried to fill it. Their cry has been education, more education, and still more education—plus a little medicine to keep the students alive. The UN has not given the right kind of medicine.

Another generalization can be made about the Young Effendis. For the most part they are oriented, by education and by example, toward the West. While most of them have drawn heavily upon their own national past, and many specifically assert that the original teachings of Islam and of the Arabic golden age have been their greatest inspiration, a number of them have felt that to achieve progress a radical break with the past is necessary. And almost all have looked outside their own civilization, outside the world of Islam, for at least some guidance and direction.

Many of them are the most ardent nationalists of all. But they feel that to attain full measure of independence and the highest expression of national spirit, it is not necessary to reject everything that has come from the West. They are, essentially, moderates, progressive as distinct from revolutionary. In the Middle East a moderate may be defined as a man working for the advancement of his country along Western liberal lines, one who is not a xenophobe.

Times of strife are hard on moderates. When you condemn outsiders, it is easier to condemn them *in toto*. When you are fighting invasion from the West, it is less complicated to hate everything Western than it is to distinguish between some things that are bad and others that are good. Too much has happened, too many concepts have been absorbed, too many products of Occidental civilization have been adopted, for the impact of the West to be eliminated root and branch. But events are making the new nationalism anti-Western by the very occasion of its being, and by the food it is fed upon. The average inhabitant of the Middle East, like so many of his brothers in other parts of the world, is naturally inclined to hate foreigners and distrust their works. This inclination for the time being is being strengthened by the Palestine conflict; for the time being it is a regional characteristic.

There are two corollaries: First as this inclination grows the strength of moderates and progressives is diminished. So it follows, second, that our own position in the area is deteriorating, both from the weakening of our natural friends (moderates and progressives should be our allies everywhere) and because the United States has pursued a wavering but generally pro-Zionist policy. We have been the most bitterly attacked of all Western powers.

This is ironical, because American education and American ideals of democracy played a vital role in the development of Arab nationalism. But it is true.

In addition to Arab nationalism, there is also Syrian, Egyptian, Iraqi nationalism, to say nothing of Turkish, Iranian, Kurdish and other varieties. The countries do have problems of their own, interests of their own, special attributes which might be described as national. Naturally this is more true of those that have had a longer separate national existence—Turkey and Iran, for instance. The Arab countries, with the exception of Egypt, have existed as units in their present form for only a brief time. It is true that, as states, they do not always co-operate as closely as might be expected. But the differences which tend to separate them are clashes of dynastic interests (Hashemite vs. Saudi or the House of Mohammed Ali,* or personal conflicts, rather than clearly established national rivalries. The rivalries between the great cities, particularly in Iran, have more tradition and body to them in many cases than the rivalries between nations.

The world says confidently of the British that they are phlegmatic and that they muddle through; of the French, that they are frivolous, logical, or immoral; of the Americans, that they are crude, boastful or frighteningly efficient. Of the Middle Eastern countries, most are too young to have had time to develop such generally "recognized" national traits. The Lebanese (the Swiss or hotelkeepers of the Middle East) say that the Iraqi are penurious, that five or six of them will sit at a table admiring the view and sipping water until pressure from the management impels them to buy one cup of coffee for the six. Egyptians regard all Syrians as hard bargainers and smart businessmen, and Egyptians, in return, are thought to be rather gross. Persians are indolent liars, fond of poetry and of gardens; Saudi Arabians fierce puritans, as befits men of the desert.

Those are some of the casual remarks you hear applied to the different nationalities. But they are not widely current or well established as are our own equivalent bromides. The significant bromides of the region

* The Hashemites, descended from Sherif Hussein of Mecca, rule Iraq and Transjordan; the Saudi dynasty is established in Saudi Arabia, the house of Mohammed Ali rules in Egypt.

are about nomad, peasant and townsman—still the most important categories and cleavages of the area, more so than those of nation or even race.

When we think of Middle Eastern peoples we think chiefly of nomads. Numerically they are becoming less and less important. Yet our thoughts do not mislead us in this instance, for the nomads have stamped their image upon the land. The settled peasants and the city-dwellers have taken language, religion and, in many instances, manners and code of honor from them. Townfolk still look with respect to the man from the desert. I remember asking a Palestinian Arab lawyer what he thought of King ibn Saud and he said quickly, "He's a *desert* Arab. He hasn't been corrupted by the city. He is strong and proud."

There is also, of course, hatred and fear. The settled have good reason to hate disturbers of the peace; tribesmen have raided and plundered the villages, even the kingdoms, of the settled. The history of much of the region is a history of periodic waves thrown up from the Arabian desert—waves of invading nomads who conquered, and eventually settled, and were finally conquered in their turn by a later wave. That history helps to explain how the townsman's fear of the nomad, and even his occasional contempt, is tempered by nostalgic admiration. My ancestors, he thinks, were once like that—bold and harsh and strong.

That is why many Egyptian peasants, attached to the land for centuries, adhere to a desert code of honor which, in its insistence upon personal retaliation for injury, is not suited to their lives or temperaments. (The result is that in many villages it has become customary to hire a professional killer to execute the punishment required by the desert code—that injury to any member of your family or tribe shall be repaid in blood from the family or tribe of the offender.)

If you meet a Bedu in the desert and ask him who he is, he will reply "el homdul illah, I'm a Moslem." You will have to ask him specifically what his name is to get the reply which we would normally give to the question, who are you? The average nomad may be careless in the practice of his religion, but if you want to reach him with any appeal besides his tribe, it has got to be religion. No political appeal is meaningful.

The tribes of Iraq, Syria, Transjordan and Saudi Arabia have more in common with each other than with their fellow citizens, the townspeople of, respectively, Baghdad, Damascus, Amman and Jidda. The Shammar tribe, for example, has branches in Syria and Iraq, and the tribal loyalty transcends any feeling of loyalty to the state. For the Bedu, blood relationship is the most important factor in society. It binds families together in clans, and clans in tribes. It unites small groups and stamps them distinctively, apart from all other men. Identity is complete; injury to any member of a tribe can be avenged by anyone in that tribe upon any member of the tribe of the man who committed the injury.

Thus blood relationship binds together the most individualistic of peoples. For it is completely erroneous to regard, as is commonly done, the Beduin as antisocial or asocial. He is and must be primarily a social being, an integral member of one of the most extreme forms of group life, analogous to the group life of an army. At the same time, blood relationship gives him the occasion to express his individuality, which might be described as extreme egotism, where those outside the blood tie are concerned. Traditionally the Beduin owes nothing to anyone (except a guest) outside the family. He recognizes no loyalty to any leader outside the tribe. One of the desert prayers says "God have mercy on me and Mohammed and no one else beside."

Within the tribe all its members have the same rights and the same obligations which come from the blood relationship. They are obliged to stand by their fellow members in bad times as well as in good, without questioning whether their brother may be right or wrong. The leaders of the tribe are men selected on the basis of their personal qualities and abilities. Their position rests upon their moral strength and on their physical strength as well. They have no legal power to enforce any of their decisions. Since there is no constituted authority, it follows also that there is no tribal law. Against thieves or murderers private justice is the only recourse, and since a murderer's family usually takes his side, according to tribal custom, a blood feud is the common result. These feuds can continue for generations. Payment can be made in atonement for blood guilt and the tribal leaders must attempt to see that some sort of compromise payment is agreed to. However since they cannot normally enforce their decisions, payment is usually agreed to only after long and protracted blood letting. One of the greatest difficulties ibn Saud has had to overcome was in the establishment of his own position as dispenser of justice over all the tribes of his kingdom. Still, in many areas, a man must depend upon himself and upon his family, rather than upon law or law-enforcement officers to protect his rights. Inevitably, in such a society, the greatest of importance is attached to personal honor.

There are still places and tribes in the desert where the modern world has hardly penetrated or made itself felt. Its one important contribution has been the rifle. Raiding continues, as it has since the beginning of time, but the rifle has made it somewhat more efficient—if you have cartridges that fit your rifle. Daggers are still worn, the hooked, ceremonial ones and the straight sharp working knives hanging from the belt. The costume is unchanged, a shift-like undergarment, the camel's hair *abba*, and the white (occasionally red or black-checked) *keffiyeh* held in place over the head by a plaited *agal*. In some tribes the women are not normally veiled, but it is a serious discourtesy to the man to take any note of his womenfolk.

My wife and I once visited a tribe in the desert near Beersheba in which we thought views would be very liberal. The traditional forms were of course observed. A fire was made, coffee ceremoniously ground, the polite phrases spoken and, when food was brought, we dipped into the great dish of sheep and rice using only our right hand. (The left hand serves in various connections with the toilet, and is therefore considered unclean. To eat with it would be a shocking breach of manners.)

In the course of conversation we discovered that the sheikh's three sons had attended the university in Cairo, and one of them was hoping to continue his studies in America. They would not let us take their picture in Bedu costume, for they said Zionists used such pictures to make propaganda against the Arabs. But they gave us pictures, taken in Cairo, showing them in European clothing. They were, obviously, cultured and knowledgeable young men. But when my wife, hearing sounds of movement in the next tent, asked if that was where their sisters lived, there was uncomfortable silence. She repeated her question thinking it had not been heard, and one of the boys replied with embarrassed politeness: "It is not proper for me to speak of the women in the company of men!"

To a stranger, the problem of how to treat the wives and daughters of Middle Easterners he meets is often perplexing. In many cases, of course, the question does not arise because you do not meet the women. Most of the time you will be safe if you do not mention them or take any notice of them. Yet in some homes that would be considered rude, just as it would be if a visitor did the same thing in this country. In many Lebanese families, for example, the girls are treated much as they are here. As a general rule, the greater the contact has been with the West, the more liberal is the treatment of women. The U.S. Army *Soldier's Guides*, issued during the last war, advised: "Never make advances to Moslem women or try to attract their attention in the streets or other public places. Do not loiter near them when they are shopping. If a woman has occasion to lift her veil while shopping, do not stare or smile at her. Look the other way. Do not try to photograph women. These rules are extremely important. The Moslems will immediately dislike you and there will be trouble if you do not treat women according to their standards and customs. These rules apply both to the cities and towns and to the villages and the desert. The village and desert women go unveiled more often than the women in the cities and *seem* to have more freedom. But the rules are still strict." This is no longer as universally true as it was. But you can get into plenty of trouble, even in Cairo, by taking a picture of a woman. Many of them like it and will simper sweetly for the camera. But if you run into one who doesn't like the idea, my advice is to skip it quickly. Or first thing you know there'll be so much fuss you might think you had raped her.

The tribes, and the nomadic life, are on the way out. But it would not do to underrate their strength or the contributions they can yet make. It is the standards, and not the abilities, that are so far removed from other more modern forms of society. To take one example, we consider that the illiterate is an abnormal, generally useless member of society. But that is to some extent a matter of context. In a literate country, where the reading of newspapers, books, magazines and so forth is essential to community life, the illiterate is left out, a misfit and incompetent who cannot participate adequately in society. But in some societies still remaining in the world, including many nomadic societies, the illiterate is normal. The local culture is based on widespread illiteracy, with memory taking the place of ability to read. The illiterate may be extremely clever, a pillar of society. (The Beduin are not, of course, wholly illiterate; the sheikhly families are often well educated. The poet al Mutanabbi summed up Beduin life in verse: "I am known by the night, the horse and the desert, By the sword and the guest, the paper and the pen.")

Toynbee remarks that nomadic civilization is in some ways higher than agricultural civilization. Their difficult life allows nomads no time or strength to struggle for anything but survival. But it also develops fine qualities—independence, pride, a high sense of honor, close family loyalties.

Adjusting the nomadic tribes to the new way of life is one of the fundamental problems facing the Middle Eastern countries. Relations between tent, village and town are difficult, and often threatening. In later chapters they will be discussed in more detail. Here we are concerned only with the fact that these relations cut across national lines and create many of the characteristics which differentiate the Middle East from the West.

☆ VII ☆

"There is One God"

E L HOMDUL ILLAH—Praise be to God, I am a Moslem."
The religion of the Moslem, Islam, is simple, austere, specific
in the beliefs and actions it requires from its adherents and capable
of an unusual degree of toleration. Islam is obviously one of the greatest forces in the molding of the Middle East "character." It is the faith
of most of the area's inhabitants, the most pervasive single influence
in their lives.

Many of us think of this religion, which we usually and misleadingly
call Mohammedanism after its major prophet, as a wild cult which
promises a heaven filled with dark-eyed and very affectionate damsels
to men who are killed in battle against the infidel. Whirling dervishes
are a part of the setup, too, though we are a little vague as to just
where they fit in. We also know that "Mohammedans" flop up and
down on prayer rugs, uttering queer chants, several times a day. This
is a reasonably accurate picture as far as it goes. Similarly, it would be
accurate to describe Christianity as a religion which teaches that the
world was created in six days, whose heaven is filled with harp-playing
angels, and whose holy men sit on top of pillars fasting in the desert.

Actually, Islam is a plain, puritanical faith. There is no priestly
caste, because Mohammed and his followers believe that no one else
can intercede between the individual and God (Allah). Mullahs, muftis,
Imams, and other religious leaders of Moslem society, are primarily
the expounders of Islamic law, although they may also have responsibilities in the administration of the Wakf (charitable funds) and care
of the mosques. They may lead the faithful in prayer but so may any
Moslem of good character. They may chant the call for prayer, they

may preach on the holy days. But they are not in any way an essential link between man and God: their services, or the withholding of them, cannot affect a man's salvation.

One day a few years ago my wife and I, together with a Western-minded Egyptian friend, paid a visit to one of the great centers of Islamic learning, the al-Azhar University in Cairo. Mustapha, as I shall call the friend, is a plumpish young man who manages to combine great decorum with a well-developed sense of the ridiculous. He comes from a prominent family, received most of his education in France and England, and is a professing Moslem who seems to find no difficulty in reconciling his religion—or, as he chooses to put it, his "faith" —with his Western learning. "Stripped of a lot of complicated language," he used to tell us, "my faith is simple, far simpler than most denominations of Christianity. I believe there is One God, Allah, the Creator and Ordainer. I do not have to bother with such complications as a Trinity! And yet my God is the same as yours."

Now Mustapha was taking us to call upon a very learned and holy man, a professor of the university, Sheikh Hassan, who was to explain the doctrines of Islam to two friendly "unbelievers." After the formalities essential to politeness had been observed, my wife opened the discussion with some preliminary questions: What, she wanted to know, is the meaning of the different words we use, Mohammedanism, Islam, and Moslem? Before she could make any sense of words like Shia and Sunni, she thought she should know the more general terms.

The old sheikh smiled at her. He was a fine-looking man with serene eyes and brown skin, smooth and glowing like well-finished vellum. Inevitably, he had a long white beard and wore a turban wound around his red tarboosh.

"Islam is the name of our religion," he explained. "It means, in your language, 'submission.' Moslem, or Muslim, is the word for 'one professing submission,' a practicer of Islam. Our creed is, There is no God but Allah and Mohammed is His Messenger."

"You usually translate 'Mohammed is His Prophet,'" interposed Mustapha, "but actually the word used means messenger. And we never use the word Mohammedan which among you is the common way to refer to Moslems."

"You know," said Sheikh Hassan matter-of-factly, "we believe that

Christians and Jews worshiped the One God, but their doctrines became corrupted. Allah was also worshiped by Arabs before Mohammed came, but the religion needed purifying. That was Mohammed's great task."

"Then you wouldn't regard us as absolute pagans," said my wife.

The sheikh nodded agreement. "You are what we call 'people of the Book.' Your Bible, like the Hebrew Torah, has much true religion in it. We feel that the Jews went astray when they rejected Jesus, who was a true prophet. But you Christians seem to us at fault in that you make Jesus a God. We believe that he was an inspired mortal, just as Mohammed was."

This reminded me of an old theory of mine, that the cleavage, theologically, between Moslem and Christian is more serious than that between Moslem and Jew. To a Moslem, as I realized from many conversations with Mustapha, the doctrine of the Trinity is at best confused and idolatrous. More likely, it is a denial of the cardinal belief of Islam, the unity of God; those who adhere to it cannot be regarded as monotheists. But the Jews are guilty, in Moslem eyes, of no more than the repudiation of a prophet. This is a crime, to be sure, but a far less serious one than the blasphemous fragmentation of the Holy Indivisibility of Allah. I put my theory to Sheikh Hassan, who nodded gravely. It was a most ingenious theory, he told me, his eyes twinkling. Then, seriously, he said: "We have no quarrel with Jews over religion. We think they are wrong on some things, but not as wrong, nor wrong in as many things, as a lot of other peoples. Do not ever think that the fight in Palestine is over religion. It is simply a resistance to invasion."

Islam is a very *practical* religion in the sense that its tenets are simple to grasp and its rules of life are clearly laid down. Having accepted the unity of God and the revelations of His Will as reported by Mohammed, the believer, Sheikh Hassan explained, has four other main obligations.

"He must pray in the prescribed manner the prescribed number of times each day, wherever the hour of prayer shall find him. In the street, his home or place of business, he must drop what he is doing, free his mind from worldly thoughts, and go through the eight postures while repeating the Holy words and facing in the direction of Mecca."

(At the sheikh's suggestion, Mustapha illustrated the different postures for us.) "The hours of prayer are dawn, midday, midafternoon, sunset, and the hour of retiring."

In addition to this regimen of prayer, the believer is required to fast between dawn and sunset during the month of Ramadan, and to make, if possible, the pilgrimage to Mecca. (This latter gives him great merit and the title of haj or hadji.) He also has to contribute one tenth of his income to charity, that being the Poor Rate established by religious law. To give less than that is a sin, and the tithe does not count as alms, for it is a set obligation. To give over and above that is a charity to which all believers are urged.

The Poor Rate is an example of the matter-of-fact way in which Mohammed approached his problems. He set great store in charity; as a practical matter, some sort of communal care for widows and orphans is necessary if more than a fortunate few of them are to survive the hardships of desert nomadic life. Actually Mohammed himself provided for the widows of his fallen comrades by going through the form of marriage with them and providing for them himself, and this is a common procedure for brothers to follow in nomadic society. The necessity for community action in hardship cases has markedly tempered the fierce individualism of the desert Arab on other scores.

A practical man, however, was bound to recognize the difficulties involved in administering a charitable program if the funds available to it were uncertain, depending upon the unpredictable if generous whims of men. And so Mohammed set a fixed Poor Rate. It may be argued that this makes the contribution no longer charity but a tax, and thus discourages generosity of spirit. But it does keep the widows and orphans from want, and the number of beggars in Moslem countries who live off alms given over and above the tithe suggests that the well-springs of charity have not gone bone dry under this system.

Others of Mohammed's regulations and prescriptions were motivated by concern for public health. His stress on the virtues of running water, the ablutions required before prayer, the prohibition of pig's flesh (which spoils very easily, and is generous host to worms) and of wine are cases in point. So is the way he went about limiting sexual license. He forbade adultery, but recognizing that monogamy would be too difficult to enforce, he allowed a regulated polygamy. His marriage and divorce laws, and the property rights he guaranteed to women, represent a very successful effort to improve conditions as he found them.

One feature of Islam which deserves mention is the importance attached by the faithful to holy places. For a while, Sheikh Hassan told us, in the early days of Islam, Jerusalem was the holiest city of all, and it was there that Moslems turned in prayer. Moses and Jesus are conceived to be the two great predecessor prophets to Mohammed, and Mecca obtained its present importance only after Mohammed had been infuriated by the Jews of Medina. Since he acknowledged Moses and the Torah, he expected that the Jews in turn would accept him and his revelations. But they did not, and he turned against them. Reconsideration of the matter led him to name Mecca as the holy of holies, for it was there, according to Mohammed, that Abraham and Ishmael had erected the Ka'ba as a temple to the one God.

Then there is the tomb of Mohammed in Medina (next to Mecca the holiest of cities), and, of special veneration to the Shiites, the tombs of Hussein at Kerbala and Ali al-Rida at Meshed.

Also, there are the Holy Places in Palestine, including the rock from which Mohammed is supposed to have taken off on his magic steed for a visit to heaven. For the eclipse of Jerusalem, in spite of Mohammed's anger against the Jews, was temporary and relative. Palestine was conquered by the Moslems in 636, and a land already holy to two of the world's great religions became venerated by, and under the domination of, a third. Now contention over that same land threatens relations among the same three bodies.

Moslems, like Christians, are divided broadly into two main branches, the Sunnites and the Shiites. The former, whose name means "traditionalists," are the orthodox majority, stricter theologically but practically more tolerant than the Shiites. The latter, the "legitimist" party who supported the claim of the Prophet's cousin and son-in-law Ali to the caliphate, insist that to be authoritative a tradition must be traceable back to the family of the Prophet. They attach considerable importance to the Imam, whose coming was foretold by Mohammed, and who must be by very nature without sin and error. Many Shiites believe that Ali, who was the first Imam, never died; many more cling to the same view on Mehdi, the twelfth Imam; others believe in the transmigration of souls. There is general belief in a "Concealed Imam," but this doctrine means different things to different believers. To some, Ali is the only Imam and is being hidden by God until the time is ripe for his return. To others there have been a series of Imams among the descendants of the Prophet, but their identity is known only to a small circle; at the right moment, the true Imam will be revealed to the whole world.

As Mustapha told us later, many of the wilder offshoots of Islam have developed from versions of the Imamist doctrine, and the Shiites are in general more fanatical in their views and practices than the orthodox Moslems. In the Middle East, Saudi Arabia, Egypt, Turkey, Transjordan and Syria are Sunnite countries. Iran is Shiite, Iraq has a Shia majority, and there are significant Shiite elements in southern Arabia, Lebanon and northern Palestine.

There was one particular doctrinal point about which I wished to ask Sheikh Hassan, the importance of fatalism in Islam. Submission to the Will of God is, of course, emphasized in the very name of the religion. Before our visit I had carefully read up on this point.

Actually the predestination of Mohammed, doctrinally, is far less severe than that of Calvin. God does not predoom some to damnation; rather He allows those who will not listen to Him to wander to their ruin. Of hypocrites, Mohammed said "They forget God and He forgets them."

"The preaching of predestination is not meant to make the sinner feel his helplessness, but to warn him of his peril if he rejects the message."* It appears to have appealed to Mohammed largely as an explanation of how it was possible, in view of the unquestionable revelations he had received, that there could still be those who rejected his claims. One answer could be that God had ordained that some men should believe and be saved, but that others should perish in unbelief.

A number of Moslem theologians after Mohammed went beyond his predestinationism to a determinism of the most rigid kind. According to some, God not only creates man but, one by one, each of their acts; man does not act voluntarily, as he believes, nor does he make choices of himself; "the power of choice is created, the choice determined, the act affected, by God; man's participation in it is solely

---

* George Foot Moore, *History of Religions*, Vol. II, New York, 1928.

that of appropriation [*kasb*], by which, in his own mind, he makes the choice and the act his."* Thus the principle of causality, of a natural order of events with one deriving logically from the other, is completely denied. Moslems who follow this teaching are theoretically in doubt from one moment to the next whether the sun will continue in its path, whether water will be wet or ice cold, or whether their arm may not fly away from their body or themselves from the earth. (As a matter of practice, we can assume that very few Moslems live in such a state of philosophic uncertainty.)

Other philosophers of Islam rejected this doctrine, and held that men have the ability and the obligation to choose between right and wrong. If they sin, it is their own fault and they are punished justly. It is difficult to reconcile this view with that of a God who foreordains the fate of each individual (you can of course argue that He foresees but does not foreordain—i.e. that He is omniscient but not omnipotent). However, many theologians have succeeded, at least to their own satisfaction.

This problem of why an omnipotent deity should allow some men to go, for lack of faith which He could give, to eternal damnation, is a knotty theological issue which has taxed the brains and consciences of many. Mohammed's solution is not an original or an uncommon one. It has, if accepted literally and interpreted rigorously, obvious dangers to the further development of a community. That was what I wanted to ask the sheikh about—a touchy subject but one which didn't seem to me to involve too much technical theology.

I was wrong in the latter theory. The sheikh's reply was difficult for Mustapha to translate with any confidence. We did gather, beyond any possible doubt, that Sheikh Hassan was convinced that belief in the immutability of God's will need not hamper man's natural efforts to improve his lot on earth. The subtleties of the argument were beyond us all, including Mustapha. But Mustapha had some arguments of his own which we could understand. Recalling his study of English and American history, he asked,

"Weren't the Calvinists the most prosperous, hardest-working people in their communities? Weren't many of the founders of America

* Ibid.

Calvinists? And wasn't Calvin one of the strictest predestinarians of all time?"

He was right on all scores. We sat and thought for a while. My wife remarked that Bunyan was a stanch Calvinist. Yet *Pilgrim's Progress* is not the work of a man who thought that, since all was predetermined, there was no use in man's striving. Many believers in predestination seem to have been spurred on to greater efforts in the practical world by a desire to prove to themselves and their neighbors, by worldly achievement and upright living, that they were (at least likely) members of the elect. Belief in that particular doctrine need not necessarily, we must agree, be a bar to progress.

That was true. But I made one mental reservation. If Islam is to be blamed, as it must to some extent be, for the lack of progress of the Moslem world, it is far more plausible to argue that responsibility lies not with the doctrine of predestination but with the fact that Mohammed, who was a great reformer and who probably made over his own society as effectively as any man in history, made the mistake of labeling what he did as revelations, the final word of God. Therefore, to many pious Moslems, what was right in Mohammed's time is right today— twelve centuries of change to the contrary not withstanding.

Sheikh Hassan, who had asked Mustapha to repeat for him in Arabic what he had been saying to us in English, turned to me again.

"If you look for explanation of the backwardness of our countries," he said earnestly, "you should look not to religion but to nature and disease. We were speaking of the Prophet's interest in public health. He had the vision to go right to the heart of our problem. How can men be active in citizenship when they are so eaten away by parasites that they have barely the strength to get a little food to keep a little life still in themselves?"

"But," I inquired, "mightn't fatalism be partly responsible for that? I have heard Egyptian social workers complain that when they try to get mothers to keep the flies off their infants' eyes, the mothers shrug their shoulders and say 'What can we do? It is the will of Allah.' "

"That is because the mothers themselves are so weak from bilharziasis or some such thing that they haven't the energy to do otherwise," said Mustapha quickly. "Until we can educate doctors who can train the people to observe the rules of health, we can expect no progress. And how will the doctors be trained until we are healthy enough to impose our will upon our government and *insist* that they be trained? Our trouble now is that we are trying to obtain *through* democracy the training and abilities *without which* democracy cannot exist. And our liberal friends in other countries encourage us in our folly!"

Sheikh Hassan clapped his hands for coffee, and for the rest of our visit we talked of less unpleasant things.

VIII
The Past was Promising

MANY Arabs argue that though they are divided into several national states, the ties which bind them together are actually stronger than the ties binding a Texan to a Rhode Islander. Americans have had at most a few hundred years of common background, while Arabs are linked in a past which stretches back for thousands of years. The reader will already be aware that this argument is not wholly convincing. There are some forces which have tended to unite the diverse peoples of the Middle East, including the Arabs. But even religion—as for instance in the Sunni-Shiite controversies—has had a divisive effect as well as a unifying one, among Arabs as elsewhere.

Nevertheless the Arab argument, though exaggerated greatly, has some substance. In spite of the failure of every attempt so far to achieve union, a strong community of interests and background is widely recognized. Language, and the sense of history, have contributed to this.

The dominant language is Arabic. Remarkably rich and flexible, it lacks any established modern scientific or technical vocabulary. In some countries the attempt has been made to adapt or compound classical words to meet this lack. Mostly, however, it has been met by incorporating English, French or German words into the Arabic. For example, the words "radio" and "telephone" are in general use. A classical word, *hatef*, meaning "to make repeated calls" or "to holler," exists for telephone, but is rarely used. A phonograph, however, is generally known as *haki*. Automobiles are called automobiles in Palestine and Syria, but in Iraq the classical *sayyarah*, meaning "thing that moves by itself," is used.

The fact that today Arabic lacks a modern scientific vocabulary does not mean that it has always lacked one. A thousand years ago it was the most important scientific language of all. Through Arabic the thoughts of Aristotle and other great Greeks were transmitted to European Christendom. Some masterpieces of Greek scientific thought survived, in fact, only in Arabic translation. The tongue which developed to meet the requirements of the desert Beduin (it has some two hundred words for camel, according to the beast's age, sex, color, speed, and other attributes) also met the scientific, classical and religious requirements of empire. For next to Islam, the Arabic language was the strongest cement, and most lasting effect of the Arab conquests. It took permanent root in many of the conquered lands which later gained their independence. It is today the chief reason why peoples who are not racially of the same stock as the Arab of the Arabian peninsula do nonetheless regard themselves as Arabs. At the height of Arab power, Arabic was more widely spoken than any language save the Latin which had preceded it. Moslem culture produced in Spain the finest civilization in Europe of the time.

It made itself felt beyond the limits of conquest too. The English language owes, in addition to its numerals, many words to Arabic. To take only a few of those beginning with "al" (many of them do) there are: alcohol, algebra, albacore, alcazar, alchemy, alfalfa, and alkaline. None of them, sad to say, are of much help to an American trying to speak Arabic. If you asked, for instance, for alcohol firmly, loudly and long enough your listener might eventually (if he were very imaginative yet without knowledge of European tongues) bring you a kind of powdered antimony known as *kohl*, from which our word came. But it is used, rather like mascara, to darken the eyelids; properly applied it may intoxicate others, but not the consumer.

Arabic is a hard language to master. There is a common saying that most words in Arabic have four meanings. The second meaning is the contrary of the first; if the word commonly means "coming" it will also, in some circumstances, mean "going." The third meaning will relate to camels—perhaps, in this imaginary case, it will refer to the gait of a white female three-year-old bred in the Nejd and blind in the left eye. The fourth meaning will be unprintable. (Among serious students of the field, a number assert that Arabic possesses the richest treasury of obscenely insulting phrases of any language, living or dead, known to man. Thus it does not always serve as a force to bring people to-gether.)

Turks, Persians and Afghanis, of course, do not speak Arabic as a native tongue, though most of them do venerate it as the language of the Koran. And some groups within the "Arab" lands, such as Kurds, Druzes and Copts, speak Arabic but retain a very strong sense of identity as people not of Arabic race or nationality. Yet on the whole the Arabic language must rate as one of the great common heritages of the Middle East.

Many Middle Eastern peoples also have in common a sense of past glories—some further in the past than others. The Pharaonic glories of Egypt and the great achievements of the Persian Empire have at least remoteness in common. The later triumphs of the Arab conquests under the caliphs are more closely a shared glory, but even from that many of the Middle East peoples are excluded.

Arabs everywhere, however, look back to it with pride if not always with complete understanding. The Arab conquest—the great moment in Arab history—did not offer a new civilization. The desert did not have that to offer. But the Arabs did bring new life, some new ideas and new ways of expressing ideas, to older civilizations then on the decline.

Professor Sarton of Harvard University says: "One may speak of the miracle of Arabic culture as one speaks of the miracle of Greek culture, the meaning of the word being the same in both cases. What hap-pened was so extraordinary that there is no way of accounting for it in rational terms." The birth and the rapid development of Arabic science is almost without historical parallel. And the Moslems were not mere imitators and transmitters. In mathematics and astronomy they con-tributed a new arithmetic and a new trigonometry. Omar Khayyam, known to us for his witty, fatalistic verse, was also a great mathe-matician. His algebraic system was the first to succeed in solving cubic equations by algebra and geometry. (Omar, like many other great Mos-lem contributors to knowledge, was not an Arab but a Persian.)

In philosophy, Arab scholars did more than translate Aristotle, though that in itself was a great service. Philosophers of history, up to and including Professor Arnold Toynbee, owe much to their work, par-ticularly to the great fourteenth-century political philosopher ibn Khaldoun. Lawyers too have benefited; early Moslem laws of evidence and contract were far ahead of anything of their kind in Europe. The mercantile laws of the Arabs introduced bills of exchange into Europe; words like "check" and "douane" (French for customhouse) were derived from Arab practices. Much of the Code Napoleon and other Western law codes is drawn from medieval Arab law and legal commentary. Moslem architecture produced some of the masterpieces of world history—the Moorish Palace of Alhambra, the Giraldo Tower of Seville, the al-Azhar Mosque in Cairo, the great *midan* (public square) in Isfahan, and the Taj Mahal are a few that spring to mind. The dome and minaret, particularly with the pure quick colors of the best Persian tiles, is surely one of the most breath-takingly beautiful combinations men have ever developed. At its height Islamic culture and life was a fair flower of the world.

Unfortunately its collapse was almost as sudden as its rise. After the fourteenth century science and philosophy declined rapidly. For a period the Middle East under the Arabs served again in what should be its natural cultural role—that of bridge between East and West. It preserved the heritage of the West for the West; but the Western Renaissance, which owed so much to the East, made almost no impression in the Moslem world. In fact, in Islam, theology reigned as the integrating science and dominating cultural and intellectual force. Authority and tradition, rather than observation and experiment, were the proof positive to an Islamic student, just as they had been to the Christian scholastic.

It was the growth of Islamic dogmatism which was the main cause of the decline and eventual collapse of Arabic science. This is not an unusual situation. The theologian who knows the whole truth and knows that he knows it can have very little patience with a man who is always searching for the truth; a scientist who is never satisfied with the amount of truth already available to him, is always questioning to eliminate error and to enlarge upon what he knows and is always ready to discard something even if it has been accepted for generations when evidence or experiment shows it to be wrong. This is the very antithesis of an orthodox reliance upon tradition and written authority.

The supremacy of theology as a science always means the death of other sciences. This was true in medieval Europe and it was true in

Islam. It is the danger of any revealed religion. The Book always tends
to become the great authority backed by tradition. It took the West a
long time to shake off the domination of the Book. The Moslem East
has not yet succeeded in doing so, although in the last few generations
the hold of strict orthodoxy has been badly shaken and new ideas have
been penetrating even such fortresses of tradition as al-Azhar University in Cairo.

One thing about the Middle East likely to surprise Americans is the
tremendous respect, amounting almost to awe, in which learned men
are held. In our country, outstanding scientists may command such respect; their words even on subjects far removed from their field will
command a hearing. The college professor in general, however, is popularly dismissed as a faintly ridiculous, absent-minded impractical
creature. Not so, among Moslems. The first time the difference was impressed upon me was during the war, when I was preparing a report
upon Arab attitudes toward the United States. I found that well-
informed Arabs were deeply concerned by Zionist petitions on Palestine
circulated among American university and schoolteachers. In fact those
petitions aroused much more attention in the Arab world than they ever
did, in my experience, at home. The Arabs assumed that if teachers
signed such documents, the American government would immediately
respond by adopting the policy advocated by their most influential and
important citizens. As an ex-teacher myself, it embarrassed me to recall
how many of us had signed almost any petition presented if casual reading indicated that it was at least harmless. It was less trouble to sign
than to argue, and in the days before the Un-American Affairs Committee no one paid any attention to what a professor signed anyhow.

In addition to the treasured memory of past glory, the Middle Eastern
peoples share other, more recent, memories. These are bitter memories
of domination by outside powers, and of intensifying struggles against
such domination. Mongols from east Asia, Crusaders from Europe and
the modern imperialisms of Russia, England, France and Italy have at
different times ruled different parts of the Middle East. There have also
been local imperialisms; at the outbreak of World War I the Ottoman
(Turkish) Empire held sway over most of the Arab areas, Anatolia, and
much of the Balkans. The history of the modern Middle East really begins with the breakup of the old Ottoman Empire.

That breakup began before 1914. The European part of the empire had been drastically shrunk, and even in the Middle East the Turks had suffered losses, particularly in North Africa. Egypt, under the founder of its present royal house, Mohammed Ali, had gained practical independence from the Turks though still owing them formal allegiance. (Egypt found, however, that she had shaken off the Turks only to receive the British in their place.)

In other areas Turkish rule at the outbreak of the war was still in fact effective. Areas which now make up Syria, Lebanon, Palestine, Iraq, Transjordan, and Saudi Arabia were administratively part of the Ottoman Empire, though the effectiveness of the Turkish administration varied according to the distance from Constantinople. Arab nationalism and the desire to overthrow Turkish rule had been on the rise in these areas for several generations. Secret societies were active and educated opinion was aroused. The war offered an obvious opportunity for Arab national aspirations to be achieved.

The British, who were hard pressed in the area, expressed sympathy with these aspirations. Negotiations for Arab support against the Turks led to the making of certain "promises" which gave concrete expression and aims to Arab nationalism. One of these "promises," made by Sir Henry MacMahon in correspondence with Sherif Hussein of Mecca, has received attention and been the subject of much debate in connection with the controversy over Palestine. Actually MacMahon's correspondence has far broader significance than that. In it the British assured Sherif Hussein of their readiness to recognize Arab independence in territories bounded by the borders of Persia, the Indian Ocean, the Red Sea and the Mediterranean. A reservation was made, excepting those parts of Syria lying to the west of the districts of Damascus, Hama and Aleppo. These regions, according to MacMahon's note, "cannot be said to be purely Arab." In a later note, MacMahon specified that the reservations of Great Britain with regard to these areas were because of the interests of their ally, France.

MacMahon's promise, made in 1916, has been interpreted in many different senses by various British spokesmen. Many of them have held that Palestine was intended to be an exception, but Arabs deny that anyone would have gathered this from the wording of the promise. In 1939 the British government formally recognized that the Arab case based upon the MacMahon correspondence was 'far stronger than had previously been admitted.

However, the British had also made other commitments in 1916. In the Sykes-Picot agreement with France, the heart of the Ottoman Empire was divided into five areas. Two were to be under such administration or control as Britain and France respectively might desire. The French zone ran north from what is now Lebanon well into Anatolia. The British zone included the Tigris and Euphrates valleys from Baghdad to Basra. Two other, larger zones were established in which British and French influence respectively might predominate. The French sphere ran roughly from Damascus to Mosul, the British from Kirkuk to Aqaba. A fifth zone, made up of what corresponds roughly to modern Palestine, was to be under some form of international administration to be agreed upon by the Allies and representatives of Sherif Hussein of Mecca.

It was difficult enough to reconcile the Sykes-Picot agreement with MacMahon's promise. But the following year (1917) the British added still another conflicting promise (or what has, at least, turned out in execution to be a conflicting promise). That was the famous Balfour Declaration, in which it was stated: "His Majesty's Government view with favor the establishment in Palestine of a national home for the Jewish people, and will use their best endeavors to facilitate the achievement of this object, it being clearly understood that nothing shall be done which may prejudice the civil and religious rights of existing non-Jewish communities in Palestine or the rights and political status enjoyed by Jews in any other country." (The reader who is interested in the negotiations which led up to this declaration, and the promises with which it is in conflict, will find an excellent account in Nevill Barbour's book, *Palestine Star or Crescent?*.)

In the meantime, on the strength of the MacMahon correspondence, the Arabs revolted against the Ottoman Empire and fought the famous campaign with which the name of T. E. Lawrence is so widely associated. A high value was placed on their military assistance by General Allenby and other British leaders. Toward the end of the war, as success was apparently within their grasp, seven Arab leaders addressed a memorandum to the British government requesting more specific assurances of British intentions. This "Memorandum of the Seven" brought a most reassuring response. The British pledged themselves to work for liberation of Syria, Palestine and Iraq, which were to be assured freedom and independence. No regime would be set up in any of those areas which was not acceptable to their population. In November 1918, the British and French together issued a declaration stating that their aims in the Middle East were the complete and final liberation of the populations living under the Turkish yoke. They promised the Arabs that they would have "national governments chosen by themselves in the free exercise of their will."

Almost immediately, however, it became apparent that these promises were, at best, disingenuous. Not only in Palestine (where further explicit promises had been made to the inhabitants by General Allenby) but also in Iraq, Syria and Lebanon, the British and French set up administrations which were not in any sense "national governments chosen by the Arabs in the free exercise of their will." Feisal, son of Sherif Hussein of Mecca, reviewed the Arab case at the Peace Conference, but to no avail. A "National Assembly" was elected by the Arabs and met in Damascus, where it asserted the independence of Syria (including Palestine) and of Iraq. Feisal was chosen as King of Syria and his brother, Abdullah, as King of Iraq. Their "rules" were short. The Peace Conference and the League of Nations assigned to the French mandates over Syria and Lebanon, and to the British mandates over Palestine and Iraq. The French forces entered Damascus and forced Feisal to leave. With his departure, the prospects of Arab independence in a single state or a federation of states came to an end for the time being. Abdullah had not even taken up his crown in Iraq.

The bitterness engendered by what the Arabs could only regard as a complete betrayal was deep seated and long lasting. It has been directed, naturally, chiefly against the British and the French, but most of all, against the British. From time to time in different parts of the Arab world, the British appear by subsequent actions to have vindicated themselves and to have earned, if only temporarily, the right to be considered as the Arabs' friend. But always under the surface, and usually not far under the surface, there is bitterness—available to demagogues (and the Russians) for whatever purpose they may choose.

The drive for Arab union has been gaining in intensity over the last years, although it suffered a severe setback as a result of the British-

French betrayal. The types of union advocated have varied considerably. Adherents of the Pan Islamic movement urge that a single state be created to include all the Arabs from North Africa to Iran, as a first step toward a state to include all the Moslems of Asia and Africa. The Pan Islamists are reactionaries who oppose all Western influences, cultural or political. Other forms of union advocated include a federation of existing Arab states to be linked together in close economic, cultural and perhaps political ties. Federation has received the backing of most progressive Arabs.

The Arab League, which began formation in the fall of 1944, represents the latest and most concrete move toward that goal. Its establishment was encouraged by British and American representatives. (It was actually a statement by Anthony Eden in the spring of 1941 which brought on the first movements to establish the League. Eden stated that Britain would favor Arab unity if the initiative were taken by the Arabs themselves.) The Anglo-American Middle East Supply Center, a wartime joint undertaking to plan over-all import programs and production schedules for the area, also contributed to the movement for Arab union by emphasizing common economic problems.

Although there are strong motives behind the drive for Arab unions, there are also serious difficulties in the way of its achievement. Many Arabs, as well as other observers, have remarked that Palestine seems to be the only issue which holds the Arab states together (and not too closely together at that). The forces which separate them are partly personal or dynastic issues between leaders, partly the volatility and irresolution of present Arab societies, and partly normal conflicts of economic and social interests. Some of the leaders whose rivalries have hampered closer union have already vanished from the scene, but more fundamental conflicts than personal differences remain to be overcome. Many of the problems that each country faces individually must be faced by all collectively if union is to be achieved.

One such already mentioned is the wide rift between the nomad and the townsman—which has been called "the problem of the tent and the town." This involves a disparity of economic and cultural interests within —and among—the Arab states which must be rationalized if effective union is to be attained. Economic rivalry among the different states, although it has not been much of a factor to date, may become more important in the years to come. Arab oil, for instance, may come forth in such abundance as to create rivalries for different markets where such rivalries do not exist today. And the maintenance of markets may create bonds between individual Arab states and outside powers which are not conducive to Arab unity.

Signs of this have, as a matter of fact, already appeared. A special relationship exists between Saudi Arabia and the United States, for example, resulting from the presence of the Arabian American Oil Company and the interest, on the one hand, of the United States in Saudi Arab oil and, on the other, of Saudi Arab reliance upon American dollars. This has created tensions and jealousies in Saudi Arabia's relations with her neighbors. Even more serious are the rifts caused by the utter dependence of Transjordan upon Britain. The attitudes and actions of the great powers will be as important as the desires of the peoples in the success or failure of Arab attempts at union.

✿ IX ✿
The Case of the Vanishing Veil

NEXT to Palestine, the things in Arab life that apparently have the most lively interest for most Americans are romance and the place of women. In our thinking the two are identified. In Arab thinking, they are rarely so. Women play a large part in the Arab's life, but romance, in the common sense of the word, plays little if any part at all.

Romance and beauty are, of course, words with an infinite variety of meaning and, therefore, inexactitude. Writers of the West have devoted lives and books to analyzing them. Arab writers have not. The Princeton University Bicentennial Conference on Near Eastern Culture and Society concluded:

Arab writers never developed a theory of beauty. We find no trace in their writings of esthetics as an independent science. On the whole the enjoyment of beauty was determined by the Aristotelian concept of form as distinct from content. The view was mechanistic; beauty was something added from outside by a technician. Poetry illustrates this view. The poetry of the ninth and tenth centuries shaped the poetical compositions of the following centuries. Down to the present time there has been no marked deviation from this pattern.

The point is that while the stories and verses of the Arabs seem vividly romantic to us, they are so primarily because of their strangeness. To the Arabs, they are seen to follow a well-established traditional pattern. Even the grotesquerie is formalized; there is none of that wild and unpredictable element which makes for a truly "romantic" literature.

As in their literature, so in their life. Because of their strangeness, deserts, camels, the Nile, flowing garments and veiled women—all these are romantic symbols to us and possibly, through reaction to West-ern culture, to some city Arabs as well. But the average Arab, who lives with them all his life, sees them with a strictly unromantic eye.

There is, of course, something else which we commonly include in "romance"—romantic love. Love and sex are so basic to human nature that each people is almost bound to assume that what has become cus-tomary to it must be natural to all. Not only sexual customs but emo-tional patterns are thought to be universal.

Modern cultural anthropologists have demonstrated how far this is from true. But the lesson has not yet been widely grasped. Differing conceptions of love can still seriously hamper understanding between peoples—as we saw during the war in spite of all the orientation lec-tures and *Soldier's Guides*.

Literature may be misleading too. Shahrazad does tell an occasional story of romantic love, but the very setting of her tales, while extremely romantic in one sense, does not often reflect any great belief in "true" love between man and woman. The majority of her stories fall into the category of Chaucer's "Miller's Tale" rather than his "Knight's Tale." Classical Arabic love poetry is also romantic in a sense, but that is chiefly due to a traditional language and form going back in ancient Semitic literature to such masterpieces as the Song of Solomon, most of which are, properly speaking, passionate rather than romantic.

I kiss the prints of your feet in the sand with the same fervor that the Imam feels when he kisses the holy book.

When I see no more than your eyes over the veil, I do not know whether you smile, or look at me distrustfully.

When you let me have your hand, I do not know whether you give it to me to lead you towards love or towards friendship.

When you speak to me of my roses, I do not know whether you are thinking of their beauty, which must pass, or my love for you—which must pass?*

Other poems follow the traditional recital of charms, as in the fourth chapter of the Song, beginning "Behold, thou art fair, my love. . . . Thy hair is as a flock of goats, that appear from Mount Gilead. . . . Thy

* Robert Laffort, *Chants d'Amour et de Guerre de l'Islam*, Marseille, 1942, pp. 92, 76-7.

lips are like a thread of scarlet, . . . Thy two breasts are like two young
roes that are twins, which feed among the lilies."

Thus Fadl al Hagiri:

> She is pliant as a willow branch, her gaze gives the rapture of wine, she is
> a gazelle bounding across the desert of my eyes, a moon to lighten my soli-
> tude. . . . Her neck has the warm glow of amber, her soft lips are wine-
> colored, like the wine of Karman', her cheeks are perfect roses.*

Fadl concludes that he would be happy who could drink morning and
evening of the saliva of her mouth. This detail is not considered in good
taste by Western poets, but is not offensive to Arabs, who would in turn
be shocked by certain of the details upon which some Western writers
commonly dwell. Another Arab love song runs: "Her saliva is more
tasty than date syrup, her tongue is like a rose-colored fish, her neck is
like a silver vase, her breast is firm and white like a marble jet of water,
her heels are round like small saucers, she is my life and my death."†

These poems are sensual, but the language and the magic are so well
established as to have lost intensity. There is more pungency in the
folk song:

> Daughter of the sheikh trimming ribbons round your neck
> You had better tell your father to stop you going for water
> I shall change my favourite hack for the butcher's snicker-snack
> And learn the art of slaughter on your slack ungodly father.‡

And you get a better idea of Arab capacity for love from the tenth-
century story of Salama and "The Priest." Salama was one of the half-
slaves of Medina, a well-educated, talented and witty singer. "The
Priest" was a scholar of Medina renowned for his piety.

> "The Priest" was living in Mecca, and the way in which he came to love
> her was this. He was sitting with her owner, Ata Ibn Abu Rabah, and heard
> her singing, and was deeply moved. The host observed his reactions and said
> "Shall I bring her out to you, or shall we go inside to listen to her?" But
> he refused. Then her owner said "I will put her in a place where you can
> hear her singing without seeing her." But he refused. Her master persisted,

---

* Ibid, p. 100.
† Ibid, p. 165-6.
‡ *Images from the Arab World,* item 22. Herbert Howarth and Ibrahim Shukrallah,
London, 1944.

and took him inside, where he heard her sing. After that the host asked "Shall I bring her out to you now?" And though he again refused, she was brought out and seated before him. She sang, and he fell deeply in love with her and she with him. And all the people of Mecca came to know of it.

She told him one day "By God, I love you." He answered "I love you, too." She said, "I would love to put my mouth on yours." He said "By God, I too." And she said "What prevents you, for the place is empty." He said "I heard God say 'Emptiness will rise against you, making you enemies.' And I would hate our friendship to be enmity in the next world." And he left her and returned to his devout life.*

Another side of the picture can be reported by women only—those foreigners who have been able to see something of the vanishing life of the harem. The following is my wife's description of her visit to the harem of King ibn Saud in Riyadh, during August of 1947.

"I was received by three of the queens, a daughter and granddaughter of the king, and a Syrian woman doctora who did the translating for us. The women, in spite of the heat, were all elaborately dressed. The senior queen, Um Talal, who had been married to ibn Saud for over fifteen years, wore a black veil edged with a wide border of gold sequins. Her outer garment was a long printed silk dress, under which could be seen pantaloons, also covered with sequins. Henna reddened her hands and the soles of her feet, and her eyes were darkened with kohl. Although she had on only one ring, there was a diamond in her nose. Two of the queens wore lipstick, and several of the ladies present were chewing gum vigorously.

"I sat beside Um Talal on a sofa and answered questions. Did I like Riyadh? Was I 'content' there? Didn't I find it hot? When did I come? Did I have pictures of my husband and children? The queen fanned herself vigorously, and black serving girls standing around the edge of the room also fanned. We were served fragrant, bitter coffee, about a spoonful at a time, in tiny cups without handles. Everyone in the room listened, laughed, and made remarks about our conversation, including the servant girls. There was much excitement when it was discovered that my second son, then seven, was just the same age as one of the queen's young sons.

"Every time the Syrian doctora left the room, whoever was talking to

* *Images from the Arab World*—item 74.

me went right on asking questions, repeating them louder and louder. They just couldn't believe that I didn't understand *some* Arabic. I felt very stupid.

"The sitting room had many Turkish rugs, and the furniture was in heavy Turkish style, with many cushions. In one corner was a telephone on a stand. A queen sat by it, occasionally turning the old-fashioned crank, speaking a few words, and concluding the conversation by more cranking. The stand on which the telephone rested was part of a Playskool set, of the same kind my children used to drive pegs into and mash their fingers on.

"I was asked if I would like to see the king, and soon Um Talal, her oldest son and the doctora led me off to a small room, quite dark, where ibn Saud was sitting alone. Um Talal said, 'His Majesty,' and I walked up and shook his hand. The doctora, partially covering her face, remained to translate but the others withdrew. I sat by the king, who talked to me in a grave, friendly manner for five or ten minutes. With my husband, he was often very animated, showed a quick sense of humor and a gift for making a visitor feel like one of the family. But that would obviously not be proper with a female guest. During our conversation, he was quiet, and scarcely moved.

"When I left the king, the corridor outside was filled with princes (ibn Saud has twenty-three sons and thirty-three daughters, according to his wives). I started back along the way I had come, but servants were throwing water in the passageway to make the rooms cooler. While we were waiting, the doctora told me that one of the princes I met had been in America with the king's second son, Emir Feisal, but he could not speak any English.

"Back in the sitting room once more, we were served tea, with much mint and sugar, in little glasses so hot I couldn't touch them for a long time. Then Um Talal shepherded us in to lunch, with endless but delicious courses. We finished with three desserts, the last being ice cream in my honor. Each time the handsome black manservants passed them food, the queens modestly veiled their faces with one hand while helping themselves with the other. There was a large ceiling fan overhead, and four black girls stood at the corners of the table waving large fans, but it was still very hot. Beyond the barred windows I was facing, servants came and went continuously, staring at me with unabashed curiosity.

"After lunch we went to another parlor, hung with many mirrors. Two queens, each in front of a large mirror, adjusted their headdresses and prayed, bowing their heads gently to the carpeted floor. I felt shy, but the doctora assured me my presence was no embarrassment. Then the questions resumed. When I said I could fly an airplane, Um Talal exclaimed how much she would like to fly with me, and see something of the world! They asked about New York, Washington and San Francisco. Was it cold in San Francisco? I noticed, irrelevantly, that the servants all wore expensive gold wrist watches but the queens didn't, unless they were hidden beneath their flowing sleeves. We discussed marriage customs. 'It must be nice,' mused one queen, 'to have a husband all to yourself.' I agreed that it was nice.

"Driving back after my visit to the guest palace, I thought over one thing Um Talal had said. I asked what the queens did all day, and she replied, simply, 'Nothing. Just sit around like this and drink coffee and tea, and talk. We have many servants to do everything.' How would a girl brought up in the West ever stand the horrible, endless, stifling boredom?"

The position of women in Moslem society is widely thought to be due to its religious precepts. This is to a great extent true, although Mohammed himself intended to—and did—do much to improve the status of women. Judge Crabites, an American judge in the Egyptian Mixed Tribunals, has in fact argued that Mohammed was probably the greatest champion of women's rights the world has seen. His outstanding contribution was the bestowal of equal property rights upon women, and of an inalienable right to a share of a relative's estate. The regulation of polygamy set forth in the Koran was designed to correct existing abuses, and feminist monogamists point out that the verses limiting a man to four wives at one time specify that he can marry more than one only if he can be equally just in his treatment of them all. The Koran then goes on to say that this is impossible. Therefore, it is argued, Mohammed intended that man should have one only. But this argument has not gained wide currency; although polygamy is indeed upon the decrease, the decrease is taking place chiefly among progressive, educated people who are not strongly traditionalist in their religion. (The other great cause for decrease is economics. Extra wives may, it is true, be an asset to a peasant. To others they are likely to be an additional expense which they cannot possibly afford.)

The story also is that the veil became obligatory for most Moslem women by an error in tradition. The Koran does of course forbid exposure of those portions of the female anatomy which might arouse lascivious thoughts; and Moslems would, in view of the determined lewdness of men, be justified by that instruction in covering their women completely—were it not for the fact that covering provides no guarantee against lasciviousness. At any rate, the veil is not specifically required in the Koran. According to some authorities* the tradition came about because Fatima the Prophet's daughter, had some pretty, saucy slaves, the sight of whom called forth familiar chaffing from the men of Mecca. Some were unable to distinguish mistress from slave, so Fatima took to wearing a veil when she went out. The custom was seized upon and developed far beyond the original intent. An eleventh-century caliph imposed the veil by law, requiring that women must wear one when mixing with men or in mosques and other public places.

Soon after the harem was introduced. This, together with the veil, has been the symbol of the low estate of women in Islamic society. The harem, which enforces seclusion of women, was adopted from the Persians. It never applied to all elements of society, but only to the higher classes. The freedom allowed to women varied inversely with their rank.

Although Mohammed discouraged it, divorce under Islam is extremely easy, requiring nothing more than formal expressions of the intent to divorce. In many cases this represents a grave injury to the woman, particularly among poorer people, where an unscrupulous husband may turn out his wife after he has had all the work and children out of her he is likely to get. He has, it is true, to pay her the sum of her original dowry, or more if he has grown wealthy since he married her, but there is no continuing alimony. Actually divorce is far less common than might be expected. King ibn Saud, of course, presents a notable exception, the number of his wives and divorces being generously estimated in the hundreds. But, as a king, his marrying has been in part at

* Others hold that the practice of veiling was Persian or Byzantine in origin, and was adopted by the wives of the Baghdad caliphs.

least political. His ex-wives have been very well provided for, and have been the objects of envy rather than scorn.

Certainly the divorce laws are one aspect of Islamic life which could stand immediate and drastic reform. At present, all you have to do to be rid of your wife is to say to her, "I divorce thee, I divorce thee, I divorce thee," in front of witnesses. Even in America where divorce has become easier and more fashionable than it was a generation ago, that hardly seems like adequate protection against abuse.

In all except the best-insulated regions of Islam there have been in recent years strong feminist movements, attracting more and more prominent support. Particular progress has been made in Turkey, Egypt, Iran and Iraq. In the latter three, the women of the royal families have taken the lead. In Lebanon, with its large Christian population, conditions have been far more favorable for women. And Palestine likewise, with its mixture of religions, has been more open to liberal views on the place of women in modern life. Many Moslems are coming to agree with the young Palestinian Arab who said to me, "Naturally we want more education for our women as we ourselves become better educated. How else are we going to find the kind of companionship we want out of marriage?"

The most drastic measures to change the conditions of women's life were introduced in Turkey and Iran as part of conscious state policies to modernize—that is, to westernize—their national patterns and to diminish the influence of Islam in extra-religious life.

In Turkey the modernization, under the direction of the "Gray Wolf," Mustapha Kemal (or Kemal Ataturk), was widespread and apparently lasting. The Latin alphabet was substituted for the Arabic, the wearing of veil and fez was prohibited, the power of the mullahs was undercut, and the dictator tried to introduce democracy by fiat. An opposition party was created at the government's demand—the politics, the clothing and the secularization of Western society were imitated with equal assiduity. Reform had, in fact, begun under the Young Turks before World War I; it gained momentum during the war, when women were needed to do work hitherto reserved for men. Ataturk gave them political equality as well. In the elections of 1935, for the first time, seventeen women were elected to the Turkish Great National Assembly.

The action of Ataturk set an example which other Eastern political leaders have, with greater or lesser vigor, attempted to follow. What happened in Turkey was watched elsewhere with interest—whether of approval or repugnancy. The most thorough-going imitation was undertaken by Shah Reza Pahlevi of Iran. Shah Reza forbade veils, fezzes and other local headgear, trying to substitute the "Pahlevi" hat of his own choosing. He conducted a vigorous, not to say harsh, drive to crush not only the power of the mullahs but of the tribes which existed then as more or less independent principalities within his kingdom. Anything which symbolized separate tribal existence, such as the distinctive tribal costumes, he sought to abolish. To westernize his capital, as his own countersymbol, he tore down the old gates of Teheran and destroyed buildings in order to broaden its streets. But the limitations on his westernization program were pointed up by his handling of Teheran's water system. The German engineers he employed told him that the town's water should run through pipes, not open ditches by the side of the street. The shah thought that was all right, and instructed them to build him one set. They objected that two sets would be required, one for incoming water and the other for waste and sewage. The shah couldn't see this. It would be, he felt, an unnecessary extravagance; all you had to do was have the pipes carry water for drinking and washing in the morning, and take off the sewage, etc. in the evening. Any fool could see that. But his German engineers couldn't, and were stubborn in their refusal. So the "modern capital" of Teheran still gets its water from open ditches.

The shah's reform program had, in many fields, only a temporary success. The tribes regained much of their power, and many women resumed the veil, after his forced abdication. But there is no doubt that, after his efforts, the country of Iran has a more secular society than it did before.

In other countries, such as Egypt, Syria and Iraq, the drive for secularization was never to the same degree a formal government program, but nevertheless great progress has indeed been made. In Egypt, for example, the feminist movement started at the turn of the century with the books of Qasim Amin. Even in the university of al-Azhar, students engage in sports (unheard of for students of religion!) and take courses in modern physics and chemistry. In the Arabian peninsula, the last stronghold of Islamic isolation, the schools now being operated by foreign oil companies are imparting an outlook on life which cannot be in complete conformity with that of traditional Islam.

Even some religious leaders have been encouraging a degree of secularization of national life. For it must be recognized that secularization is not, in Arab eyes, a goal in itself but a means to a goal. Ideally, the goal is threefold: complete independence, unity, and progress in economic, social and cultural fields. Others set less ambitious, or less worthy, goals for themselves. Some politicians, for instance, are interested in breaking the grip of religion upon all phases of life chiefly to increase their own power. Whatever the motives, their efforts have apparently become far more difficult as a result—suggested already in the discussion of the Young Effendis—of increasing antiforeign feeling and the rise of fanatically Moslem groups such as the Ikhwan al Muslimin.

The improvement in the position of women has gone hand in hand with the movements for social progress carried forward by the Young Effendis. It is also associated with the West. Reaction in political or religious circles will mean a setback to the progress made in this as other fields. Restoration of the veil and the harem might seem an odd reaction to the Arab defeat in Palestine, but in many quarters it is quite possible.

﹡ X ﹡

"Waiting is an Occupation"

THE bars to understanding between East and West cannot be shrugged aside lightly. Some seemingly trivial issues can create lasting resentment. For instance, the different values attached to time.

Americans and, to a lesser extent, Occidentals generally, regard time as a commodity that should not be wasted. We consider that time and efficiency (that magic word) are closely related. Other people do not always agree. To them energy, not time, may be the important, and scarce, element. It may seem better to them that a thing should be done in ten days, or weeks or months or years, rather than in ten minutes. This different sense of values causes, in many instances, impatience, scorn, and even acute hatred. There is no sound reason that it should, but it does.

Edward Crankshaw, in his excellent book on Russia,* remarked:

When we talk of Russian idleness, of the Russian's apparently total lack of time-consciousness, we should remember that for him waiting is not, as for us, an irritating interruption in a swift sequence of activities: it is itself activity, as real and as valid as any other. It is a definite occupation, with its own laws and its own very prominent place in the general scheme of life. We should remember that the ancestors of our present Russians have for centuries under direct compulsion developed the art of doing nothing, not merely for days and weeks, but for the whole winter through.

The Russians were snowed in, with nothing to do but feed their cattle and their stoves with fodder and fuel they had already gathered. What snow has been in the life of the Russian peasant, sand, wind, and drought have been for the Arab. A herdsman is bound to have a different sense of time from a department store executive; a nation which

* *Russia and the Russians,* Viking Press, 1948.

is or has been predominantly herdsmen will view things differently from a nation of merchants.

There are other differing concepts which cause trouble. Oriental and Occidental ideas of courtesy are in many ways far apart. For example, an Oriental thinks it polite to tell you what you want to hear and this can be very annoying, particularly when what he thinks you want to hear has only the most remote connection with actual facts. I remember a boar hunt in Iran, when a friend and I were clambering over what seemed to me the steepest mountains in the world. Obviously we wanted to be told that there were lots of boar near by, and the villagers we met obliged most charmingly. Always, it appeared, there were many boar just a little further on. It did not occur to our informants that while, for the first time or two at least, it gave us pleasure to be told of nonexistent boar, over the long run it would have been kinder, and more appreciated, to have been told the truth.

On another occasion I was planning a visit to King ibn Saud and inquired of his consuls in Jerusalem and Beirut when would be a convenient time. "Any time you want," I was told most graciously. It happened that my wife, who was anxious to make the visit, too, was to return to America shortly, so I suggested a date just before her departure. Realizing that this would be during the month of Ramadan, when all pious Moslems fast strictly throughout the day, I specifically asked if it wouldn't be a nuisance to have foreign, unbelieving guests at that time. I was assured it would be perfectly all right; when I persisted in my questions one consul told me the king had telegraphed that we would be welcome whenever we could come. By then I had had many lessons in Eastern courtesy, so I remained somewhat skeptical. However, we went ahead, planned a hasty trip to Turkey after Riyadh, and reserved space on a plane from Istanbul for my wife.

Needless to say, when we arrived at Dhahran we learned informally that while of course his majesty would receive us at any time, it would be much more "convenient" after Ramadan. We had to rearrange plans, cancel air reservations and scurry frantically for new ones. My wife has yet to see Istanbul.

There was, of course, no ulterior purpose behind this particularly inconvenient manifestation of politeness. But sometimes courtesy is hardly distinguishable from guile. You can't tell whether an Arab is agreeing with you because he doesn't want to hurt your feelings, or because he wants to deceive you—it is hard to believe, for instance, that King Abdullah of Transjordan seeks to be all things to all men out of politeness, rather than as a deliberate, if ill-advised, policy to advance his own interests.

One must distinguish as well between the strict Occidental view of truth and the far more lenient Oriental one. We often violate our own concept; either consciously or unconsciously, our statements may leave truth far behind. But when that is pointed out to us we are embarrassed and apologetic—or sometimes jailed. The Oriental is not so easily persuaded by others, and far more easily persuaded by himself, of what truth is. Christopher Sykes quotes a friend of his as saying, "Persians are Christian scientists upside down." What they *feel* is true to them, even though to a prosaic Westerner it may seem totally unrelated to fact.

Another difference in view between East and West, closely related to time and to courtesy, concerns bargaining. The Westerner rather resents the necessity of bargaining in the West if, indeed, he recognizes it as a necessity; it is to him a waste of time, undignified, a damn nuisance. But to an Oriental it is an essential and enjoyable part of life. It is unthinkable that the first price mentioned or the first position stated should be regarded as final—or even seriously intended. Yet failure to recognize this has led to great confusion in many quarters; for example, the Palestine controversy, in which both sides have followed the traditions of Oriental bargaining.

Palestine has, of course, been a focus on which misunderstandings between East and West have centered. Arabs have concluded bitterly that the West is either completely unscrupulous or that democracy does not mean what they have understood us to say that it means. The course backed by the United States is, they feel, a direct violation of majority rights and the self-determination of peoples, both of which they assumed to be cardinal principles of democracy. Moreover, having little experience of the actual working of democracy, many Arabs who do believe that Americans *have* meant what they said now conclude that democracy is not such a good thing after all. As one Arab representative at UN said to me, "This has given us a poor opinion of your system. If it is possible for less than a million Zionists to lead more than 140 million peoples into an act which is contrary both to their principles and to their interests, there must be something wrong with democracy."

If the Arabs don't understand our democracy (and right now they feel they don't or, cynically, that they understand it too well) the lack of understanding is certainly mutual, and very hampering to solution of the Palestine problem. To take a comparatively minor point, we draw a clear-cut distinction between peace and a state of war, regarding the latter as incompatible with negotiation. The Arabs, and other Orientals, do not. They see no reason why you shouldn't fight and negotiate at the same time. The difference in view makes the task of a Western mediator even more difficult than it otherwise need be.

The Palestine conflict is certain to continue aggravating the already severe inferiority complex the Arab states suffer from—another regional characteristic. (This will be discussed further in the chapter on Egypt.) One aspect of this is an almost total inability to take criticism, and a sensitivity which suspects criticism where none is meant. Thus after having overcome their superstitious fear of being photographed, many city Arabs fiercely resent it for another reason—they are convinced that the pictures will be used to make anti-Arab propaganda. Five or ten years ago you could take all the photographs you wanted in Cairo, provided you showed reasonable care in avoiding obviously objectionable subjects, and no one was likely to object or question you. Now, for a foreigner to show a camera on the streets is to invite trouble. As early as 1947, when tension between Britain and Egypt was high and feeling over Palestine was on the rise, this change began. That summer my wife, in the first few days of her first visit to the Middle East, got an unpleasant taste of what a city-Arab mob can be like when she was arrested by the Egyptian police and led off to the station through a horde of angry, shouting Cairenes. Her offense: taking pictures of some children in the park near Shepheard's. The crowd, and the police, thought that the children were too dirty and ill-dressed to be photographed.

During the same trip I wrote an article for *Harper's Magazine* in which I reported that an Egyptian doctor estimated that over 90 per cent of the population suffered from trachoma. I gave other gloomy statistics as well, but also gave full credit to the Egyptians for having made notable progress, since 1936, in overcoming bad conditions. At the time the article was published, the Arabs did not have any great number of friends in this country. Of the few they did have, I was reputed to be one. The article was, I should say, objective and quite fair. Some Zionists liked it, and so did various Arab friends who are not Egyptian. But the Egyptians hit the ceiling. They called the article prejudiced, full of inaccuracies if not downright lies, written just to vilify Egypt. "That man says 90 per cent of us have trachoma, but everyone knows that not more than 80 or 85 per cent actually do," they complained!

The Middle Eastern peoples look upon the Western world with a curious combination of distruct, cynicism and childlike faith. Long, unhappy experience leads them to suspect the motives of foreigners, to fear Greeks bearing gifts. More recent experience, during two world wars and the present "cold" war, has led many to place a very high price upon their nuisance value. Turks, Iranians and Afghani, not to mention a number of Arabs, have come to feel that their continuation in the anti-Russian camp is so important to us that we should, without further question, be glad to pay anything to assure it. Such a view can lead to no relationship satisfactory to them or to us; the dispelling of it must be one major aim of American diplomacy in the area—a delicate task requiring more finesse than we have recently been displaying.

I mentioned a childlike faith as characterizing many a Middle Eastern view of the Western world. Perhaps the past tense should be used, though in some areas this faith may still prevail. Everywhere it has been badly shaken. Its object was, pre-eminently, the United States, and we have therefore suffered more damage to our reputation than countries with less to lose. The reaction of many Arabs to American policy on Palestine was comparable to that of a small child who had idolized a parent, thinking him far far above all wrong, and who finds him lying, tricking, cheating for his own gain. I have seen elderly Arab villagers and Beduin, who could speak no word of English and had probably never seen an American before but who had idolized America because their respected leaders were American educated, speak of the American "betrayal" with tears running down their cheeks.

In any case, as far as Westerners are concerned, the most important and most universal characteristic of the Middle East is this growing disillusionment and hatred of the West. The danger is not so much that we have, by making enemies from friends for ourselves, made friends from enemies for the Russians. That is, of course, a real danger, but so obvious that we cannot fail to see and guard against it. The long-range danger, which we are more likely to overlook, is that we encourage the creation of an isolationist, fanatically reactionary and xenophobic force which will dominate an important segment of the world and constitute an always-festering wound in the side of peace.

PART TWO

The Countries

Note

THIS part deals with the Middle East country by country. Needless to say, I have made no effort to give the *whole* picture of any one country, or even a well-rounded picture. Rather, I have tried to use each chapter to make a point about one country which is valid also for others.

Thus, in Iran I have dwelt on the tribes, not because the tribes present a peculiar problem there but, on the contrary, because the tribal problem is at least as important, though with slight variations, in Iraq, Syria, Transjordan and Saudi Arabia as well. In Egypt, for similar reasons, I have analyzed the sense of national insecurity—"Egypt's inferiority complex"—at a length which would be wholly out of proportion if my concern had been simply to present a balanced view of Egypt. So in Syria, where emphasis has been placed upon the difficulties faced by progressive new leadership because of religious and antiforeign popular prejudices. It would be particularly unfair to Syria and Lebanon to assume from this that the reactionary forces were especially strong there because of the attention paid them in that chapter. Quite the reverse: it is possible to get a clearer understanding of this struggle precisely because the progressive elements have grown stronger in Syria and Lebanon than in many other sections of the Middle East.

☊ XI ☊

Egypt: Cakes for the Fat, an Onion for the Thin

IN A few years there will be only five kings in the world—the King of England and the four kings in a pack of cards." That, at least, is what Farouk I of Egypt is fond of saying. And coming from a king it makes interesting hearing.

So far, the Arab world has been kinder to royalty in the twentieth century than have other parts of the globe. In the rapidly dwindling stock of ruling kings, four are from countries of the Arab League. The old Lord of the Desert, Abdul Aziz ibn Saud; the boy King Feisal of Iraq; his great uncle, Abdullah of Transjordan; and Farouk himself. (The Imam of Yemen might almost count as a fifth.)

Of course, it may be that Farouk means his remark as a joke. He has a pronounced, and occasionally far-fetched sense of humor. Other prophets who agree with him may be dismissed as professional Cassandras (by equally professional Pollyannas). But in the setting of Egypt, his speculation makes more sense than humor; what there is of the latter comes from the wry acceptance of unpleasant fate, like that of an aristocrat who dresses for dinner every night and toasts the revolutionaries already planning his execution. The chances are that as a prophet of his own fate, Farouk may prove too accurate for his own happiness. For Egypt is a land of unhealthily violent contrasts where the rich grow richer, the poor grow poorer, and everyone grows more nervous. In the classic tradition, the government sought foreign adventure to distract attention from domestic trouble. The attempt has boomeranged. Public enthusiasm for the Palestine venture was crushingly disappointed and its disillusion may be dangerous.

The King of Egypt makes a good point of departure for study of his country. He is a heavy-set, balding man who looks far older than his twenty-nine years. He has been king for a dozen of those years, but until recently his political life has been one of almost complete frustration. Perhaps to compensate, his social life has been active, notably unmarred by frustration of any kind. Both lives are reflected in his appearance but rarely in his photographs, in which the royal physiognomy receives most favorable presentation.

Farouk is the only son among six children. His father, King Fuad I, believed that "F" was a favorable letter for him, so Farouk's older half-sister is named Fawkiya, and his four remarkably beautiful sisters are called Fawzia (once Empress of Iran but now divorced from her husband), Faiza, Faika, and Fathia. Farouk's ex-wife changed her name to Farida upon marriage. Their daughters are named Ferian, Fawzia and Fadia.

Like most wealthy Egyptians, Farouk has traveled much in Europe; he was at school in England when the death of his father brought an end to his education. Also like many wealthy Egyptians, Farouk is not of Egyptian origin; the royal family descends from Mohammed Ali, an Albanian in the service of the Turks who successfully revolted against the decaying Ottoman (Turkish) Empire.

Particularly indicative of his country's problems have been Farouk's relations with the British. These have played an important part in the development of his character, and in the character of present-day Egypt. King Farouk as a boy was a proud youngster, intelligent, very much aware of his kingly status and of his country's recently won independence. This "independence" was recognized by the Anglo-Egyptian Treaty of 1936, already in negotiation when Farouk came to the throne and signed formally a few months after his accession. As one result of this treaty the British high commissioner in Egypt, who had played a very active role in the ruling of the country, was to be replaced by an ambassador who would presumably serve as other ambassadors do.

Unfortunately—so far as Egypt *and* England were concerned—the British kept on the former high commissioner (Sir Miles Lampson, later Lord Killearn) as their new ambassador. Killearn never grasped, or at least never accepted, the implications of his change of status. He went on treating Egypt, and particularly Egypt's king, as though nothing had happened. Farouk might have been a young schoolboy in the hands of a bluff and hearty but, when necessary, severe tutor.

The climax came on the fourth of February, 1942, when Rommel was threatening to sweep through the British armies to the Suez Canal and beyond. Killearn rightly or wrongly attached great importance to the appointment of Nahas Pasha, leader of the Wafdist party, as prime minister. Farouk refused to appoint him. Killearn didn't hesitate. The schoolboy flouting his tutor? Rap his knuckles! British tanks rolled into Abdin Palace courtyard, trained their guns on the doors. In walked Killearn with a paper in his hand, a royal decree appointing Nahas, all prepared for signature. It was signed. But Killearn in particular, and the British in general, have not been forgiven by Egyptians. And even though Farouk, now Killearn has gone, is personally friendly with the new British ambassador, his hatred of Nahas is unflagging.

The king was not allowed by Killearn to be a king on big affairs, so he took it out by being extra arbitrary in small things. Not that his behavior was always aloofly regal. During the war, for example, he was on occasions very "democratic" and hail-fellow-well-met in his relations with foreigners, particularly Americans. But apparently he had to show that laws were for ordinary people, not for him. If he couldn't appoint his own prime minister, at least he could drive as fast as he liked. He had a collection of great shiny new cars in which he tore around the country at fantastic speed—thus demonstrating his kingship. Or if he saw something he liked, he *must* have it. Cairo, one of the most extravagant, imaginative and uninhibited gossip centers of the world, was full of stories about what happened when somebody else's cigarette case or electric razor happened to strike the royal fancy.

Since the departure of Lord Killearn and his replacement by Sir Ronald Campbell, King Farouk has somewhat relaxed. The British ambassador's behavior is scrupulously correct; British forces have evacuated Alexandria and Cairo (the English Bridge in Cairo is now popularly known as Evacuation Bridge). If these developments had occurred earlier, the attitude of Farouk and Egypt might be even more relaxed. As it is, stories of the king's wildness still sweep Cairo. A few years ago the gossip reported that Farouk killed a man at the palace. According to the story, the king and a companion had been held up and robbed one night outside Cairo. A clear case of *lèse majesté*—violation of the royal person or prerogative. When the police brought a group of suspects to the palace, the king identified one and, with his own hand, shot him dead upon the spot. The story may not be true. Most Cairo gossip isn't.

But it does indicate a general impression that the king regards himself as above, or perhaps, *as,* the law. The words *"lèse majesté"* get immediate reaction in Cairo; sometimes a rather nervous silence, sometimes a supercilious titter, depending on the listener.

The king's personal reaction to British pressure and its sudden relaxation has been shared, though in different, nonregal form, by many of his subjects. Old-time foreign residents of Egypt, particularly Britishers, speak of antiforeign feeling, and newspaper correspondents write about Egyptian xenophobia (which is the same thing). This does not tell by any means the whole story.

The fact is that foreigners were used to being treated like masters in Egypt. The readjustment which results from being treated more or less as equals is hard for many of them to make. It is also true that some Egyptians, exuberant in their newly found "equality," express it by rudeness and adolescent arrogance. The worst excesses, the outbreaks of brutal violence, have resulted from feeling over Palestine, incited in many cases by agitators deliberately promoting hatred of foreigners. A number, including at least one American, have been killed in the streets of Cairo by mobs.

This is a new development and one that, presumably, will not last. When I was last in Egypt, in the early summer of 1947, I noticed little difference in the way I was treated then and during the war, four years earlier. Street urchins occasionally made rude remarks or gestures, but that was neither new nor peculiar to Egypt. The horde of dragomen and beggars around the big hotels was infuriating, but it always had been. Individually, the Egyptian seemed unchanged. He was still a friendly fellow, especially if the foreigner made some effort to speak his language and observe his customs. And certainly many of the measures of which foreigners complain are, in the light of modern Egyptian history, quite understandable. For example, the requirement that firms operating in Egypt employ at least 90 per cent native personnel may work hardship on individual foreigners, and will almost certainly be an economic handicap to Egypt for some period, until local people can receive more training for technical tasks. But business has for so long been almost exclusively in the hands of foreigners that drastic action was necessary if Egyptians were to take over. A government regulation that accounts be kept in Arabic has also caused complaint from foreigners. But imagine the reaction of American tax inspectors to a firm operating in the United States which kept its books in Arabic only!

However, the friendliness of the average Egyptian, the new regulations such as those discussed above, and the spasmodic violence of the mob, do not tell the whole story. The government is even shakier now than then. The Palestine situation has grown worse. We have seen how nationalism is rising in the Middle East generally, and new nationalism, lacking self-confidence, is often touchy and extreme. Moreover, political parties in Egypt have for years vied for popular favor chiefly by expressions of anti-British, and in some cases generally antiforeign, sentiments.

A mild and bloodless story of two years ago illustrates the feeling. A Belgian woman, whose father had bought up and developed what became one of Cairo's best residential suburbs, was sitting with an Englishman in a cabaret she had inherited from her father. The son of a prominent Egyptian politician joined them, and a political discussion ensued. In the course of the argument the Belgian woman said that Egyptians were foolish to force the British out of their country. The Egyptian took offense, asked by what right she made such a statement. "You are a foreigner yourself and have no more right here than the British," he told her. She replied that, on the contrary, she had more right than he did, she owned the land, and the building in which they were sitting; she could have *him* ejected if she wished. As the argument continued she made a gesture as if she might have the Egyptian thrown out. He rushed to a telephone, called Abdin Palace (the King's official residence in Cairo) and the Belgian woman was expelled from Egypt within twenty-four hours.

This incident shows the extreme sensitivity of the Egyptians as well as the arbitrary action which may follow any offense to that sensitivity. Certainly in a country whose independence and national pride were assured, such remarks might have aroused contempt, or even rage; but except in a nervous police state, say in Soviet Russia, they would be regarded as too trivial for official notice.

The incident also illustrates the ill-advised, unnecessary provocation which some foreigners, resentful of the Egyptians' change in demeanor, continue to offer. The violence of the 1948 riots has undoubtedly changed this. But Palestine, which occasioned those riots, does not explain the whole situation of which the riots were only a recent manifestation.

The question remains: why is it that Egyptians, particularly the "ruling classes," are so lacking in confidence in themselves? Surely it is not only because they recall that they have been under British domination since 1862. Another answer can be found by consulting some of Egypt's staggering statistics.

At the time of Farouk's forebear, Mohammed Ali, little more than a century ago, Egypt had a population estimated at two million. Now its population is around 19,500,000 and is increasing at a rate of over 20 per cent every ten years. Yet the arable land in Egypt has increased but little, and most of the population lives and depends upon the land. For Egypt, though it looks big on the map, is mostly uninhabitable desert. Only 1/125 of it is covered by water; only 3.5 per cent of Egypt's land —8,600,000 acres—is fertile; and only 5,350,000 of these acres are under cultivation. Thus Egypt, for practical purposes, consists of the Nile valley; it is the most densely populated country in the world, far exceeding Belgium and Bengal. Egypt's density of population is now estimated at one person to each third of an acre of arable land.

Just because a country is densely populated does not necessarily mean that its people are destitute. Belgium, for example, is a comparatively wealthy country. But Egypt is, unfortunately, more like India than like Belgium. In Cairo you can find one of the world's most ostentatiously luxurious societies, but it does not represent Egypt. The pashas, beys and effendis, the 1,200 big landholders, the rich merchants, even two million government officials, they are most of them comparative newcomers—Turks from the days of Turkish rule; Greeks, Italians, Albanians, a motley collection of Central Europeans who, generations ago, found Cairo a good place to make a fortune; Syrians who settled there when Egypt was governed as part of Syria, and well-born Moslem families from other lands, whom Ibrahim Pasha,* dreaming of a Pan-Arab empire, brought in and settled in different parts of Egypt.

It is the fellah, the peasant-farmer, the villager, who is the original Egyptian and who makes up the great mass of the population today. The fellah is lucky if he earns ten piasters (forty cents) a day. If he is fortunate enough to own some land, it is usually less than an acre. The yield per acre is about ten Egyptian pounds a year (forty dollars),

* Son of Mohammed Ali.

whereas the average cost of living is $120 per year for a family of five. (The average family consists of husband, wife, two children and an adult relative living with the family.) So the peasant landholder gets into debt early in life and rarely if ever gets out. Even so, he is better off than the tenant farmers, the landless odd-job workers, the porters or donkey drivers.

Most of the fellahin live in villages in which the sanitary conditions are, to Westerners, unbelievable. Their food consists of a little black cheese, green vegetables, an occasional onion, and perhaps some bread. Inside their insect-ridden huts they have a few water pots, cooking vessels and perhaps an earthen plate or two. Their bedding is straw covered with gunny mats.

Ninety-five per cent of the population lives in this kind of extreme poverty. Eighty per cent are illiterate. They treasure blue beads to ward off the evil eye; blue tattoo marks are thought to be the cure for toothaches. And, as one might guess, it is when one gets into the field of public health that the statistics become really shocking.

Diseases which are endemic in Egypt include worms and other parasites, amoebic dysentery, malaria, and, in some localities, filaria, a worm transmitted by mosquitoes, which causes elephantiasis. Eye infections are almost universal—their omnipresence is one of the facts of Egypt which impresses itself first and most strongly upon the visitor. A doctor on the medical faculty of Fuad I University in Cairo told me that he estimated roughly 90 per cent of the population suffered from trachoma —and that other eye infections were also prevalent. The most serious public-health problem is presented by bilharzia, a worm whose life cycle carries it from human to water to snail and back. While in the human body it settles in the portal veins which carry blood from the intestines to the liver. There the worms mate. Their young secrete a poison which dissolves the human tissue so that the bilharzia can pass from the veins to the intestines themselves, and thence to water to continue the cycle. The destruction of tissues creates wounds and internal bleeding, and though it is not likely to be fatal itself it is extremely debilitating and lowers resistance to other infections. The incidence of bilharziasis in rural districts is 75 per cent. For the country as a whole it is 60 per cent. Ancylostoma, a hookworm, is another widely prevalent parasite. One out of every two rural Egyptians suffer from it. Fifteen per cent of the country's inhabitants suffer from pellagra as well.

Now return to the king and the ruling classes, which constitute less than 5 per cent of the population and hold probably 95 per cent of the country's wealth. The fellah lives with his family, his *gamoos* (water buffalo), his donkey or camel and goats, and whatever other livestock he's lucky enough to have, all in one little mud hut. (The animals, being more valuable than humans, usually get the best quarters.) The king, on the other hand, with an income of about one million Egyptian pounds a year, has two palaces in Cairo, two in Alexandria, one in Inchass and one in Helwan, as well as other properties which, as one member of the palace staff put it, "are too numerous to mention." A pasha may leave untouched on his table after one evening's entertainment enough to feed a peasant and his family for several weeks. Surely contrasts of this sort are part of the explanation of the lack of confidence shown by so many educated, well-to-do Egyptians.

Moreover the wealthy Egyptian without social conscience is now losing, with the departure of the British, his standard, infallible excuse for the miserable conditions of his country, which were easily blamed on foreign occupation. As long as issues remain unsettled with the British —such as the presence of troops in the Canal Zone, the future of the Anglo-Egyptian Sudan, and so forth—unscrupulous demagogues will continue to seek popularity by berating the British instead of trying to grapple with the real problems of Egypt. They will use Palestine as the matador uses his red cape. The efforts of workers to improve their lot will be dismissed as Communist agitation. But all these excuses are going to wear thin very soon.

At the moment, Egyptian political parties are a pretty meaningless lot. The present government of Ibrahim Abdel Hadi Pasha is a coalition of middle-of-the-road parties. Like his predecessor, the assassinated Nokrashi Pasha, Abdel Hadi is an honest and able man, but his government is weak. The chief issue of interparty debate has been the manner in which Egypt's differences with the British should be pressed. It is a senseless debate in which the shades of opinion are often hard to detect and the inadequate basis of Egyptian "democracy" is clearly shown. In a *free* election, without coercion of any kind, so small a section of the population would vote that it is difficult to talk of the popular backing enjoyed by any one party. The masses are indifferent; the interested fraction is so volatile that the real following of any party may vary from o to 100 per cent in a few days. In such a situation, strong party organization is at a premium.

The Saadists and Liberals, who have combined to back Nokrashi, have no such organization. Together they would probably be unable to corral as many votes as either of the two well-organized parties in Egypt —the Nationalist Wafd and the Ikhwan al Muslimin or Moslem Brotherhood.

The Wafd was once, under the leadership of Egypt's "liberator" Saad Zaghloul, a great party. But Zaghloul is dead, his colleagues have died or fallen away, and only Nahas Pasha remains. Nahas has been hated by the king ever since Killearn forced his appointment as prime minister on the famous fourth of February incident. After several years in power the Wafd government became so notoriously corrupt that the censors would not allow newspapers to print any kind of cartoon showing thieves or highwaymen because they knew the public would immediately regard them as antigovernment satire. Eventually, after protracted difficulties with the British, Farouk was able to dismiss Nahas. Subsequent governments, if more honest, have been no more effective. People have forgotten their grievances against the Wafd and Nahas has kept the party machine together. Some observers claim that in a fairly free election the Wafd would get as much as 60 per cent of the vote (presupposing, in a "free" election, a very light vote). This seems far too high a figure; it is probably safe to assume that the Wafd would get a plurality—if not a majority—say at least 35 per cent of the votes cast.

However it would require pretty desperate circumstances to persuade Farouk to appoint Nahas premier again, and there is no one else in the Wafd he could appoint. Moreover the Wafd is growing old. There is a young extremely leftist wing which keeps the name Wafd, but otherwise the leaders are elderly men who have made small fortunes and who aren't feeling aggressive. They will not, in an old Paris expression current in Cairo, *descendre dans les rues*, go into the streets and demonstrate—or fight. The Wafd is unlikely to get in power while Nahas lives, and will probably break to pieces when he dies.

The Moslem Brotherhood, on the other hand, is only too eager to *descendre dans les rues*. It is a young aggressive party whose first leader was the fiery orator-demagogue, Sheikh Hassan el Banna. Its members are mostly students and laborers. Fanatically religious, antiforeign and reactionary, it is well organized and growing in strength. Nahas always opposed it, but its development was assisted, only a few years ago, by the Saadists as a counterbalance to the Wafd. After the assassination of Nokrashi Pasha, in which it was deeply involved, the party was outlawed. In February 1949, its leader Hassan el Banna was in turn assassinated. In spite of that, forced underground, it continues to expand, and the Saadist successors to Nokrashi must already look on the brotherhood as the inventor of Frankenstein looked on his handiwork.

The nature of the Communist danger in Egypt is discussed later, in the chapter on Soviet strategy in the Middle East. But it may be noted here that there is no open Communist party, and that the so-called Labor party is led by a Prince, Abbas Halim, whose connection with the working classes is tenuous at best. Prince Abbas is a sporting gentleman who fles airplanes and fought in the German Air Force during the First World War. No one takes his party very seriously, though it has been suspected of Communist affiliations. More important, similar suspicions have arisen over the leftist element in the Wafd. And it seems likely that Soviet gold has got behind the Ikhwan al Muslimin as well. This may strike Americans as surprising because it would be difficult to find any group more fanatically opposed, on ideological grounds, to Communism. But it is standard Soviet procedure in the Middle East to finance any antiforeign movement, whatever its ideology. More unusual, so far as the Middle East is concerned, is the discernible growth in Egypt of Communist sentiments among students and white-collared unemployed.

It is obvious that Egypt is not, and cannot immediately become, a democracy in any real sense of the word. Aside from anything else it is too much to expect that a people 80 per cent illiterate, infested by parasites which sap the very blood from their veins, and often so close to starvation that they can scarcely work—it is too much to expect that such a people can spare the energy or develop the skills necessary to effective democratic rule. It is obvious also that, although Communism has made comparatively little progress in Egypt to date, conditions are such as to be an open invitation to Soviet propaganda.

So much for the black side of the picture. It is not by any means the only side. There is plenty of white to be seen too. (Cairo is a city where everyone talks pitch black or dazzling white; one who listens and looks hard is likely, after some time, to see everything in pale muddy brown, the color of the Nile.)

The Egyptians argue that their present low estate cannot be blamed on them. For centuries they have been under foreign rule. When, in the early nineteenth century under Mohammed Ali, they gained practical independence from Turkey some progress was made—particularly in irrigation projects. Foreign interests soon intervened; in 1882 the British took over effective direction of the country, which they retained, in spite of gestures to the contrary, at least until 1936. It was not until 1923 that Egypt gained a constitution which gave it a pretense of democratic self-rule. By this constitution (which is still in effect today) the king, who appoints or dismisses the prime minister, governs in conjunction with a Senate and a Chamber of Deputies. Two fifths of the former are chosen by the king, the remainder, together with all the deputies, are directly elected by the people. (Though of course the British until recently still retained the effective power.)

In discussing the social progress Egypt has made in the last few years (since the elimination of British influence), Egyptians point to the early budgets in contrast to those of the present. In 1924, for example, one-half million pounds (an Egyptian pound equals about four U.S. dollars) was allocated for public education. Now the Ministry of Public Education has an annual budget of almost ten million pounds. Two million of these are, however, not in the regular budget but part of a Five Year Campaign against Poverty, Disease and Ignorance.

In this and other campaigns, such as that for village improvement, Egypt has in the last few years made considerable progress. Water works are being built to bring the fellahin pure drinking water for the first time in history. New primary and secondary schools are being built and staffed throughout the country. Hospitals, dental and maternal clinics, social welfare institutes, agricultural education centers and health propaganda units are making their appearance in villages that had never before seen a sign of outside interest in their welfare. Little advance, however, is being made so far in what might seem the most important field of all in the long run—namely, birth control. So far disease and poverty limits the family. If they are overcome temporarily, unless some means of restraining population growth is developed, poverty and disease must return soon. Overpopulation crops up as a basic problem of the East, from China and Japan to Egypt.

The most important progress has been made in public health. A vigorous campaign is being waged against the bilharzia, including drives to exterminate the snail which plays an essential part in the life cycle of the parasite, the draining of marshes and ponds and provision of pure water and sanitary toilet facilities, public-health instruction, and the treatment of those already diseased, who are themselves a source of further infection. This latter phase has been running into difficulties on two scores. The treatment requires one month of intravenous injections of antimony (tartar emetic) which produce painful symptoms. The fellahin, disliking those symptoms and anxious to devote all their energy to their work, are likely to stop the treatment as soon as the active signs of bilharziasis disappear, even though the disease is by no means conquered. Another problem is that the full-strength treatment proves fatal in about one case out of a thousand. Since the death of a patient undergoing treatment is damaging to the doctor in charge, many doctors do not risk the full treatment nor achieve the full cure.

Apart from the cholera epidemic in the fall of 1947, Egypt has been remarkably healthy in the last few years by comparison with earlier periods. Doctors attribute this chiefly to the systematic widespread use of DDT. Beginning in 1947, the villages—people, clothing, houses, etc.—were thoroughly dusted once every two months. As a result, for the first half of 1947 there were 54 cases of typhus as against 1,201 for the first half of 1946. (In 1943 there were over 40,000 cases.) For relapsing fever, the figures were 166 as against 77,519.

Though she has a terribly long way to go, Egypt has made some real strides in the right direction, and the Egyptian Young Effendis have set a mark which their colleagues in other countries will strive to attain.

At the moment, Egyptians not only have an inferiority complex, but at the same time a grossly exaggerated notion of their own importance. Here again, King Farouk reflects his country's tendencies. His aspiration to become champion of Islam has been shown on many occasions, most notably in the reception he has given to the grand mufti and the old anti-French Riff leader, Abd el Krim. These intentions are doubtless praiseworthy, but sober counsel might suggest that Egypt has enough problems inside her own borders without taking on those of Palestine and North Africa as well. However, her desire to do so is symptomatic of her condition.

Egypt is the richest of the Arab countries. She is also one of the most important in terms of strategic location. Culturally she is the leader as well. Egyptian newspapers have wide circulation in other Arab countries, and their journalists have replaced the Syrians as the models from which other Arab journalists adopt their standards. The best Arab universities and technical schools are in Egypt, and al-Azhar, the ancient religious seminary in Cairo, is regarded as the fount of Islamic learning. Politically also Egypt has recently taken a leading position. For years the Egyptians held aloof from Arab politics, aware of their own economic and cultural superiority. Their own nationalist aspirations were more important to them than Pan-Arabism. But as those aspirations have one by one reached fulfillment, it became evident that something else was needed to make Egypt healthy. That something else, as anyone can see, is sweeping internal reform, which is a difficult and undoubtedly painful operation to undertake. Many Egyptians prefer to shout about what is wrong with the rest of the world, rather than settle down to clear up their own mess. It is a human, but not particularly admirable or effective, reaction. It leads to the conviction that the world owes you a living—with a minimum of effort on your part.

An American comes to Egypt with the idea that the country *is* important—as a communications center, close to oil, as a key state in the Arab world where democracy and Communism meet face to face. But after a few weeks in which Egyptians go all out to make a pusillanimous piker of the Persian who coined the phrase "Isfahan is half the world," reaction sets in. One would think that foreign troops had never evacuated a country before. You get tired of being told that the United States must prove thus and so by doing thus and so. Americans throughout the Middle East are upbraided because of United States assistance to Zionism. When I was there, Egyptians made great capital of the recent visit of Senate committee members to Palestine, pointing out—unfortunately with truth—that the senators spent their whole time with the Jewish Agency and did not even call upon the representative of their own government—let alone the Arabs. "Is that," they ask pointedly, "an example of American open-mindedness?" But in Egypt, in addition to the issue of Palestine, we are criticized for backing the

British everywhere, and for not supporting Egypt on the issue of evacuation and the Anglo-Egyptian Sudan.

So far as evacuation is concerned, the question was purely one of timing. The Anglo-Egyptian Treaty of 1936 provided that British troops could remain in the Canal Zone until 1956. Egyptians argue that this treaty was negotiated under pressure and is contrary to the terms of the UN charter. They demanded immediate evacuation. Recent negotiations for a new treaty, during which the British offered to remove their troops by 1949, were broken off without conclusion. British forces remain in the Canal Zone, and Foreign Minister Bevin has stated that Britain will adhere to the old treaty. Conclusion of a favorable economic agreement has relieved the tension on this score, and it is unlikely that there will be further serious trouble over this particular issue.

The future of the Sudan is likely to produce far more headaches. According to Egyptians, the Nile is indivisible; the Sudan and Egypt, living literally upon and out of the Nile, must be united. The British are proud of the job they have done in the Sudan, which is indeed a model of colonial administration. They say that the Sudanese do not wish domination by Egypt and that they, the British, are morally obligated not to "sell the Sudanese into bondage." As a matter of fact it is hard to prove just what the Sudanese *do* want. Any rejection by them of union with Egypt would be attributed by the Egyptians to British pressure and propaganda.

On both these points the Egyptians are in a curious frame of mind. They insist that justice is unquestionably on their side, and that no fair-minded person could oppose them. But when, in 1947, they brought their case before UN, they did not really expect to win. Justice means nothing in international politics, they said, pointing to Palestine. Why, then, did they appeal to UN? Partly because the maneuvers of internal politics forced the Nokrashi government to make an appeal. Partly because it was hoped that an appeal might force concessions from the British. And partly because when the appeal should fail (as it did) Egyptian politicians would again be able to point outside Egypt—away from themselves—to explain why things go wrong. A foreign scapegoat is useful, and once you become accustomed to it, you miss it very quickly when it's gone.

﹫ XII ﹫

Iraq: Russia Loves a Vacuum

IN SPITE of, or perhaps because of, the coffee my host had so lavishly served, I had a coppery taste in my mouth as we went to the door. The sky was copper too, and heat rose dully from the dusty street. To my right, fifty yards up and across the street, a wormy-looking individual crouched in the meager shade of an equally wormy tree. My host pointed scornfully: "From the secret police. Our Gestapo." (I could not help wondering if Harun-al-Rashid's famous secret police had been no more impressive.) He swung to his left and gestured. "And there you see—hovels. Even animals have better houses than these." He was not exaggerating; though he spoke with the flourish which Arabs, like Latins, love, he was obviously sincere. "Iraq is one giant prison and poorhouse. I tell you, they will drive us all to Communism!"

That afternoon I went to a palace—nothing very special as palaces go, but a perfectly presentable palace. There I was received by the regent, an amiable, smooth, slight young man with a thin mustache and a superior British accent. There everything was for the best in the best of possible worlds.

The contrast is typical of the Middle East. Other things also are typical: the threat of Russia, looming huge and mysterious just beyond the horizon; the reasons for Russian interest, shared by the other great powers, a compound of strategic location and the black wealth of oil; and, noticeable above all else in Iraq, the *weakness*, the political and economic weakness which comes close to being a vacuum, the absence of all strength. Broadly speaking, the story of the Middle East today is the story of Russian efforts to create, by spreading chaos and violence, a power vacuum which only the Soviet Union could fill. That story should be accompanied by another, telling of sustained Anglo-American efforts to build order against chaos, to prevent the vacuum. Unfortunately the second story is heard only in snatches, disjointed, occasionally brilliant, occasionally clouded and obscure.

Iraq is a new state, consisting chiefly of the area formerly known as Mesopotamia—"Between the Rivers." There is in addition the Mosul region which Iraq, itself a former Turkish province, obtained from Turkey with the strong diplomatic support of Great Britain. It is there that the immensely rich Kirkuk oil fields are located and, near by, half a million Kurds create a continuing problem for the Baghdad government.

Iraq has an area of about 116,000 square miles, largely of desert, although much of the land is fertile when watered. Its population is about four million, of whom one-tenth live in the capital, Baghdad. During the First World War, many Iraqi joined with the revolt of Sherif Hussein of Mecca against the Turks, and Iraq was included in the territories promised independence in the negotiations between the British and Sherif Hussein which preceded that revolt. However the San Remo conference which gave France domination over Syria assigned Iraq to British "influence." An Iraqi revolt in 1920 was subdued, but only at considerable cost in British blood and money. In 1921 Feisal, son of Hussein, was chosen King of Iraq by a referendum in which he received strong British backing. Three years later he adopted a constitution which provided for a Chamber of Deputies (150, chosen by popular vote) and a Senate (20, appointed by the monarch). Independence was granted soon after, and by 1932 Iraq was accepted as a sovereign member of the League of Nations. However, Iraq remained bound to Great Britain by treaty, British advisers dominated the government, and the RAF was allowed to maintain air bases there.

From my 1947 notes on Iraq: "The British have most of the politicians, especially that hardy perennial among prime ministers, Nuri al-Said, thinking their way. The Regent, Abdul Ilah, is *plus royaliste que le roi*—more British than the British. What the British want done is done without instructions by eager guesses on the part of the ministers and the regent. As an illustration: a young Iraqi friend of mine, well educated, etc. has been refused employment by the Foreign Office because his father had been indirectly involved in an anti-British affair. The Foreign Office *thinks* that the regent wouldn't approve his appointment because he might *think* that the British wouldn't like it. Actually it appears that neither the regent nor the British have anything against this particular youth. Government by guesswork of this sort has its disadvantages."

Again: "The British have the politicians, but that is not much— they are a sorry, shaky lot, hardly worth owning. If the British want to retain influence in Iraq, as they obviously do, they had better find better friends. The Hashemites—the most British-dominated of Arab dynasties, rulers of Iraq and Transjordan—the Hashemites and their hangers-on are *hated* by the Iraqis. If it weren't for British protection (which allowed them to build up their own secret police and army) Abdul Ilah and the others would be murdered in two hours." The present Iraqi state cannot, unaided, fill the vacuum. If one side withdraws support, the other will rush in unopposed.

During the last war Iraq was the scene of the one open outbreak against the Allies in the Arab countries. Iraq had been the heart and soul of the Arab nationalist movement and anti-British feeling had been increasing by leaps and bounds. In 1941 this feeling, agitated by the efforts of the grand mufti who had reached Iraq in 1940, together with German propaganda, combined to force the resignation of the pro-British Nuri al-Said as prime minister. His successor was Rashid Ali Gailani, whose anti-British enthusiasm far exceeded his discretion. In May of 1941 Rashid Ali, the mufti and a small group of top army officers decided that the time had come to strike against the British. Their move was to be, in their estimation, the signal for the rising of the whole Arab Moslem world. Although Colonel Grobba, the German minister, had been very effective in mobilizing anti-British feeling, this seems to have been a purely Arab nationalist movement inspired by desire to get rid of British influence rather than by support of the Nazi cause. Whatever its intentions, its preparation was extremely inefficient. Although it had more backing from public opinion in Iraq than the British have ever been willing to admit, Rashid Ali's revolt failed to gain the support of any important Arab leaders outside his country.

And if it were designed to help the Germans, it was equally unsuccessful.

I once interviewed a Nazi intelligence officer on the subject of this revolt. His rage was a pleasure to behold. The Germans had, indeed, been scheming for a revolt in Iraq, but felt that it required careful planning. Rashid Ali, however, acted first and informed them afterward. As it happened, there was little the Germans could do to help at the time. As it also happened, one of the relatively few foreign casualties inflicted in the revolt was suffered by the Germans. The son of Marshal von Blomberg was flown in from Turkey to be German liaison officer with the rebels and, arriving over Baghdad, his plane was greeted by bursts of erratic but enthusiastic rifle fire. The pilot landed the plane successfully but it was found that young von Blomberg had been damaged in transit. A stray bullet had killed him instantly, ending the liaison before it had properly begun. The whole revolt ended, equally ignominiously, soon after.

Now at that time the British strength was at a very low ebb. If ever a move to throw off British control were to be successful, the time would seem to have been then. The fate of the revolt—because of the failure of German support—has suggested to many observers, Iraqi, British and Russians, that Iraq is not yet strong enough to determine its destiny without support from abroad. The fiasco in Palestine has confirmed this theory.

Another significant feature of the crushing of the revolt was the role played by the Arab Legion of Transjordan. The revolt had naturally been opposed by the Regent, Abdul Ilah, and by his uncle, Emir Abdullah (not yet at that time elevated to the rank of king) of Transjordan, for both are utterly dependent upon British backing. There is evidence that among some elements in Transjordan, at any rate, the Rashid Ali movement was able to gain considerable support, but the loyalty of the legion to its commander, the famous Glubb Pasha, was not in any way shaken. The part that the legion played in putting down Rashid Ali's movement served to consolidate Iraqi opinion against the Hashemite dynasty in general, and against Abdullah in particular. The position of Iraq as a natural leader of Arab nationalism was also compromised, not only because of the failure of Rashid Ali but also because of the position taken by the regent and by Nuri Said, who has been described both as "the architect of the Arab League" and "the conductor of the Hashemite orchestra."

The Western visitor to Iraq is likely to be gravely disappointed at first. He has heard Mesopotamia described in our history books as the "cradle of civilization." Four thousand years ago the first written code of law was drawn up by Hammurabi, King of Babylonia.* Ur of the Chaldees is reputed to be the original home of Abraham; about 140 miles south was Babylon, the political and intellectual center of west Asia, the most civilized part of the world down to the Christian era. The land, watered by the Tigris and Euphrates, was rich and Mesopotamia was known as the "granary of the world." Now the land and the people seem exhausted, though both are capable of being restored to life. An English writer, Robert Byron, described the flat land between the rivers: "It is a mud plain, so flat that a single heron, reposing on one leg beside some rare trickle of water in a ditch, looks as tall as a wireless aerial. From this plain rise villages of mud and cities of mud. The rivers flow with liquid mud. The air is composed of mud refined into a gas. The people are mud colored; they wear mud-colored clothes, and their national hat is nothing more than a formalized mud pie."

To readers of *A Thousand Nights and a Night* who have not visited it, Baghdad is still a city of romance and adventure where Harun-al-Rashid wanders disguised from his subjects and veiled beauties make dangerous trysts. It is the city of the terrifying magical garden of James Elroy Flecker's vivid verse play *Hassan*—where Rafi and Pervaneh were tortured for a day of love. But Baghdad's period of great glory was over a thousand years ago. Then it was renowned for learning, famous for its silks and for its tiled buildings, and for the glory of its rulers. Its downfall, however, came in 1258, when Hulaku, the Mongol, overran Mesopotamia and destroyed the remarkable irrigation system which had made the land rich. This destruction turned the agricultural land into a waste of steppe. After that Baghdad was rarely independent. It has been ruled by Mongols, then by Turks and Persians and Turks again, until finally, after the First World War, it was re-established as an independent capital.

* Recently archeologists report finding in Iraq evidence which suggests that the same kingdom of Babylonia had a written legal code which antedates Hammurabi's by about two hundred years.

The Arabian Nights are not a reliable guide to modern Baghdad. The great rivers are still there, the golden domes of Khadimain will be no disappointment to the reader of Flecker, one of the hotels is named after Sindbad, and the main street is called Rashid—though it is not the sort of street on which we would expect to meet the great caliph. Even the most determined romanticist is likely to be somewhat disappointed, and the tourist who looks and runs will not find Baghdad exciting. The bazaars, it is true, are interesting, but they cannot compare to those of Isfahan or to the famous souks of Aleppo. The city is hot, drab and dirty, and the hotels leave much to be desired. The climate is one of the most trying anywhere in the world.

Nevertheless Baghdad has its lovers, including many Americans and British. Its society is friendly and easy; there, unlike Cairo, it is possible to go to a formal party without feeling the need of dark glasses to protect your eyes against the glitter of diamonds. And aside from its other attractions, for the serious student of Middle East problems, Baghdad is one of the best observation posts. Air and water routes have diminished the commercial significance it had in the days when the desert caravans between East and West used commonly to pass through its gates. But in Arab politics, and in world oil politics, it is still a center. And it seems likely that Iraq will take Iran's place as the main testing ground for the strengths of East and West.

Moreover, if shakiness is to continue a characteristic of Middle East governments, Baghdad is a good place to study shakiness. All the causes are present: maldistribution of wealth; the faulty British tactics which rely upon stability imposed by a small, selfishly interested clique; the lack of a middle class and of a politically educated electorate; and the lack of any coherent *national* society.

The three-cornered society of the Middle East, made up of nomad, peasant and townsman, is as sharply divergent in Iraq as anywhere else. The desert herdsmen, gathered in huge and powerful tribes such as the Shammar, are almost kingdoms within the kingdom (as in Iran) and owe complete loyalty to their sheikhs. The nomads of the north are hillsmen, moving the year round, living in goats' hair tents. Those in the south are desert nomads, living off the camel (they are sometimes called "camel's parasites")—breeding camels and horses, eating camel's meat and drinking camel's milk. These dwellers in "the house of hair" are hardy, independent and fierce, healthier than the settled Iraqi because their life of movement in the open keeps them free from many of the diseases which affect the town.

The settled agriculturalists of northern Iraq live in houses of mud with timber roofs, two rooms and an outer courtyard enclosed by mud walls. They live on bread and curds, with an occasional treat of meat, and a little tea and sugar. In the south the settled tribes live on the rivers and the canals. They form the largest single group in the country, and live in mud huts which have evolved gradually from tents to the detriment of the health of their inhabitants. (The tents were movable, and the sanitary habits of the people did not change when their dwellings became immovable.) The diet is chiefly dates, lentils, and barley or rice.

The townspeople of the big centers, Baghdad, Basra, and Mosul, are dominated by local political bosses. Many of them have adopted European-style clothes with the exception of shoes, which are not common, the lack of which contributes greatly to the spread of hookworm. The poorer classes live chiefly on dates and bread, supplemented for those who can afford it by rice and vegetables cooked with meat.

The conflict between peasant villager and nomad tribesmen, and the way in which tribal allegiances cut across national lines, was illustrated in a rather bloody incident of August 1946.

Members of the Shammar tribe in Iraq had a difference of opinion with some villagers. Contemptuous of the villagers' fighting spirit, they gathered two hundred riflemen and charged straight across the fields against the mud walls protecting the mud houses of the village. The Shammar had underestimated their opponents. Ambushes had been prepared, the walls were well defended, and the villagers made surprisingly good use of their motley collection of rifles, pistols and an occasional hand grenade. Perhaps they used their knives to finish the job. The only Shammar who escaped alive did not wait to see.

Word of this shocking defeat got around. Seven sheikhs, with far-reaching family connections, had been killed. The tribesmen of Iraq and Syria were horrified, and the Syrian Shammar sent immediate promises of help—followed by men. Reinforced, the Shammar returned to the village which had resisted and humiliated them; this time, their attack did not fail. Every living thing in the village was wiped out.

Altogether, including Shammar, 1,200 people lost their lives. The Iraq government, which takes an understandably dim view of such incidents, tried to play it down, admitting only a loss of eighty lives. But this story was confirmed by Iraqi and American sources.

A Baghdad Jew, commenting upon it, told me that the Shammar were saying that they would fight in Palestine. "I don't want to wish evil upon my co-religionists," he remarked unhappily, "but I just hope they don't decide to take it out on us here instead of making the long trip to Palestine."

The word "feudal" has been much used to describe Middle East society. This is not a correct use of the word for there are fundamental differences between it and the feudal society of the Middle Ages in Europe and Japan. At first glance, it is true, one might take the independent Bedu for the equivalent of the knight-vassal of feudal Europe with his sheikh corresponding to the feudal lord, and the fellah to the serf. The townsman, of course, is always the townsman in any society, in rivalry alike with Bedu-knight and fellah-serf. However, important differences appear immediately. The Bedu does not constitute a professional military class as did the European knight and the Japanese samurai. Moreover, historic feudalism was essentially a system of land tenure. The vassal, or seigneur of the manor, held land from the great lord in return for certain specified obligations—the swearing of fealty, provision of military service and the like. The serfs, who belonged to the land and could not leave or dispose of it, wrested their sustenance from it in return for other kinds of obligations—labor, a portion of their crops and so forth. The situation in Arab lands is not quite the same. There is not the hierarchical system, from serf to small seigneur to count to duke to king, that marked medieval feudalism. The peasant, if he owns land, may dispose of it; or, if he can raise the money, he may purchase land. The fellah's lot may be every bit as miserable as that of the medieval serf; but his lot falls within the framework of a different kind of society. It might be more accurate, for instance, to compare Arab agricultural society, so far as the system of land tenure is concerned, to that which has prevailed in our own south. The categories of sharecropper, "poor white," small landowner and independent farmer as well as large absentee landholders are all to be found, widely differing in proportion, of course, in different parts of the area, in the Middle East as well as in the American south.

The alternation of extreme pride and acute shame characterizes the insecurity and instability of Iraqi life as Arab life in general. It is marked in the rapid shifts in governments and in cabinet posts, in the concurrent susceptibility of the fleeting governments to foreign influence and the accompanying fanatical rejection of anything foreign. The same speaker in the course of a comparatively short conversation may assert with pride Iraqi leadership of the Arab cause and, despairingly, confess Iraq's inability to stick to any given course of action.

Underlying Iraq's recent moves with regard to the Arab League is a definite sense of inferiority and hurt pride. Iraq was a leader in the move toward the league, proposing actually something far stronger and more binding than what was finally accepted. Iraq also was a leader in support of the Arabs in Palestine. But recently Egypt, not hitherto interested in Pan-Arab matters, has turned to the East. Egypt is stronger and richer, with more educated men, than Iraq, and has inevitably taken a commanding role. (So also Syria, now its independence is won.) Moreover the inclusion of Saudi Arabia in the League (at Egypt's insistence, backed by everyone except the Hashemites, but including the Iraqi delegate, Tewfik Suwaidi) annoyed the Hashemites, and the "conductor of the Hashemite orchestra," Nuri Said. Supporters of the government policy—who seem few in number—emphasize that since she has concluded separate treaties with Transjordan and Turkey Iraq's delegate to the league is heard with more respect, and that Iraq plays a valuable role in winning the support of Turkey, Iran and Afghanistan for league policies in UN. Those three countries are already linked with Iraq in the Saadabad pact; the party line is that Iraq must extend her special relationships outside the Arab League to include Pakistan, India, and possibly Greece as well. It is notable that all of the countries named have supported the Arab cause in Palestine, so closer alliance is a distinct possibility.

The party line also included, however, a renewal of the treaty with Great Britain. In January 1948 Prime Minister Saleh Jabr announced the signing of such an alliance, providing for a mutual defense pact, in the event that either nation was threatened or involved in war, and the relinquishing by Great Britain of all but nominal control of two British-built airfields in Iraq. The terms were remarkably favorable, and London was confident of their acceptance.

Instead, rioting began, continuing for two weeks and costing thirty-four killed, three hundred injured. Saleh Jabr fled the country by plane in disguise, to find refuge with pro-British Abdullah in Amman. The treaty was repudiated by the regent for failing to realize "the national aims of Iraq." And extreme nationalists elsewhere in the Arab world, such as the reactionary antiforeign Moslem Brotherhood of Syria, took exultant note of what had happened. Nationalist pressure had overthrown a government. With Palestine likely to grow more rather than less explosive, they could look forward to good hunting.

Meanwhile the British, shocked at the fate of their defense alliance, are hanging on. The old treaty, which the new one was designed to replace on terms more satisfactory to the Iraqi, does not expire until 1955. The Iraqi government is less predictable than before, the production of oil has been interrupted, but the RAF is still at Habbaniyah and British advisers still hold key positions. And Baghdad is more than ever a city where politics and revolution are the most common, the most heated and the most frustrating topics of conversation.

I remember with a sneaking sense of guilt an evening at the house of some charming Baghdadi friends, whose hospitality I repaid by promoting a rather heated political argument. (A reporter does not want to become involved in argument himself, but often there is nothing more helpful to him than a vehement argument between others.) On this particular occasion the up-and-coming nephew of an Iraqi prime minister was justifying to me the government policy on the league and Transjordan. By luck and some good management I had collected in the same circle a rabidly anti-Hashemite doctor and a young "revolutionary" just back from an English university where he had been studying, presumably, how to overthrow the British. Like almost all the anti-Hashemites, meaning almost all politically conscious Iraqis, they support the Arab League with passionate intensity. They began, quietly at first but with growing ferocity, to needle the young politico—whom we'll call Haidar.

Haidar is a swarthy fellow with patent-leather hair, a neat, rather British black mustache and dark liquid eyes of, I should judge, considerable romantic appeal to the other sex. His control of his temper is not complete, nor is his discretion. Both were sorely tried. The doctor, a deceptively mild person until the argument warmed up, placed the most outrageous interpretations upon everything Haidar said, until he had needled young Haidar into saying some pretty outrageous things. The revolutionary, a thin youth of great intensity and rapidly shifting moods, supplied the chorus.

The details of the argument do not matter now. But there were several interesting aspects. For one thing, there was the claim of Haidar that Iraq could not rely upon all the members of the Arab League. This produced a moment of silence while the growing audience tried to divine his meaning. Ironically the doctor inquired whether he feared some of the members might be under British domination, and Haidar flushed but kept his temper. With a polite inclination toward me he said,

"There are some who feel that Saudi Arabia is no more than a puppet of America and that the league can do nothing in which ibn Saud will not agree."

There was a ripple of laughter, and the revolutionary gave me a faintly mocking smile. But the doctor returned to the attack.

Did the government propose to wreck the league just to satisfy the family ambitions of the Hashemites? Haidar angrily answered that Iraq had taken the lead in forming the league and in upholding the Arab cause in Palestine, but what was the outcome? It was time for Iraq to look to her own interests, which were being upheld by her rulers. Let Egypt or Saudi "America" (another laugh from the listeners) look to the league.

The point that struck me was the implicit recognition on Haidar's part that Iraq could not stand by herself without British support. His only defense was that other Middle East governments also had to rely upon foreign backing. It was easy to imagine anti-British elements reaching the same conclusion—and looking to the Soviet Union to provide what has been accepted as necessary.

Another intriguing aspect was the story-book, faintly unreal atmosphere in which such apparently bitter enemies could eat and drink and mingle together. There are genuinely revolutionary elements in Iraq. Perhaps some day the doctor and his young ally will be driven into the arms of those elements. But on that evening the differences between them and Haidar—in fact the convictions of either—seemed very insubstantial. Much Baghdadi talk of politics has a dreamlike—or at most, nightmarish—quality to it. It is not planted in sordid reality.

If it were, you could be sure that Haidar would have reported to the secret police the next morning.

As it was, before tempers grew too hot our hostess arrived with glasses of lemonade and instructions for us to "circulate." The doctor drew me aside for a parting word. "Now you see what we are up against. We shall have," he said dramatically, "to get rid of traitors like that." I tried to imagine either him or the revolutionary "getting rid" of Haidar, but couldn't quite picture it.

Another weakness of the Iraqi state is that while the political system, modeled on the West, seems to require strong political parties, there are in fact no such things. Iraqi politics have been more personal than anything else. There has been a small group of men who have proven acceptable prime ministers, more or less, to the Hashemite monarchs, the ruling clique, and presumably the British. They held office in rotation; when the government became too unpopular, there would be a "change"—or, more properly, a reshuffle. The current prime minister would retire, usually into the Senate, for a while to enjoy in relative peace the fruits of his last term of office. And another of the hardy perennials would take his place. Obviously, this system had its conveniences, but was not notably democratic.

In the summer of 1946, as a result of pressure and complaint from various quarters (including British), a step was taken to reform this situation. At that time Tewfik Suwaidi was prime minister. Suwaidi is a sincere man, who has stood up to the British and the Hashemites on many occasions, but who has been around long enough so that when things get bad, and an opposition prime minister is pretty definitely demanded, he is the logical candidate. He has been used to lend an air of respectability to many a dubious cabinet but he had to wait a long time for the customary appointment to the Senate. He has a position, but he was not a man on whom the powers could rely. He had ideas of his own.

So he was a good person to introduce this reform—the official recognition of five parties in Iraq. This was done early in April of 1946 and the parties were allowed to publish newspapers and pamphlets, and to organize on a national basis. However no one—government, parties, press or people—was apparently ready for such radical steps. At least so the government thought. And though Americans are quick to criticize such a thought we should, in all fairness, recognize that we have traditionally established standards of at least minimum responsibility for parties, and press, and people; these standards take time, education, and experience to establish, and do not exist in every part of the world.

We talk, for example, of the *free* American press. A free press is not remarkable in the world. If we want to do ourselves justice, we ought to talk of the *responsible* American press, for our newspapers are, with few exceptions, remarkably responsible. In many parts of the Middle East, the press is as free as could possibly be desired. It is free to attack the government, or anyone else it chooses, as viciously and as slanderously as governments or individuals can be attacked any-where in the world. Recently one of the Teheran newspapers offered a million riyals' reward to anyone who would assassinate the Iranian prime minister. That is, in a sense at least, freedom of the press. But it is not responsible democratic procedure, any more than the subsequent assassination of the editor who made the offer was responsible demo-cratic procedure.

On the other hand, opponents of the Iraqi government say: How are the Iraqis ever to get experience in democracy and party politics unless, in spite of temporary abuses, parties are allowed to operate? It is a good question. It poses the dilemma of democracy in a politically backward country, a dilemma that confronts us in Greece (to our open dismay), in Argentina, in Germany (where the Nazis took advantage of democracy and destroyed it), in China, in the Orient generally, and everywhere that Communists or other antidemocratic forces are organ-ized to seize power through legal means if illegal means fail at first.

Yes, say the Iraqis. But Communism was not strong here. If it has become strong, it is because the government, which described all opposition as Communist, has made it so. And that is, I believe, quite true too. It is the natural instinct of a ruling class, in Iraq, Egypt, Argentina, Greece, Spain, or where you will, to wish to hold its power, and to label anyone who wants to take away that power with the dirtiest name possible. And what are liberal outsiders to do about that? What is the anti-imperialist United States to do? Intervene, say some enthusiasts, intervene to help our friends. It is an easy answer, as imperialists have found throughout history. A few cautious individuals will wish to wait at least until democracies may develop some better method of identifying their friends. Otherwise we may find that we import into our own land the conflicts of the other lands in which we intervene—as we have done, to a limited extent, in the cases of China, Greece, and even Palestine.

These are serious, important questions. If we can't solve them here, at least we can recognize them as questions, and important. We might go a step further, and decide at least this much: that before we take sides in the internal problems of any foreign country, we should be satisfied that we know what the different sides are, what they stand for; and that this isn't always as easy as it looks, or as we are told it is.

So. We return to Iraq, spring of 1946. Less than a month after Suwaidi recognized the existence of five political parties, he was dismissed as prime minister. His successor declared war on the parties, and particularly on the party press. Only the progovernment press was allowed to continue. The new prime minister announced his intention of holding free elections—obviously a laudable intention—but in order to win, or for some other urgent reason, he found it necessary to outlaw all political parties (the government did not have a party). Apparently the Iraqi, in spite of their lack of political background, have a sound sense of the ridiculous. They could see that it was pretty silly to talk of a free election when you have discouraged opposition by putting your chief opponents in jail. At the last minute the government realized this, and called the election off. The old reliable, Nuri al Said, was called in to get the government out of the hole.

Nuri collected a "national" cabinet for the purpose of holding the elections. He even released the more eminent politicos who had been languishing in jails and invited one representative each from two of the five outlawed parties to join the cabinet. They agreed to join on condition that the parties should be allowed to carry on electioneering and that there should be freedom of the press. Shortly they resigned, convinced that neither condition was going to be met.

Meanwhile the ruling clique had decided that maybe it too should have a party of sorts. A special group was formed within the government known as al Kutla (the group), for the purpose of fighting "bad opinions"—by which they seem to have meant "opposition to the government." A month before the election a list of candidates to be supported by the government was published, and an al Kutla newspaper announced that the group had one thousand armed members in Baghdad to "protect" its candidates. Almost all of the government-backed candidates were elected. In one place an independent won, and received a letter certifying his election from the election committee. But soon armored cars arrived, the election was declared illegal, and a new one resulted in victory for the group's man. On the day scheduled for voting, most of the five opposition party candidates decided to boycott the election.

The al Kutla government, once installed, continued its campaign against "bad opinions," amending the press act so that cabinet appointees had judicial powers; so that the police, rather than civil courts, could dispose of censorship or subversive propaganda cases. One of the opposition party leaders, predicting that he would soon be in jail, told me that a third of the budget was being spent on the secret police and army to guard against uprising. "If this were spent on education or irrigation, uprisings would not be necessary," he commented.

This man had been a successful lawyer, a member of Parliament, a magistrate on the high criminal court. The government had asked him to detain a man without evidence and, when he refused, had stopped assigning him cases. So he resigned and formed an opposition party. (Later, he discovered that the man the government wanted detained was a police spy to be planted in prison.)

Since then, of course, his finances had not prospered. One of his schoolmates, he told me, whom he used to help with his lessons, was now a wealthy individual with two fine American cars. "He has no ability, but he has gone along with the government." Not long ago, Nuri Said had spoken to my friend, saying he mustn't "grumble" so much; if only he'd settle down, he could go a very long way.

Not long after I'd left Baghdad he was, as he had expected, put in jail. He was not, I am sure, then a Communist. But what he is now, Lord knows. As I left, he told me: "Just before the last war, people in Iraq turned to Germany, simply because of desperation over the present regime which they regarded as British-run. They felt they had no place else to turn. In case of another war, they would turn to Russia or to the devil himself—to anything that offered a change from present evils."

Logically, the Iraqi have nothing to gain and everything to lose from closer acquaintance with the Russians. Even if the British were as bad as the Iraqi think they are, and as responsible for Iraq's ailments as is charged (they are neither), logical people would recognize that the Russians are far worse. But when have people been logical?

The Iraqi are not the only people to be illogical about Iraq. In general, it is easy enough to see what should be done there by the Iraqi, the British and the Americans. We all have at least one strong interest in common, that of keeping the Russians out. This should lead the Iraqi to welcome assistance in becoming strong enough to stand on their own feet, and diplomatic backing until they are strong enough to be independent. It should lead the British, who cannot provide all the assistance needed, to welcome the provision of assistance from other friendly nations. And it should lead the United States to provide such assistance.

It is not such a tough job, nor would it cost the American taxpayer much. As ex-President Hoover has pointed out, irrigation projects could make Iraq agriculturally wealthy. These projects would be self-financing. In addition, education, public health and other technical missions could provide Iraq with badly needed assistance. There have been such missions already, and the results have not been all that might be desired. One explanation has been friction between British and Iraqi, and reluctance on the part of the British to allow other foreigners to "poach on their preserves."

If Iraqi, British and Americans should decide to co-operate, there is nothing to block success. There is now no place, not even the Far East, where the Russian menace is more serious.

Maybe that is because, in Iraq as elsewhere, the Russians are working logically toward their own aims. Their opponents have better aims but, so far, sadly deficient logic.

⚉ XIII ⚉

Transjordan: A Legion, a King and a Joke

TRANSJORDAN, with an area of 4,700 square miles, has a population of somewhat over 300,000, of whom almost half are nomads. It has no industry and little agriculture, and must import most of its requirements in food as well as goods. It is a vagrant country, without visible means of support. Without a subsidy of two million pounds a year from the British, its government would be unable to make ends meet.

British interest is responsible for the creation and continued existence of Transjordan. Control there gives them control of the oil pipe line from Iraq to the Mediterranean, of the Baghdad-Haifa road, and (should it ever be restored to service) of the Hejaz-Damascus railway. Since the British have given up their bases in Palestine (and with their bases in Egypt and possibly Iraq soon to go) this little artificial impoverished country finds that its one negotiable asset—its strategic importance to the British—is of increasing value. (Realization of that fact by both parties is shown by the terms of the revision of the treaty between them in 1948.)

Because of British interest, there are two forces which keep Transjordan a going concern.

The first, the *sine qua non*, is the Arab Legion, a British-trained body of approximately fifteen thousand men with about fifty British officers and noncoms. It is made up of one mechanized brigade (equal to a U.S. regiment) plus garrison companies. The brigade has British armored scout cars, South African armored cars (rather ancient) and Bren gun carriers. Artillery consists of 3.2 inch pack howitzers, and seventeen- and twenty-five-pound guns. The military capabilities of the legion are subject to dispute, though it is generally agreed that it was never fully committed in the 1948 Palestine fighting, and that it is the most effective of existing Arab military forces.

The second "force" which keeps Transjordan going is its king, and the question is, from one minute to the next, which way will he make it go?

The radio announcer spoke most impressively of this desert warrior, picturing a hard, fierce man who, astride his Arabian steed, might lead his legions against the Zionist Haganah. Mildly puzzled, I asked myself: who could that be? Then the speaker identified his subject—King Abdullah of Transjordan. And I could not help laughing at the contrast between the radio word picture and my own memories of the man who was being described.

These memories are of many different kinds. Some are firsthand memories of Abdullah himself, others of Abdullah as reflected in the eyes and minds of those who have dealt with him—Arabs, Jews and Britons. The scenes vary, from kings' palaces to small dusty offices, from the peace of Galilean hills to the unrest of narrow streets, cleared of their crowds by spreading gunfire. One thing holds these scenes together: a personality apparently as diverse as they, with different meanings for different men, but consistent in ambition and in a capacity for being surrounded, always, by trouble.

First there is the picture of His Royal Hashemite Majesty, Abdullah ibn Hussein, a plump, expansive little man receiving me with gracious hospitality at his palace in Amman in the summer of 1947. This king was never the warrior type. His well-rounded five feet four inches are obviously no more suited to combat now, at the age of sixty-seven, than they were more than thirty years ago, when Abdullah sat back to let other members of his family lead the Arab revolt against the Turks; or a few years later, when he was ignominiously defeated in his father's kingdom of Hejaz by a young chieftain, ibn Saud, who later took over the Hejaz to make it part of his own kingdom of Saudi Arabia. But although Abdullah is pudgy and not warlike, he can carry himself with regal dignity. He has a grand manner, a smooth tongue, and the self-confidence to speak with certainty upon an infinity of subjects—a self-confidence common to kings, and some presidents, who need never fear contradiction.

Abdullah has kingly ambitions, too. He considers that his family was promised, by Lawrence and other British representatives, rule over an Arab state which would include not only the Arabian peninsula but Mesopotamia and much of the Levant as well. The Hashemite family has lost its kingdom in the Arabian peninsula. Abdullah's grand-nephew, young Feisal II, is King of Iraq which includes most of the area known in the past as Mesopotamia. The Levantine lands were split up, Abdullah receiving, eventually, only the barren, thinly popu-lated area now dignified as the Kingdom of Transjordan. But Abdullah has never given up his claims. Officially he still asserts his rights to the Hejaz. Actually, he would settle for as much of Palestine, Syria and Lebanon as he could get. He knows, too, that his time is short. What he is going to get, he must get quickly.

When I visited Amman it was during the Moslem holy month of Ramadan and the king, like other pious Moslems, was fasting from sunrise to sunset. I arrived just before the evening gun which marks the setting of the sun. The king received me under a finely woven canopy in his garden and then excused himself to break his fast and pray in private. Later, as we dined (European style, on chairs and from individual plates, as distinguished from the Beduin fashion of squatting around a common dish) he spoke of Arab poetry, of world geography and politics, of his early life in Turkey and the Hejaz (which he still regards as his kingdom), and of chess. Abdullah is noted as a poet in his own right; also as an enthusiastic chess player who feels it undignified for a king to lose and who resorts, if necessary, to his royal prerogative to stave off such an indignity. He would not talk to me of Arab politics, probably because he had heard that I was opposed to his own "Greater Syria" ambitions, and because he suspected me of being too friendly with his old enemy, ibn Saud. But on world politics and politicians, he was fluent; the great mistake, he felt, had been made when Churchill and Roosevelt had insisted upon a policy of unconditional surrender from the Germans and had not made peace with the Germans before their defeat in order that all three powers might concentrate upon the Russians. "Churchill," said the little king grandly, "was a fine orator, but he lacked the penetration to discern his real enemy." I appreciated this note of condescension from a man who had gained his own throne at Churchill's personal instigation.

That is my direct memory of Abdullah in person—a cheery fellow

inescapably of Soglow's "Little King." Glib, rather than sound, on
with twinkling eyes and a demure, speckled gray beard who reminded me
international affairs, putting an arm around me and calling me friend,
though he never really thought me such. He knew that I did not
believe, as he did, that the Middle East would benefit from the extension
of his rule to include Palestine, Syria and Lebanon.

It was late when I left the king's palace, but the evening was not
over yet. At the Philadelphia Hotel, across from the ruins of the
Roman amphitheater which commemorates the importance of Amman
in ancient times, a man was waiting for me. A mutual friend in
Baghdad had written of my intended visit and Rashid—that is not his
real name—wanted to make sure that I did not leave thinking all was
sweetness and light in Transjordan. Obviously we could not talk in
the hotel, so we climbed into his ramshackle car and drove around the
outskirts of town, through narrow, steep, rocky streets lighted chiefly
by a waning moon, while Rashid talked inexhaustibly, with only an
occasional glance at the road for appearance sake. I found it hard to
concentrate on what he was saying.

Rashid was a graduate of the American University of Beirut, and a
dentist. Only the scarcity of dentists in Amman kept him from exile,
for his disrespectful attitude toward his king was but thinly disguised.
Abdullah, in his opinion, was a British stooge who allowed his
personal ambition to blind him to his patriotic obligations as an Arab
nationalist. This opinion, common among Arab nationalists, is of long
standing and was confirmed by Abdullah's acceptance of the British
treaty of 1929. Before then, the financial administration of his country
had already been removed from Abdullah, and the three most important
ministries in the government given to British officials. The treaty
removed his last pretense of power, and was greeted by storms of indig-
nation from his subjects—storms which had to be put down by British
bombers. Rashid told me that Abdullah also got into trouble in 1933
by leasing land to Jewish settlers. Other great landholders in Transjordan tried the same thing, but the "People's Representation" (the
nearest thing to a popularly elected body Transjordan has seen) immediately passed a law forbidding the sale or lease of land to Zionists
or other aliens.

Opposition to Abdullah among his own subjects is still active. The leader, a little doctor named Abu Ghannima, is now in exile in Damascus, but is said to have considerable backing within as well as from outside the country. One rumor has him receiving financial backing from Russia, but I have been unable to confirm this. He is surely assisted, however, by members of the Syrian government who distrust Abdullah's ambitions.

What, I asked, do the Beduin tribesmen think of Abdullah. "They despise him," was the quick reply. "They feel that he was corrupted by the Turks, by the luxurious, idle life of Stambul. He has abandoned the strict code of the desert."

But, I objected, doesn't he rigorously observe the fasts and prohibitions of Islam? Rashid, rather grudgingly, admitted that perhaps he did. That wasn't what he meant. He would tell me a story, or rather, two stories.

Some years ago, a niece of King Abdullah fell in love with a Greek who worked in a hotel. Not only that; she ran away with him, she even married him, bringing officially into the family a man of distinctly dubious origins. "I," said Rashid proudly, "am an educated man. I know one should be reasonable about such things. But the Hashemites are descended from the Prophet, and the decencies must be observed." Yet the man was, so far as anyone knew, still alive. King Abdullah had protested, threatened, bewailed the family disgrace—but he had done nothing. This the Beduin could not understand.

I made the sympathetic noises obviously required of me. "Now," said Rashid, "here is the other story. There is another famous family, the Sa'adoun family, also descended from Mohammed. Their head is Abdullah Falih Sa'adoun, an old, very holy man, gentle and pious, who lives a life of asceticism and meditation in the desert of Iraq. A cousin of his, an educated girl, fell in love with a man named Achmed Sani, who was director general of the Interior Department of the Iraqi government. He was an able man, holding respected office. But unfortunately he was descended from slaves. It was unthinkable that the blood of Mohammed should be mingled with any but the finest blood of Islam.

"So the girl's relatives warned her and Achmed Sani that their marriage was impossible. But they went ahead and married anyhow. Now it was up to the head of her family to protect and preserve the Sa'adoun honor. Unlike Abdullah ibn Hussein, he did not shout forth his disgrace to the world. Instead, he took leave of his lonely tent and his contemplations, and traveled to Baghdad. Arriving there, he went straight to the office of the director general of the Interior. Achmed Sani received him politely, and offered coffee. But the old man, equally politely, declined. 'I am very sorry,' he explained regretfully, 'I shall have to shoot you. Please believe that there is nothing personal in this. But I have no choice. You must know that.' Achmed Sani said that he did. And Abdullah Falih Sa'adoun pulled out a revolver, with which he shot Achmed Sani dead. Then he gave himself up to the police.

"By tribal law, of course, Abdullah Falih was within his rights; was, in fact, obliged to do what he did. King ibn Saud and others intervened on his behalf and he was released. The Beduin respect and revere him. And they often contrast the two Abdullahs. One, they say, is a man of honor who can stand up proudly in the sight of Allah. The other is a Turkish dilettante, not a serious man, unworthy to uphold the honor of his family, worthy only of being a tool for foreigners."

I caught another glimpse of Abdullah through the eyes of an Englishman, a blowsy, kindly giant of a man, redfaced, clad in moist white, dripping in the Arabian heat. Not at all what you'd expect a British officer to be. But he had known the great Lawrence and had a sentimental attachment to the Hashemite dynasty. He particularly admired the late King Feisal of Iraq, Abdullah's brother and Lawrence's stanchest ally.

"That was a man, Feisal," he told me. "If only he were alive today the Arab world would be a lot better off. But Abdullah is all right. A bit erratic, of course, but a sound fellow at heart. And these Arabs need a king, you know. This idea of separate Syrian and Lebanese republics— that's a lot of nonsense. This all used to be one country, Syria, Lebanon, Transjordan, and what we call Palestine too. It was all Syria. Wasn't till the Versailles peace conference and all that stuff came along that it was split up. One kingdom for the whole area could stand up to Soviet penetration where three or four small states can't possibly. Abdullah's the man to head it up."

In a darkened office in Damascus, capital of the Syrian republic, which Abdullah aspires to take over, a stocky young man in khaki took a different line. He had just returned from a tour with the Rualla, one of the most powerful of the Syrian tribes, and had come back with badly inflamed eyes as a result of incautious exposure to the sand glare. Hence the darkened room. He had also come back with some definite notions on Abdullah's ambitions. "Even the tribes are against him," he said, "and they were by far his best hope. The townspeople wouldn't want any part of him. Remember Transjordan is small and poor. It has to have an outside subsidy to keep it going. Syria, on the other hand, is comparatively rich and prosperous. To think that Transjordan could take over Syria is like expecting the flea to rule the dog. All Abdullah has is Glubb Pasha and the legion, and I doubt if the legion would obey him if he ordered an invasion of Syria."

Glubb Pasha (Major General John Bagot Glubb) is a small, mild-voiced British officer who had part of his jaw shot away in the First World War—a wound that does not make him any more impressive looking. He speaks excellent Arabic and has built the Arab Legion into one of the best fighting forces of the Middle East. Like a sheikh, or even a king, he holds his *Majlis* (court) in Amman to hear the grievances of the tribesmen. It is said, though I have never seen him in the act, that he scratches himself publicly to make insect-ridden visitors feel at ease. Glubb's aggressively prosaic name has not kept him from a romantic and remarkable career.

I don't know what Glubb Pasha really thinks of his Arab king; I haven't asked, and wouldn't expect an answer if I did. But I do know what the late Colonel Lawrence thought. (Glubb has been called the Lawrence of the Second World War.) In his remarkable account of the Arab revolt of 1916-18, *The Seven Pillars of Wisdom,* Lawrence wrote: "despite his kindness and charm, I could not like Abdullah . . . . The leaven of insincerity works through all the fibres of his being . . . . his indolence marred his scheming, too. The webs were constantly unravelling through his carelessness in leaving them unfinished." Lawrence recognized his ambitions, but doubted his ability to achieve them.

Abdullah was also the subject of conversation in the modern Jewish City of Tel Aviv. The population center of Israel seems, and is, far removed from Arab affairs. The town resembles a Central European dream of a Riviera resort, and entering it one enters a world wholly different from the essentially eastern culture of Nazareth, Hebron or Beersheba. That summer (1947) it was easier in Tel Aviv than it is, unfortunately, now to forget the Arabs. And Zionist leaders there apparently had not read, or did not believe, Lawrence's critical analysis of Abdullah. Most of those I spoke to felt that "Abdullah is a man we can do business with."

I had an interview with Israel Rokach, mayor of Tel Aviv, who assured me there was nothing to fear from the Arabs. "They are unorganized and infirm of purpose. We can handle them easily. The only army they have worth anything is Transjordan's Arab Legion and"—he dropped a heavy wink—"we have assurances that the king is well disposed toward us. He is a sensible man." It was common knowledge that "secret" negotiations had been taking place between the Jewish Agency and Abdullah for some time. (In fact, I am sure that such negotiations went on all through the fighting.) Secrecy always adds spice to political palaver, even if it is the kind of secrecy which cloaked these talks but did not conceal them—any more than you conceal a chair in the center of a room by draping a great black cloth over it.

Later, in the north of Palestine, I talked with a "trouble-shooter" for the Jewish Agency's agricultural projects, one of the unfortunately small number of Zionists who have made a serious study of the Arabs. His work, of course, unlike city work, had brought him in constant touch with them, he spoke Arabic fluently, and had traveled widely in the Arab countries bordering Palestine. He was, like so many experts, a prophet without honor in his own country. And his position was in no way improved by the fact that British and American officials valued his opinion highly.

"I hope our leaders don't make the mistake of taking Abdullah seriously," he said gloomily. "He seems to offer an easy way out, but I don't think for one moment that he could keep his promises even if he wanted to." We were riding on horseback along the crest of a bare hill above the Sea of Galilee. My companion, who had studied at an agricultural school in our southwest, spoke good American English. For all I could see or hear, I might have been on a pack trip in the foothills of Southern California, and it seemed unreal, like being part of a Douglas Fairbanks movie, to be talking of a king's intentions toward an ancient land.

But it was a matter, possibly, of life and death for my companion. He spoke soberly of late reports he had received that King Abdullah had proposed to issue a statement implying that he might agree to the partition of Palestine under certain circumstances. The statement wouldn't have been worth much anyhow, my friend thought, but the king couldn't even issue it. His cabinet threatened to resign if he did, and advised further that he had better have a plane ready for his getaway as soon as his subjects should hear of it.

"Abdullah might risk his throne to gain something," my friend continued, "but he wouldn't risk it to give something up—even something that isn't his! Our best chance in dealing with him is to recognize him for what he is—but everyone who meets and talks with the man has a different idea, and each one is convinced that *his* idea is the right one. He is certainly an elusive little guy. So far as pinning down character is concerned, I'd call him the Scarlet Pimpernel of the Arab World."

Shifting from the crisp air of the Judaean hills to the heavy, tangible heat of the Arabian interior, my next talk of Abdullah was with Abdul Aziz ibn Abdur Rahman al Sa'ud, better known to Americans as ibn Saud, King of Saudi Arabia and hereditary foe of the Hashemite dynasty. Ibn Saud bears little resemblance to his brother Arab king. He is tall and massive; his beard, despite his age, is still dark; although one eye is almost closed by a cataract and he limps from an old battle wound, the Lord of Arabia is still vigorous and decisive.

Besides Palestine, the chief problem ibn Saud had on his mind was Abdullah's ambition to extend his rule over the Arab republics of Syria and Lebanon. Ibn Saud was inclined to agree with many Zionist leaders that Abdullah was really on their side. He argued that Abdullah's pretensions to rule over Syria and Lebanon were absurd, and that to press them at that time could only spread distrust among Arabs and thus help Zionists.

Transjordan, ibn Saud observed, was indeed historically part of Syria, and should perhaps become so again. But that was for Syrians to decide, not for a foreign upstart, a minor official of the old Turkish Empire who had managed to hoodwink the British into proclaiming him King. Ibn Saud's good eye twinkled as he went on to say something which obviously puzzled his interpreter. This young man, crouched at the king's feet, turned to me for assistance. "His majesty says this scheme is not based on reason or history. It is the fantasy of one man's ambition. His majesty says Abdullah is sick-mindedly greatness mad—I cannot translate it, but his majesty says there are words for it in English."

After much discussion, we concluded that ibn Saud was describing Abdullah as a "morbid megalomaniac"!

When we pronounced the words to the king, he was very pleased. "That sounds good," he told the interpreter. "I want that quoted."

Early last spring a writer for one of the weekly news magazines came to me in some puzzlement. His editors had decided to use a picture of Abdullah on the cover of a forthcoming issue. My visitor was to pull together a story to go with it—but, as he pointed out unhappily, the issue wouldn't come out for some weeks.

"How am I going to know what Abdullah's position will be by then?" he asked plaintively. "Some people say he made a deal with the Arab League, others say he's promised the British to do what they want. And still others say he has come to an agreement with the Zionists. Which do you think is right?"

"Almost certainly they are all right," I told him. Abdullah loves to "negotiate," and his personal idea of negotiation is not quite the same as ours. The way he sees it, commitments on future action are made to keep people happy and friendly as long as possible. He tells the Arab League, the British, the Zionists, as nearly as he can what he thinks they want to hear. And he expects them to do the same for him.

Then when the time comes for action, he will do what seems most to his own advantage and if that happens to be close to what he promised one of the earlier negotiators, all right; if not, all right too.

The only thing that would surprise the little king in all this, would be to discover that any of the negotiators took his words, or their words, more seriously than he did himself. Then his little round face would beam, his eyes twinkle, and the royal mirth resound at such a great joke.

It would not be accurate to dismiss the Greater Syria project as lightly as Abdullah's ambitions for it. The scheme as advocated by Abdullah is indeed doomed to failure. It is opposed by the Syrians, and indeed Arab nationalists everywhere including Transjordan, on two main grounds.

First, they fear that extension of Abdullah's rule would be the equivalent of extension of British rule. They have fought too long and too hard for their independence to surrender it under such a guise.

Secondly, there is distrust and dislike of Abdullah personally and of the Hashemites in general, throughout the Arab world.

But if the complications and controversies aroused by Abdullah are removed, there is widespread Arab support for the idea of a reunion of the lands which used to form Syria. These would include Palestine, Lebanon, Transjordan, present-day Syria, and possibly Iraq as well. This might cause jealousy in Egypt, although individual Egyptians have spoken favorably of the idea to me. Ibn Saud also told me he thought that eventually a reunion of the old Syria was desirable and inevitable.

In addition to Arab support, the project has for widely different reasons the tentative backing of the big powers. The British would like to see Abdullah or his nephew the regent of Iraq as king of a Greater Syria, but even without that they welcome the idea. They believe that it might assist solution of the Palestine imbroglio, and that it would provide a strong buffer state against the Soviet Union. Moreover they think that establishment of such a state would give the Arabs more confidence in themselves, make them less hypersensitive about British influence, and thus set British relations with the Arab world on a sounder footing.

Naturally the Russians would not like to see the actuality of Greater Syria with or without Abdullah. But they are sure that it cannot come into being without splitting the Arabs and wrecking the Arab League. Therefore they like to hear the idea agitated.

The French fear that a strong Arab League will make trouble for them in North Africa. They hope, also, that Lebanese Christians would be so frightened by the prospect of Moslem domination in a Greater Syria that they would come running back to the French for protection. So they, like the Russians, encourage the talking and plotting, without actually wanting the final product.

American foreign policy officials have opposed Abdullah's ambitions. This was partly at the insistence of ibn Saud, but also because they regarded those ambitions as a real threat to peace in the Middle East. While there is no definite policy on the matter, they incline to favor the idea of a Greater Syria established not by an unpopular king but by the freely expressed wills of the people involved. American observers see no reason why a republic of Greater Syria should weaken the Arab League. On the contrary, if there is by then anything left of the league, they think it would be strengthened by the result. The problems of Palestine and its surroundings will not be solved by splitting the land into smaller units. They *may* be brought closer to solution by bringing the fragments together. Transjordan, Arab Palestine, Syria and Lebanon would be healthier economically and stronger diplomatically as one. And if Israel could eventually find a place in such a federation, so much the better for her—and her neighbors.

✥ XIV ✥

Lebanon: Switzerland of the Middle East

NOW therefore command thou that they hew me cedars out of
Lebanon." So wrote Solomon to Hiram, King of Tyre, who
gave instructions to his servants accordingly. And the great temple
which Solomon built to the Lord in Jerusalem had the finest timber the
known world could provide. The giant cedars which still grow in the
mountains back of Tripoli (Tripoli Lebanon, not Tripoli Libya) are not
the only reminders of Lebanon's rich history. The sites of the ancient
Phoenician cities are still to be seen; the modern towns of Saida and
Jebeil, for instance, are built over old Sidon and Byblos. Some of the
oldest Christian communities in the world—contemporaneous with
those of Bethlehem and Nazareth—are to be found in Lebanon and
neighboring Syria. The mountains which provided cedar for Solomon
gave refuge to the much-feared Assassins whose leaders, with the assistance of hashish, persuaded them that they were already in paradise—
and that to stay there it was only necessary for them to make an occasional descent to the world, to rid it of some presumably repulsive
person, often a Crusader. As further reminder of the Crusades, there
are a number of fine stone Crusader fortresses, notably the twelfth-cen-
tury castle by the sea in Saida in the south, and the famous Crak des
Chevaliers in the north. The Crak is regarded as one of the finest examples of medieval military architecture. From its fastness the Knights
Hospitalers inflicted severe defeats upon the Saracens; even Saladin was
unable to capture it.

Lebanon today is a small and very beautiful country. The mountains
seem to rise straight out of the Mediterranean, and there is enough rain
to keep the valleys green. Fruits and flowers grow in profusion. Every

possible speck of land is cultivated, the hillsides being skillfully ter-
raced to stop erosion and hold each drop of water. This gives much of
the landscape a quiltlike pattern reminiscent of southern Italy, although
the Lebanese prefer to compare their country to Switzerland. The comparison rests not only upon the mountain scenery but upon a tradition
of toleration; Lebanon, like Switzerland, has long been a refuge for political and religious refugees from other lands.

The physical resemblance to southern Italy and the proud comparison
to Switzerland are not the only marks which set off the little country
from the hinterland. Some Lebanese, insisting that their Mediterranean
culture has little connection with Arab Islam, refer to themselves as
"Phoenicians." This used to be fashionable; it has become less and less
so in recent years, and most of the leading Christians now flatly describe
themselves as Arab. But there *is* a cultural difference. Beirut, the capital,
a city built upon hills and looking up into the face of mountains, is more
like a French Mediterranean town than an Arab city. Entirely aside from
the recent political domination, French culture has ruled in Beirut for
generations. Most of its inhabitants speak French and in fact Beiruti
Arabic is of distinctly poor quality. There are large numbers of foreign
schools in Beirut, including the famous American University. Most are
French, American and English, in that order. But there are also Danish,
Greek and Swiss schools. Due to the large number of French convent
schools, a majority of those receiving foreign education in Lebanon are
girls, and the education of women is far more advanced than in neighboring states. Lebanon has the highest literacy rate, about 85 per cent,
of any Arab country.

Lebanon and Syria, linked through several thousand years of history,
are almost always mentioned in the same breath. The most recently independent of Arab countries, they are new creations carved from an old
unity—for the partition of Palestine is not the first partition imposed
by the West upon this ancient land. Until 1919 "Syria" included what
is now Lebanon, Palestine and Transjordan as well as the present republic of Syria. All were part of the Ottoman Empire, owing allegiance
to the Sultan and governed by officials responsible to him. We have seen
that the postwar disposition of that empire was dictated chiefly by the
rival imperial interests of France and Britain. After much bloodshed
and contention France finally relinquished her mandates over Syria and
Lebanon in 1946.

While in control, the French operated on a principle of divide and rule. Some of their divisions did not survive their departure. They separated the Druze and Alouite districts of Syria from the remainder, but these are now reincorporated in the Syrian republic. Another division they adopted remains in force. For Lebanon, the present Republic of Lebanon, was largely manufactured in France.

The process of manufacture began long before the mandate. Until France intervened with Turkey to force a halt, Christians and Moslems in old Syria were constantly at each other's throats. Individual murders and thefts were daily occurrences, large-scale massacres and pillaging were only slightly less frequent. In 1864, at the insistence of the French, Turkey granted the Christians of Lebanon their own separate administration. Thus as a small Christian state with a seaside culture distinct from that of the interior, the republic of Lebanon does have real basis apart from French designs for its existence. However the French, who regarded the Maronite (Christian) majority in Lebanon as their most effective ally, sought to strengthen it by assigning the region of Tripoli and the rich Bekaa valley to Lebanon, thus creating a Greater (as opposed to the old, now known as the Lesser) Lebanon. Unfortunately these additions, together with sizable emigration to Africa and North and South America which was largely Christian, have reduced the earlier Christian majority to an actual, though not admitted, minority. How much longer it will be able to rule as if it were a majority, how much longer Lebanon can administer itself in terms of religious communities, is very much of a question. Some Maronites are calling for a return to the Lesser Lebanon, in which they would have a clear majority. Other Lebanese, not all of them Moslem, are agitating for a Greater Syria. The most encouraging sign is the effort of leaders such as Moslem Abdul Hamid Kerame and Christian Alfred Naccache to keep religion out of politics, to appeal to large blocs of voters in terms of other interests which they have in common. Both these gentlemen will be discussed later.

Most discouraging, on the other hand, has been the failure so far of Syria and Lebanon to achieve the economic union which is essential to both. It is a reminder (which might have been heeded by the United Nations General Assembly) that only the most politically sophisticated peoples can manage to be separated politically and joined together economically. Many of the problems of Lebanon would be greatly simplified by restoration of historic Syria. Transjordan obviously cannot survive as a separate economic unit by itself. Parts of Palestine too have suffered from the arbitrary breaking up of the old pattern. Even under Turkish rule, for instance, Palestine was not an integrated administrative division of Syria, nor even a part of one larger division. Part of it fell within the Vilayet of Beirut, the remainder in the Sanjak of Jerusalem. Most of the towns of northern Palestine were linked economically and otherwise, to their north—to Syria and Lebanon. The town of Safad is a good example of a town that flourished on northern trade and declined when the artificial boundaries and border controls set up by the British and French wiped out that trade. The road network of the area is sufficient proof even now of its economic orientation. Elimination of the barriers would be a great stimulus in reviving trade, and would benefit all concerned.

I need hardly add that the political obstacles in the path of such action are, as the French have taught the Lebanese to say, *formidable.*

In spite of its beauty Lebanon is a poor country. Inflation is bad there, which makes it tough not only on the inhabitants but on the tourists—and the tourist trade is most important to the Lebanese economy. Most foods have gone up six to ten times in price since the beginning of the war. A pair of good quality shoes which would have cost four Lebanese pounds in 1937 might have cost anywhere up to seventy-five pounds in 1947—a rise of nearly 1900 per cent in ten years. (Lebanese pounds are worth about thirty cents.) For some goods, prices have already settled. New American cars, for instance, which sold for the equivalent of twenty thousand dollars in 1946 are now down to six or seven thousand dollars. But food and labor costs will never return to the earlier levels except in a disastrous deflation.

Nor is Lebanon's government notably superior to other Middle East governments, as its higher level of education suggests it should be. Lebanon has, to be sure, one unusual feature—unusual not only in the Middle East but elsewhere. That is a perennial cabinet minister who is able, honest, hardworking and disinterested politically. His name is Gabriel Murr, and he is minister of Public Works. Murr and his brother, Elias, who serves without pay as his technical adviser, have lived in the United States and studied at American schools. (Elias is a graduate of MIT, a first-class engineer and architect.) Their road and airfield programs, and plans for the harnessing of water power in the mountainous country, have been most successful. Gabriel Murr is completely non-political. His steady tenure of office speaks well for his talents, and also for the restraint of the politicos who let him stay—or the public which made the politicos leave him be. There are other able men in the government, such as the Druze Kemal Junblatt and the Christian Camille Chamoun, whose title is minister of the Interior but who has spent much time recently representing Lebanon at the United Nations, where he has been one of the most effective speakers for the Arab cause.

There is a strong possibility that Chamoun, in fact, may be the next president. The present incumbent is a rotund gentleman named Sheikh Bechary el-Khouri, familiarly known to his constituents as Abu Kirsh ("Father of the Belly"). His term expires in 1949. He holds office largely because he is a Christian; if Chamoun and the one or two other able Christian candidates knock each other out in the preliminaries, his successor may come into office for no other reason. This is one aspect of what is probably the fundamental reason why the Lebanese government is not more effective.

Behind all these political complexities is the fact that in Lebanon there was established something approximating what was so often proposed for Palestine—a binational state. It is, of course, bireligious, not really binational, but the Christians and Moslems have often hated and distrusted each other as bitterly as any national groups could. The present complicated political setup was devised by the French with that in mind. Its shortcomings are not to be taken as indications that a binational state cannot work in the Middle East. Quite the contrary, particularly since it appears that the system may be revised to minimize the shortcomings by minimizing the accent on religious differences.

If Lebanon and Syria provide lessons (too late) for Palestine, they are: (1) that a binational state *is* practical, though UN feared it was not; (2) that it is difficult to have economic union and, at the same time, political separation, which is what UN tried to establish, under impossible conditions, in Palestine.

The Lebanese electoral laws provide for election by the religious communities according to their proportional strengths. Thus in a district which is 50 per cent Maronite, 30 per cent Sunni Moslem and 20 per cent Druze, of ten deputies elected five must be Maronite, three

Sunni and two Druze even though the sixth Maronite may have more votes than his Sunni and Druze opponents together. The president must by law be a Christian, the prime minister a Moslem, and the other cabinet posts are also allocated according to religion. The intention was, of course, to protect the different religious communities by assuring them of proportional representation. Lebanon operates by what has become known in this country as PR—but PR along religious lines. The unfortunate result is that a candidate, knowing that his own religious community must elect him, is encouraged to make a strongly sectarian appeal for votes, to play up religious prejudices and antagonisms. Each election threatens to widen the gulf between Christian and Moslem. This was hardly the intention of those drafting the constitution (unless you wish, as some Lebanese and Syrians do, to credit the French with satanic cunning). Yet in spite of the constantly recurring temptation to do otherwise, the encouraging fact is that many Lebanese political leaders are rising above sectarian interests. Many Moslems have ceased their agitation for union with their Moslem brothers in Syria. While there was at first considerable opposition among the Christians to Lebanon's becoming a member of the Arab League, that has largely vanished. Christian Lebanese have taken the lead in pressing the Arab case on Palestine in the United Nations. They have recognized that their own interests, in fact their survival, demand that they be on good terms with their Moslem neighbors. The old Christian-Moslem conflict here is not settled, but it does seem to be moving toward settlement.

The careers of three widely separated political leaders illustrate the trend. First is Alfred Naccache, the last president of Lebanon to be appointed by the Vichy French.

Naccache, a man in his early sixties, is a reserved, severe, sad-looking lawyer, whose ascetic cast of countenance accentuates the impression of high-minded gloom. He is descended from an old Lebanese family, studied in a French school in Beirut, and took his law degree in Paris. Under the Turkish rule in Lebanon, he was in trouble with the authorities for his patriotic activities and was, during the First World War, condemned to death in absentia. During the French regime he had a distinguished legal and civic career. When the British and Free French invaded Syria and Lebanon in late 1941, Naccache, who had just been appointed president, called upon General Dentz (the Vichy commander) to declare Beirut an open city. This got him in trouble with the Vichy authorities and although the Allied victory saved him then, later differences of opinion with the Free French and British forced his resignation. He became head of the opposition, and in 1947 joined with the Moslem leader Abdul Hamid Kerame in demanding dissolution of the Chamber of Deputies which, it was generally recognized, had been elected in an unusually shoddy and illegal manner. Naccache and Kerame agreed on the need for a Constituent Assembly to amend the Constitution and, particularly, the electoral law, both of which had been sponsored by the French.

Thus Naccache has shown himself a Lebanese patriot who is not constrained by narrow sectarian interests. He is one of those Christian leaders who feels that Moslem-Christian co-operation is essential, and who has shown himself willing to do his share of the co-operating. That does not mean at all that he would see Lebanon absorbed into a larger Arab state.

I asked him specifically about the Greater Syria project. He replied that he, like many of his co-religionists, had no objection to it *provided* that it was clear that Lebanon could not be included. Abdullah, he told me, had promised individual Lebanese to respect Lebanese frontiers and integrity. He would agree that Lebanese ports should serve as outlets for Greater Syria—provided he could get Lebanese support for his scheme. These promises were to be made in an international treaty which would commit Abdullah before the world.

However, Naccache told me with grave legal irony, it was impossible to sign an international treaty with private groups. The Lebanese government has shown no inclinations for negotiation on the point with Abdullah. I could well understand that, and said so. If the Syrian government should learn of such negotiations, it might well lead to a rupture of Syrian and Lebanese relations, and negotiations with Abdullah are notoriously insecure. It seemed to me that Naccache and his friends were playing with fire. But that is in the best Arab—or perhaps, in this case, I should say Phoenician—tradition.

In any case, it was clear that if they could pin Abdullah down where they could be sure of him, there was a group of Lebanese Christians who would be glad to do business with him. I wondered if they knew how many people had tried to pin the little king down before, and what an unbroken series of failures had resulted. But their motive was compelling. As Naccache put it, with solemn simplicity:

"Lebanon, like Palestine, cannot be treated as if it were just another part of the Arab world. She has a distinctly separate identity of her own, which must not be drowned in a Moslem sea."

Abdul Hamid Kerame would disagree with Alfred Naccache on many and fundamental matters. Nevertheless a good part of the time they have found themselves in effective alliance. Kerame is a Sunni Moslem, a member of a family which has a long and impressive history in Tripoli, where they have supplied an almost unbroken line of muftis (religious leaders) for the region. Tripoli, it will be remembered, was not a part of the historical Lebanon, but was added to Lebanon during the French mandate. It has been a center of Moslem agitation against the Lebanese government. As recently as February of 1948 there were serious riots in Tripoli, in which demonstrators demanded that Tripoli be restored to Syria. Kerame is a younger man than Naccache (about fifty-five) but his political career is even longer and is equally distinguished. Even now, though he holds no public office, he is by far the strongest influence in the strongest Moslem section of Lebanon. A quiet-voiced man with white mustache and hair, he looks rather like a distinguished French diplomat who has been roughing it à l'Anglais on the Riviera. His courtesy and hospitality are in the finest Arab tradition, but he breaks with tradition by being more direct and outspoken than is common among Arab politicians, or for that matter among politicians of any race. Rarely have I met a person whose integrity stood out more clearly from his face, his manners and his words. It stands out at least equally clearly in his record.

Abdul Hamid Kerame was brought up, in the family tradition, to serve as the local mufti. He was elected to that office during the First World War and when the Turks and Germans were driven out by the British and the Arabs under Feisal, Kerame assumed the post of governor of the Tripoli region in the name of the Arab government then establishing itself in Damascus. Later Feisal visited Tripoli and confirmed him in his position. When Feisal was defeated and forced out by the French, Kerame became the leader of the opposition to the French in northern Lebanon. Twice he was arrested and imprisoned for his opposition; nevertheless, he persisted. Among his activities was the organization of congresses which protested in the name of the "Syrian Coast" against the establishment of Greater Lebanon by the annexation of territories which were properly Syrian. Until 1943 he remained opposed to these annexations. In that year, however, when the independence of Lebanon was proclaimed and guaranteed by the Allies and the Lebanese people were given a chance to elect their first independent parliament, Kerame, by agreement with the leaders of other Arab countries, announced that he had given up his policy of non-co-operation and accepted without reservation the policy of an Arab Lebanon—a Lebanon free from all outside ties and allegiances, sovereign within its present frontiers. He had long since given up his post as mufti in favor of a political career and now he joined actively in advancing the affairs of a country which, under French rule, he had vigorously opposed. When the French, finding a new government altogether too independent for their taste, tried to reverse the trend by imprisoning its members, Kerame was given the distinction of being the only noncabinet member to be arrested by the French.

Later he was elected prime minister and presided over the Lebanese delegation that signed the pact of the League of Arab States in Cairo in 1945. He proposed a series of sweeping reforms of the Constitution and the electoral system and when it was apparent that he would be unable to obtain the support of the president in carrying out these reforms, he resigned his office.

His weakness as a politician is a common one among Arabs—a tendency to withdraw too easily from the game if the other team won't play fair, if the referee seems prejudiced, or if conditions of play are adverse. In the case of Kerame, this comes from a nagging feeling that perhaps politics is not a gentlemanly game, and that if it can't be played cleanly he won't play at all. Cultivation of such a feeling on the part of its statesmen is a luxury few countries, and Arab countries least of all, can afford. It is to be hoped that Kerame's combative spirit and genuine, deep-rooted desire for reform will overcome his gentlemanly squeamishness.

His importance as a politician, which persists despite that squeamishness, comes from more than his reforming zeal, though that in itself is extremely valuable. (His proposed reform of the civil service is, for example, badly needed.) Kerame is a Moslem of unimpeachable orthodoxy and large personal following who combines full-hearted support for the Arab League with the conviction that Lebanon in her present form must be preserved and that Christians and Moslems can and must collaborate to that end.

He said to me: "You know I was a mufti, and I would much rather have stayed one. It is a life far more to my taste. But when I entered politics, as I felt the interests of my people compelled me to do, I realized that I could not have the two responsibilities together. A mufti's place is not in politics, which must be kept separate from religion. Some day I hope to return to the religious life, but that cannot be until I have completed my other tasks—or failed in the attempt. How could I appeal for Christian votes if I were a mufti, any more than a Christian priest could expect Moslems to vote for him? The most important thing for Lebanon is that Christians should vote for Moslems, and Moslems for Christians. We must bring this long and senseless strife to an end."

Far different from Naccache or Kerame is Antun Saadah, the *zaim* or leader of the National Syrian Social Party. Saadah claims about thirty to thirty-five thousand supporters in Lebanon and an equal number in Syria. Actually these claims are greatly exaggerated. A more accurate estimate of his following in Lebanon would be between five and six thousand and about the same in Syria. He has, however, a tightly knit organization, well disciplined and united in admiration for the leader in a manner reminiscent of Nazism and Fascism. To an American, Saadah talks democracy and says that the decisions must be made by all those affected. But one visit to him is enough to reveal the strength of the cult of the leader in the party, and it is well known that he brooks no opposition from his followers.

The Lebanese government has been consistently suspicious of Saadah and his group. When I saw him he had just returned from "exile" in Argentina, where there is a large and comparatively wealthy Syrian colony. His followers claimed that he was met at the airport by a crowd of thirty thousand people. In any case, he made an inflammatory speech on his arrival, and next day a warrant was issued for his arrest. This seems to have been pretty much of a formality and it was canceled a few weeks after I saw him; but at the time he was in elaborate, if not very effective, hiding. (The Lebanese police could not have failed to find him if they had really looked. Presumably they did not wish to create a disturbance.)

Shortly after arriving in Beirut I had let word get around that I would like to meet Antun Saadah. One day a young Druze boy, whose acquaintance I had earlier made, came to me and said that he would arrange such a meeting. We made a rendezvous where we picked up still a third individual, to whom had been entrusted the knowledge of the whereabouts of his leader. Then we drove into the country behind Beirut and, a short way beyond one of the popular summer resorts, took a road which came to a dead end close to the top of a mountain. Here we waited while the trusted one made certain mysterious explorations. Then we were told it was all right for us to come and we clambered a way up toward the summit. There were a couple of houses and beyond them some tents in plain sight. As we approached these a man with a tommygun appeared and conversed at length with our guide. After inspection we were led to a clearing with some benches, there to await the pleasure of the leader. Shortly, he came, a stocky, swarthy man with an impressive manner and compelling eyes. His costume, to my prejudiced Western eye, was less impressive. He was smartly dressed in a gabardine suit with well-padded shoulders, alligator shoes with pointed tips, a foulard tie and a green shirt. He was gracious but managed to convey the impression that conversation with him was a privilege. His two young followers who had brought me up had been most talkative en route, but in his presence they said scarcely a word.

Saadah repeated to me the claims of strength which I had already heard from his followers. He also told me that in addition to his backing in Lebanon and Syria he also had considerable support in Transjordan and in Palestine and that he was developing branches in the regions to which Syrians have emigrated in some number, mainly North and South America and Africa. His program is a simple one on the surface, but seems to be embodied in a mystique compounded of a sense of national destiny and a surrender to direction (by the leader). I found difficulty in getting Saadah or his followers to express this very plainly, but its nature was plain. The expressed goal of the party is the establishment of "natural" Syria, which would stretch from the Suez Canal Zone to the Taurus Mountains, taking in half of Iraq, part of Turkey and, inevitably, all of Palestine, Transjordan, Lebanon and Syria. It is not an unfamiliar program. Saadah is definite that in uniting these territories he wants no part of Abdullah or of British influence in any form. Although his claims of strength are undoubtedly highly exaggerated, it does seem to be true that he has as much of a following in Syria as he does in Lebanon. Yet this extreme nationalist makes a point of appealing to all religious groups. He claims that half of his following is Christian and half Moslem. He claims also that a strong part of his following comes from the Homs-Hama region of Syria, which is noted to be fanatically Moslem.

When you find three leaders of such diverse political, social and religious backgrounds agreeing that religion must be kept out of politics, that is news—very significant and hopeful news for Lebanon and perhaps for her neighbors as well.

✿ XV ✿

Syria: Troubles for the Young Effendi

DAMASCUS, often said to be the oldest inhabited city in the world, is the most colorful of the Arab capitals. It is situated in a lovely oasis, backed up against a range of sandy mountains. The usual approach to it is particularly colorful. Driving to Damascus from Beirut, you cross the ranges of the Lebanon and Anti-Lebanon and the rich Bekaa valley which divides them, an excitingly beautiful trip. It is also just plain exciting. Even if you are not traveling by taxi yourself you are bound to meet plenty of them on the road; busses and trucks too, but the latter, while solidly dangerous, are not nearly so spectacular. The taxi drivers have spirit, abandon and dash that are strongly Gallic in flavor (they are usually garlic flavored too). They have also, in my opinion, a wider field of operation than that available to the Paris taxi driver. The Parisien does, it must be admitted, an admirable job with what is available to him. But Paris does not have twisting mountain roads, is lamentably lacking in camels, and is deficient even in donkeys. Moreover the pedestrian, while showing commendable verve and supreme contempt for automotive traffic, lacks certain natural advantages possessed by the Arab. In costume, for instance, the male Arab has an edge on his French counterpart. It is possible to screen your intentions more effectively behind a full-skirted *galabeah* than in the comparative openness of trousers (a similar advantage is enjoyed by the nightgown in competition with pajamas) and this may help to account for the transcendent skill with which the Arab leads you to think he is going to run one way while, at that very instant, he is already traveling full speed in another. In the Western world, the impression prevails that the pedestrian is mildly challenged to escape the vehicle. But the harried

driver in an Oriental city often feels that the situation is reversed, that
the challenge has been thrown back in his face, and that he must employ
every human and superhuman power to escape the pedestrian. It is surprising how often he succeeds.

Having won through to Damascus, the traveler finds the effort well
worth while. Some Eastern cities have to be lived in to be loved. Baghdad, for instance. Others, which need not be named, put up even stiffer
resistance to affection. But Damascus exerts an immediate charm. The
French have built a number of imposing official buildings upon broad
avenues, but the narrow, covered streets, the old houses with their plain
exteriors and exquisite interiors (the rooms all opening upon an inner
courtyard with trees and birds and fountains), and the bazaars with
their wealth of life and contrast—all these remain in full vitality and
give Damascus, in spite of the French impact, its distinctively Arab
character.

Certainly the first impression is of color. After Cairo, the costumes
appear vivid and lively. In Egypt, black, white and brown prevail, but
in Damascus blues, reds and yellows abound. *Galabeahs* of white or
blue are held in by many-colored sashes. Even the shoes, or rather the
slippers which are usually preferred to shoes, are often bright scarlet
leather. Damascus has always been famous for its crafts. Damascus steel,
of course, was reputed to be the finest in the world, and many a Crusader from Europe returned home treasuring a sword bladed with the
product of his Moslem enemies. Syrian steel has long since lost its pri-
macy, but Damascus still offers other special products—mosaic tables
and boxes, fine leather goods, gold and silver inlay and filigree, gold
and silver brocades, silks, wood carving, finely worked brass and bronze
vessels, and candied fruits (Damascus sweetmeats are known throughout the East).

All these and countless other goods are displayed in the different
bazaars, of which there is one for each main type of work—gold, silver,
leather, jewelry, and so forth. A walk through the markets brings not
only exciting contrasts in color and texture but in sound and smell as
well. From the stalls of shining green and pale yellow melons, soft
golden apricots and bursting red tomatoes with a prevailing sweet,
slightly sickish smell, you move in a few steps to the metal workers'
bazaar with dull bronze and bright silver, the constant sound of tapping

hammers, and a heavy odor of charcoal burning from the braziers. Wood and leather have their distinctive smells, and through them all run the scents that are never far distant in Eastern life, some disagreeable (rotting garbage and ordure), some heady, tantalizing (garlic, sesame, saffron, and others of the countless pungent spices with which Easterners flavor their food and thus themselves).

There is a variety in the people too. Proud burly Kurds, fierce brown men from Homs, a redheaded Druze, the slight soft-stepping Bedu from Palmyra way, the thousand and one racial mixtures of the ancient city rub shoulders, joke, quarrel, bargain, cajole and fight in an ever-changing pattern of sounds, sights and smells which is one of the most fascinating and revealing experiences of the world.

Damascus, like Jerusalem, is a place which has powerful associations for Moslems and Christians alike. The Great Mosque of the Ommayads was built originally as the Church of St. John the Baptist. "The Street which is called Straight," known to us from the Bible and to Moslems from stories of their own, still runs, narrow and straight as ever, from the east to the west gates of the old city. It is covered, like many other Oriental streets, to provide the passer-by with protection against the unfriendly sun—a fact which, to unfamiliar Western eyes, adds to its antique charm. You can see near by the house where St. Paul is supposed to have found shelter after, as the young arrogant Saul, he had his miraculous vision on the road to Damascus. They will show you also where (it is confidently asserted) he was lowered over the city wall in a basket, when his enemies were close upon him. And then there is the tomb of Saladin, the honorable foeman of Richard the Lion Hearted, who is one of the great figures of Islamic history. Damascus also has less heroic claims to fame. In 1860, it was the scene of one of the last major massacres of Christians by Moslems, when three thousand Christian men were slaughtered in one outbreak.

With its historical and its present-day attractions, it is no wonder that Damascus should be the city which most Arab nationalists regard as their capital. Egyptians would like to introduce Cairo in its place, but Damascus has, in the Arabian Peninsula and the Fertile Crescent, the stronger hold on men's hearts and imaginations. It was the inevitable place for Feisal to choose as the seat of his ill-fated government after the First World War. His brother Abdullah, whose personal ambitions outweigh his Arab patriotism, also aspires to Damascus because of its symbolic and prestige value.

The present Syrian government is not the most stable Damascus has seen. It and its problems illustrate the difficulties in the way of progress and reform—the troubles which plague the well-intentioned Young Effendi. President Shukri Kuwatly is widely respected and his probity is unquestioned. But his cabinet is torn by strife and personal rivalry. When I was last there, in the summer of 1947, elections had recently been held which demonstrated its lack of cohesion. The government had been, it is true, determined to have a strictly free election. This may have been partly because the election in Lebanon which had just taken place was so patently the reverse of free that criticism threatened to overthrow the government which had staged it. Other motives may have been involved too, many of them praiseworthy. But, as always in Arab politics, the situation was complicated.

The government program reportedly called for a revision, after the election, of the constitution to allow Shukri Kuwatly to be elected president for a second term. The government seemed strong, able to count upon a solid victory at the polls. Ostensibly for that reason, and to demonstrate the freedom of the elections, it made little organized effort to mobilize popular support. But another explanation was widely offered, and believed, among Damascus wiseacres. The Prime Minister, Jamil Mardam, was thought not to be overeager to see all of his colleagues in the cabinet win re-election. His special target, according to the best gossip, was Defense Minister Ahmed Sharabati.

Moreover, you were told, Jamil Mardam was not averse to the idea of being president himself. Perhaps he deliberately overestimated government strength and discouraged campaigning on its behalf in order that, after the election, the government margin would be slim enough for him to explain to Kuwatly, with suitable apologies, that it would be politically impracticable to revise the Constitution. Then his friends could proceed, over his modest disclaimers, to draft as President Jamil Mardam himself.

That was the rumor. True or not, it indicates a certain lack of confidence all around. It points up, too, another difference between politics in countries which have a long-established democratic pattern and those which are new to the game. The difference is not, unfortunately, that a double-cross is impossible in the former. But a politician in England or America has to take not only himself but his party into account. Even a prime minister or a president would think twice before deliberately weakening his party, for he would almost inevitably weaken himself in the process. But the Syrian government does not represent an organized party. When the Syrians were still working for their freedom from the French, there was a powerful party, the Kutla, united in that cause. But now the cause has been won, the Kutla has broken up in numerous splinters. A Syrian cabinet now is a conglomeration of individuals with their own personal followings, rather than a party or a coalition of parties.

Parties are forming. Particularly in northern Syria, earnest groups of younger men are meeting, are discussing the necessity of party organization in the democratic system. Programs are being formulated, candidates chosen, and backing secured. The process is difficult, and will take time. As one Syrian plaintively remarked to me, if you have a program you alienate almost everyone, but you can have discipline among those who accept your program. On the other hand, if you expect to make a broad public appeal, you can't stand for anything in particular—and there's no particular basis for telling your followers what to do. (In other words, there is no solidly established platform of party patronage; jobs have been handed out on a personal rather than a party basis!)

Another problem Syria shares with other Middle Eastern countries is a problem of leadership following upon a struggle for national independence. The transition of leadership from revolutionary nationalism to constructive progressive development is difficult, particularly in a country which is as yet economically and politically undeveloped, as most areas under foreign imperialist rule are likely to be. China offers an example of the difficulties that may be faced even by comparatively advanced countries who were not under foreign rule. The difficulty may lie in the fact that while a country has been able to provide only one set of leaders in a generation, there are two very different sets of problems it must face in the same generation. First, the struggle against the old order, in Syria's case against French rule. This is a task that may call for conspiracy, terror, and ruthlessness; certainly all energies are bent toward *destruction* and overthrow of a system. If successful, the country then faces a wholly different kind of job—one of building up, of constructive development, of political education in what are, compared to revolutionary duties, the prosaic responsibilities of democracy.

Obviously, these call for very different qualities of leadership. Yet even if a country has available the right kind of postrevolution or post-independence leaders, which many do not, it is hard to expect that the leaders who have fought their way up will turn over the rewards of victory to a new group which—if it is to do its job well—must have been more aloof from the bitterness of the struggle. Time, of course, will take care of that, but politicians are a surprisingly long-lived bunch, and time is often short if the new-born state is to grow into a healthy organism.

Many politically conscious Syrians recognized this problem, and derived particular satisfaction, and hope, from the fact that President Shukri Kuwatly showed every sign of recognizing it too. There was a very promising group of Young Effendis appearing, and finding support, on the Syrian political scene. (The use of the past tense will be explained later.)

One such, for example, was mayor of Aleppo when I visited there in the fall of 1947. His name is Mejd-ed-din Jabri. He attended the American University of Beirut, and then a middle-west college here, where he was on the football team. He is a big, hearty man with a shrewd mind and an intense desire to improve conditions in his country. His wife, a charming Aleppo girl, graduated from Vassar. People whose only concept of the Arabs is drawn from the flea-bitten mendicants of Casablanca could learn much, in more ways than one, from this family —as well educated, with as high ideals of citizenship and responsibility, as you will find anywhere in the world.

Mejd-ed-din was proud of the progress made in Aleppo since the departure of the French. He had reason. In those two years, the Syrians had built three hundred primary schools and were at that time building four more secondary schools in Aleppo—two for boys, two for girls. (Mejd-ed-din and his wife Hala wanted to make sure I grasped that latter point: the education of girls was by no means being neglected!) Already they had laid nine times as much sewage pipe as the French had laid during the twenty-six years of their rule. They had built a third as much in road mileage in a thirteenth of the time, and had opened six times as many public gardens. They went on showing me figures until, it was evident, they felt their responsibility as host must supersede their responsibility as Arab patriots.

That was fine. And it was obvious that these were good, progressive, "Western-minded" people. They believe in the same kind of justice we do. Having been educated in America, and valuing their education, it was natural that they should be almost instinctively pro-American.

But unfortunately that wasn't the whole story. It left out Palestine, and Palestine refuses to be left out. It comes into the story in several ways.

First, it was clear that in spite of his good manners and cordial hospitality to an American visitor, Mejd-ed-din was bitterly disillusioned about America, that he had lost his one outside faith. There was no danger that he would succumb to Russian wiles; he hated the French and distrusted the British; he felt that the United States had betrayed not so much him and other Arabs, as herself—the ideals and beliefs for which she had stood. Mejd-ed-din had become an isolationist. And isolationists are just as unrealistic, just as dangerous to themselves and others, in Syria, as they are in China, in Hungary, or in the American middle west.

Secondly, Mejd-ed-din and Hala Jabri had begun to think new thoughts about justice. Everything they knew of justice, much of which they had learned in American schools and had heard repeated by American teachers, convinced them that justice was on the Arab side in Palestine. Democracy, majority rule, self-determination of peoples, free elections, independence for local populations from foreign rule—all the slogans of political justice supported that belief. But the country which they had looked to as the champion of justice, the land of the Statue of Liberty, seemed to have turned against the cause. Of course, unable to comprehend the variety of reasons for that turning, the Jabris placed the worst possible interpretation on it. And they became cynics, like so many idealistic, Western-educated Arabs. They said, "There is no such thing as justice in international affairs. There is just power politics. The Arabs must learn their lesson. Power is all that counts." I may say that is not a difficult lesson for Arabs to learn, for it fits perfectly well with their experience in and after two world wars. It is natural they should be increasingly and bitterly cynical. And cynicism is no more a force for good among Arabs than it is among Germans, or French, or Argentines, or Israelis.

Thirdly, Palestine enters the Jabri story because it may destroy them as effective workers for progress. I have called them "Western-minded," though they are as convinced Arab patriots as any. Their neighbors may look upon them as Western-minded too. And such is the hatred building up against the West over the issue of Palestine that Arabs are looking with suspicion on any of their group who have had any contact with the sinister, corrupting West. The most extreme, re-actionary antiforeign nationalist may triumph at the expense of the en-lightened, broadly educated nationalist. Their own nations may not be the only ones to suffer.

As I have said, Mejd-ed-din was what I have heard Zionists describe as an extreme anti-Zionist. (Arabs point out that there are no "ex-tremists"; they are all anti-Zionist period.) The last word I had of him was during the rioting which swept the Arab world after the partition resolution of November 1947. Mejd-ed-din had strapped on a brace of revolvers and had personally held off a rioting crowd from invading the Jewish quarter of Aleppo. I would not be surprised to hear that, still wearing the same revolvers, he had marched off to the recruiting office and enlisted to fight in Palestine.

While there is a tendency to discount the existence of progressive forces in the Middle East there is also a parallel if somewhat incon-sistent tendency to discount the opposition (aside from inertia) which those forces have to overcome. It is impossible to appraise the achieve-ments and estimate the future of men like Shukri Kuwatly or Mejd-ed-din Jabri without looking at the peoples on the other side.

These are commonly thought to be "effendi" and "feudal landhold-ers." The romantic and the ax-grinding world reformers agree on one point, that if only you gave the "common people" their "free choice" they would immediately unite behind "progressive, reforming" forces. Let us ignore, if we can, for a moment the nightmarish semantic confu-sion created by the words in quotation marks in the preceding sentence. Let us put beside it a somewhat more cautious historical generalization: Very often the hardest part of putting a reform across is educating the people who will benefit from it to the point where they will allow it to go into effect. Syria is not a particularly severe example of that recurrent situation, but it does offer its share of supporting illustrations. The main reason, of course, is the widespread resentment against anything foreign.

Take the Druze "problem." The Jebel Druze ("Jebel" means hill) is a black, barren land in southern Syria, not far from the Palestine border. Its inhabitants must cart away hundreds of pounds of volcanic rock before they can clear a small patch of earth for planting. The Druzes are actually a religious sect, worshipers following a secret cult which was founded in Egypt, nearly ten centuries ago, when its founder, the Caliph Al-Hakim, proclaimed himself the incarnation of God and established a reign of terror in Cairo. Since then the Druzes, who are now centered in Jebel Druze and in parts of south Lebanon, have kept themselves to themselves and are a people bound together by consanguinity as well as religion. They are hardy, proud men, accustomed to fighting nature, foreigners or—lacking all else—each other. It is popularly thought that they have much Crusader blood in their villages, for one often sees blue eyes and red hair among them. They are fierce looking, independence loving, and have demonstrated both qualities in their struggle against Turkish and, later, French rule.

For many years now, Jebel Druze has been ruled by the Atrash family. The Atrash have been wealthy, of course—that is expected of them. They have held public office, by election and by appointment. They have been leaders in the struggle for independence, and are proud of their record and their sacrifices in the cause. Sultan Pasha Atrash was the outstanding military figure of the revolt against the French, not only among the Druzes but for all Syria. His brother, Mustapha, was killed fighting the French in 1925. One of the strong grievances that the Atrash hold against Shukri Kuwatly and his government in Damascus is that they feel Kuwatly has cashed in on labors and losses which were mainly theirs.

When I visited Jebel Druze in the fall of 1947, there was perhaps a bit more than the usual amount of trouble there. I shall not describe it in detail, though I was given, orally and in writing, the most exhaustive accounts by each of the parties involved. The gist of it was that Damascus had been supporting a so-called People's party against the Atrash, that the Atrash had nonetheless carried the last election, that the honesty of the election had been questioned and that everyone was very mad at everyone else. Already there had been considerable violence. Every man I passed on the road or on the village streets was carrying a rifle or a sub-machine gun. In the course of my visit, no matter which camp I was in, there were constant interruptions for reports from villages where tension was particularly high and where the armed forces of both sides were jockeying for position.

I was taken first to call on the Atrash, and was greeted by Hassan el-Atrash, a stocky, confident man who received me most courteously and let slip no possible occasion to impress upon me the essential, undeviating, unquestionable justice of everything pertaining to the Atrash case. Our conversation was interrupted by one of the most nicely staged performances I have encountered. A servant came hurriedly into the room as the emir was pouring coffee and whispered into his ear. Hassan looked up at me and, with an air of surprise, said that a delegation of his followers had arrived to consult with him. Naturally, they did not know of my presence, but would I care to see them? I gave the reply that was expected of me.

Outside, in the entrance hall of his home, I found an assembly of bearded, turbaned notables, so jammed into the hallway that they were practically hanging from the banisters and the chandeliers. They were an impressive group, including some strikingly handsome proud younger men with most militant mustachios. Strangely enough, they seemed less interested in consulting with Emir Hassan than in telling me their grievances against the Syrian government. At appropriate intervals they would turn to the emir, shake their fists and bellow, "You are our prince. Why are you our prince? To lead us in battle!" The heart of their grievance was that the men at Damascus, with their new-fangled ideas, had no business interfering in *their* affairs. I got the point. I even felt like applauding, as at an especially effective scene at the theater. But I sat firmly on my hands.

The next day I was given a demonstration by the opposing players. They were equally fiery, equally long winded, a bit more "liberal," by our standards, in their emphasis, and a lot less impressive in their looks. Instead of talking of oppression by Damascus, they spoke of oppression by the Atrash. The election, they charged, had been controlled by Atrash terrorism. In one way they were less democratic than the Atrash meeting, at which almost everyone had had his say. In the opposition gathering (until the subject of Palestine came up) there was only one spokes-man, a fellow in European clothing wearing a red tarboosh. The vener-able beards kept quiet, the mustachios were less militant than in the Atrash camp. I got the impression that some of them felt it not quite manly to rely on outsiders (even Syrians) in a quarrel of this sort. The real enthusiasm came when the question of fighting for Palestine was raised. Then the sheikhs raised their voices and the young men's eyes flashed. It was better that Druze should not fight Druze, but should join together against outsiders, foreigners who, like the French, had come to take their lands. Who would lead them in the fight? The man in the red tarboosh said nothing, but several others answered after a moment. The logical person, they supposed, would be Sultan Pasha Atrash.

Sultan Pasha himself had told me the same thing. It seemed the Druzes could agree on something after all; later reports that Druzes were fighting on the side of Israel turned out to be vastly exaggerated for propaganda purposes.

The Druzes, of course, are not the only tribal group who are going to give any Syrian government some pretty nasty problems. The tribes are bound to resent* the efforts which any central government *must* make to diminish their independent sovereignty, their armed forces, their tribal "law," and their claim to the exclusive, or at least to the higher, loyalty of all their members. The tribes, too, in spite of the es-sentially democratic nature of many of their customs, are bound to be an anti-"progressive" force—especially if, as seems inevitable, progress is to come by direction from a central authority. Above all, the tribes are bound to be antiforeign, and sticklers for religious orthodoxy. And the tribes still constitute a sizable proportion of the total population of Syria. They form a most serious popular obstacle to social and economic progress, along Western lines at least, in Syria as in other Middle East-ern countries. (It might be possible to argue, of course, that the values of the tribal civilization and the progress achievable within its pattern might be worth more to the Middle Eastern peoples than the material progress, and the price paid for it, so far achieved by the West.)

The opponents of Western progress find popular support from other quarters as well. The various groups appealing to religious tradition-alism, such as the Ikhwan el Muslimin, have followings in the towns

* Cf. discussion of tribes in chapter on Iran.

and cities no less than in the grazing lands. The latter, the Moslem Brotherhood, has its main strength outside Syria, among the students and citizens of Cairo. It claims a total of two million supporters, most of them Egyptians, and has only recently gained any notable backing in other countries such as Syria and Iraq. For the Syrian elections in the late summer of 1947, the Egyptian headquarters of the brotherhood sent two of its election experts to Syria to help the local brethren organize their strength. The results as shown in the popular vote came as a rude surprise to some members of the government. As I have mentioned earlier, so confident were the ministerial incumbents (and so eager to conduct an unquestionably free election) that they had made a point of abstaining from any activities that might appear to be coercive. The Moslem Brotherhood was not similarly inhibited. Consequently, in the last few hours of election day the minister of Defense who, in spite of a foreign wife, an occasional drink, and a Jewish business partner, felt sure of carrying 90 per cent of the vote, had to send fleets of cars around to transport his adherents to the voting booths. By last-minute emergency measures, he barely squeaked through. But meanwhile, the strength of the brotherhood had been increasing at a most alarming rate. It may soon become the strongest single political force in Syria.

A week after I had visited the Druzes, I was driving with a friend through northern Syria. We stopped in Hama to have a look at the famous water wheels. Hama is a fanatically Moslem town. The people were polite, even friendly, but there was a feeling of underlying violence in the air which is hard to appreciate until you have encountered it. The men crowding the streets were just not quite a mob, just as a cloud of very heavy steam is not quite a liquid. But precipitation can be very quick.

As we drove away I asked my companion—an American student of Arabic—if there was anything especially wrong. He didn't think so.

"Tension is bad these days everywhere," he commented. "The people are expecting trouble and are just waiting for the sign, perhaps from their leaders, perhaps from Allah. I don't want to be around here when it comes!"

"Well," I asked, "what could these people do? Unlike the Druzes, they seem to be without arms."

My companion looked at me pityingly.

"Let me tell you a story," he said.

It seems that in the spring of 1947 there was a big rally just over the border in Lebanon, one feature of which was a parade of men who had actually fought in Palestine during the 1936 "troubles." Three or four hundred men from Hama attended. While the parade was in progress an unfortunate incident occurred. A spectator insulted one of the marchers, who pulled a pistol. The spectator was thereupon handed a tommy gun by an obliging friend and, sinking to his knees, he sprayed the marchers, emptying the whole magazine of the tommy gun. He himself was promptly shot by a policeman, but he had killed fourteen Hama men who were in his line of fire. This story reached Hama with the suggestion that somehow Palestine had been involved. Three hours later, between five and six thousand armed men were assembled in the main square of Hama clamoring for transportation. Only by broadcasting the correct story could the Syrian police restore order.

Many of these men who sprang so eagerly to arms were not, properly speaking, town folk, but great numbers of them were. Urban crowds are traditionally more volatile, more easily incited to violence, than their brothers of the open spaces. Though cities should be more cosmopolitan, they are in practice more accessible to demagoguery, to the rabid anti-foreign diatribes on which Eastern demagogues live. After all, Cairo is not only the most cosmopolitan of Arab cities but a capital seat of Arab xenophobia and the scene of some of the most violent mob action against foreigners.

In Syria, as elsewhere, Palestine is the focus, the rallying cry for anti-foreign, bigoted, reactionary troublemakers of all kinds and persuasions. If the Palestine wound continues to fester, there will be demagogues, Moslem Brothers, ready and able to incite the mobs of Hama and the tribesmen of Jebel Druze. They can turn them not only against foreigners, but against those under suspicion of being influenced by foreigners—against those who seem to us to represent the best, most progressive element in Arab life, men like the present president, and like the mayor of Aleppo. The life of the Young Effendi will be a hard one indeed.

⚬ XVI ⚬

Saudi Arabia: Revolution American Style

DHAHRAN, in Saudi Arabia, is the site of the largest American settlement between Paris and Manila. Also in Saudi Arabia are the two holiest cities of Islam, Mecca and Medina. This country, the only important political unit in the Arabian peninsula, is ruled by the outstanding Arab of his day. Neighboring Yemen has preserved the ancient ways more completely by shutting itself off almost entirely from outside influence. But Saudi Arabia offers the most violent contrast between old and new. Before your very eyes, it is skipping several thousand years of development in one quick jump. The reason is simple. On the surface it is a poor country. Although its peoples have gone out in waves to conquer and inhabit the richer lands to the north, east and west, for thousands of years its inhabitants have lived as desert nomads, existing literally on and from camels. On the surface, even now, Saudi Arabia consists chiefly of miles upon miles of sand. But under the surface, under the sand, lie what seem to be the richest deposits of oil yet discovered. As a result, above that sand, a people are being transported from the Middle Ages to the twentieth century in record speed—as if they were riding a magic carpet.

Not long ago the only wheels in the country were those on the primitive rigs over the water wells, where donkeys and camels still go back and forth or round and round hauling up skin bags full of the precious fluid. Now Arabs who have never coped with any vehicle more complicated than a camel, are driving thirty-ton semitrailers with fifteen gears. Arab youngsters who have never seen a train or car in their lives, are trained to spot airplanes. Arabs are traveling in a few hours, by a C-47 plane, over desert that not long ago could be crossed only by weeks on camel back. Palaces that never saw an electric fan now may have air-conditioning units. A revolution is taking place, a revolution by consent and co-operation, a revolution directed by a king, made possible by American private enterprise, and beneficial to all concerned. It makes an interesting contrast with Communist-inspired revolutions.

The speed of the transition produces, of course, endless confusion and many amusing incidents. Aramco, which in 1939 had seven hundred camels, no longer finds it necessary to own any. The king, on the other hand, has acquired ten planes in the interval. These planes are flown by American pilots, although many of the co-pilots and maintenance crews are Arabs. One of the pilots told me that once he had been instructed to take his plane to a town in the interior called Hofuf. He was asked how many men he could fly from Hofuf to the king's capital at Riyadh and replied that he could take twenty. When he reached the airfield, or the level stretch of desert which served as such, he found a large crowd waiting for him. It appeared that there were far more than twenty passengers expecting to go. The pilot protested. An Arab explained, "You said you could take twenty men, didn't you? Well, these men are just taking their wives along too. And some of them want their sons to have the experience of riding in an airplane. But they are young; surely they don't count as men." It was not easy for the pilot to explain that when he spoke of passengers, he meant individuals, not families—with an average weight of under two hundred pounds, not of approximately one thousand pounds.

Arab tall stories about what is being done make some of Paul Bunyan's tales seem comparatively tame. Not long ago the king himself provided a fine example. American engineers were building for him a road in Riyadh. Describing this to his neighbor, the Sheikh of Kuwait, ibn Saud is reported to have said that to help him get around on pilgrimages and hunting trips, the oil company was building him a road three hundred miles long and three miles wide!

The important elements in Saudi Arabia today are the king, the religion and the Wahhabi leaders, and the Americans. Sometimes it seems that the king's most important role is that of mediator or catalyst, between the last two.

Abdul Aziz ibn Abdur Rahman al Saud is known to his subjects as

Abdul Aziz, though Americans refer to him as ibn Saud. He makes his capital deep in the desert and my wife and I were fortunate enough to visit him there for three days during the summer of 1947. You fly in over miles of dreary emptiness and there, almost literally out of this world, you find palaces with electric light, telephones and air conditioning against the Arabian heat. And you find a king who is even more unbelievable than his capital. Ibn Saud is a huge man, particularly for an Arab. Although he believes he has shrunk with the years, he still stands at least six feet three or four. He was a great fighter and bears the scars of battle—a stiff knee, a useless finger, one eye that is practically blind. His age must be close to seventy, yet he still stands proud and erect, a bearded giant, dressed in the flowing garments of the nomad Arab, wearing a checkered red shawl and gold circlet on his head, looking for all the world like a great Djinn out of the Arabian Nights.

The Lord of the Desert is not only the most picturesque, but also one of the shrewdest monarchs left in this antimonarchical world of atom bombs and vetoes. His mind moves as swiftly and decisively as the desert raiding parties he used to lead. In his early youth, he captured the walled city of Riyadh with a force of thirty-four men though the enemy garrison numbered several hundred. He has always appreciated the importance of being well informed. Thirty or forty years ago that meant to him being well informed about the desert tribes. The king is in many ways an Arabian Jim Farley. He can call each sheikh of the desert by name, knows his family history, his strengths and weaknesses and how to call forth his loyalty. But he knows, too, that being informed about desert happenings is not, to a twentieth-century king with oil-rich lands, enough. He must know as best he can what the great powers are up to. That is why his interpreters listen in to radio broadcasts from all over the world and three times a day give the king a summary of the news as reported in world capitals—a radio monitoring service of which any ruler could be proud. Also he pumps each visitor who comes to him from the outside world with inexhaustible patience and avid curiosity. His pumping is productive, too, for he has the incredible knack of making you feel like a member of his immediate family even though an interpreter may have to translate every word exchanged between you.

He has also a flair for the dramatic. This was illustrated most strikingly many years ago, when, after near defeat and some wounds which would have incapacitated an ordinary man, the king's physical condition—specifically his virility—was the subject of many rumors. Ibn Saud descended in regal fashion upon the tribe where such rumors were most current. Selecting a bride from the tribe's most eligible maidens, he married her immediately. Their union was consummated in the royal tent within the hour and rumors ceased forthwith.

Ibn Saud is the descendant of a great line. One of his ancestors was the founder of the Wahhabi movement, a fiercely puritanical Islamic sect which swept out of the desert with the goal of purging corrupt city practices and restoring the purity of the old religion. That ancestor's grandson, also known as Saud, was another famous ruler in Arab history. The German Oriental scholar Brockelmann wrote about the earlier Saud words that might be applied to his descendant: "He was described as the paragon of an Arab ruler. He associated with the Beduin Shaykhs on a footing of absolute equality but could always impress them by his personal qualities, above all by eloquence, still very highly regarded in Arabia. . . . His administration, though very simple, restored public security, unknown in Arabia for centuries. . . . The ancient tribal prerogative of withdrawing a criminal from punishment by placing him under tribal protection was no longer recognized. The penal code was applied entirely according to the regulations of the Qur'an. The performance of religious obligations was enforced with relentless severity; a breach of the fast of Ramadan on occasion was punished with death." Ibn Saud has shown equal strictness in the execution of justice, including an occasional death penalty for breaches of Ramadan. The punishments are by our standards cruel, but the result is an almost complete absence of serious crime.

Ibn Saud's grandfather, the Emir Feisal, was ruler of the Nejd but the kingdom was lost by ibn Saud's father and uncle. In 1901, ibn Saud, then about twenty, set out with two hundred men and the ambitious project of recapturing his family heritage. Twenty-five years later, after many a setback and almost constant fighting, he had not only established his hold over the Nejd, but was able to proclaim himself King of the Hejaz as well. Now the old king can look back on a lifetime of accomplishment such as is granted to few men. He has a unique place in the Arab world today and in Arab history to come, for he will surely rank as one of the greatest of Arab conquerors and rulers. His reputation has been enhanced by his close adherence to Islamic doctrine in all his conquests and activities. The Wahhabi have been his strength. Where a weak ruler, or one less skillful, might have been overcome by the fanaticism of his backers, ibn Saud has been able to direct and control it. There is no questioning his religious sincerity. He has been fortunate in that the religion he believes in has provided the force to break down the tribal distinctions which have always divided Arabia. Under him the Wahhabi movement, more than any sense of nationality or even of loyalty to a particular ruler, has held the tribes together against their natural inclination to divide. Mohammed, and other leaders of Islam, have achieved for a time the same end. It remains to be seen how long the union attained by ibn Saud can survive his death.

One factor which may affect the answer is another policy which ibn Saud has consistently followed in his drive for unity. From the early days of his career the king has worked to create a new national Arab community by organizing groups of agricultural settlers. In recent years, with the financial and practical assistance of the oil company, he has been able to do far more in this line, but even before the oil men arrived, he had achieved considerable success in building farming villages where none had been before. Now he has a number of agricultural settlements and experimental stations which are most promising. The biggest of these is at Al-Kharj, where American agricultural experts hired by the king are training Arab farmers in the management of a farm which already supplies Riyadh with much of its needs in fruits and vegetables. Water is obtained from several large, deep openings which tap the stores of water accumulated far beneath the sandy surface of Arabia. These holes, of course, had been used for generations by Arabs as a reliable supply for themselves and their herds. Around them was settled a small community—rare in Arabia—which farmed as much land as could be irrigated by its own efforts. The installation of powerful electric pumps has tremendously enlarged the area that can be watered. Acres and acres of watermelons, tomatoes, beans and cucumbers are now grown, and the population of Al-Kharj has correspondingly increased. Ibn Saud seems to have recognized that a stable government must depend to some extent at least upon a stable population.

While the religious fanaticism of the Wahhabis has been of assistance to ibn Saud in uniting his country, it has presented many a problem to him in his efforts at modernization. Any innovation, any spread of Western influence, any employment of Western techniques has run into considerable resistance from the religious leaders. A good example of the skill with which ibn Saud has overcome this resistance was illustrated by the introduction of radio. It was natural enough that the distrust of anything foreign should be directed particularly at radio. The religious leaders pronounced it the work of the devil and forbade true Moslems to have anything to do with it. But ibn Saud called them to his palace one day and had them listen to a reading of the Koran over the radio. "Tell me," he asked, "would the work of the devil carry and spread the word of God?" They were convinced—and radio is there to stay.

Foreign companies operating in the country and assisting the king in his modernization program have had to be especially careful not to offend religious prejudice. The Arabian American Oil Company, for example, has scrupulously observed local customs. The work week of the company for American as well as for Moslem employees is geared to Islamic practice. Friday, the Mohammedan day of worship, is Aramco's day of rest. On every working day Arab employees are given time off and provided with the necessary facilities for the morning and afternoon prayer which no pious Moslem would omit. They are encouraged to accumulate leave with pay until they have a sufficient paid vacation (six weeks) to take the pilgrimage to Mecca which is enjoined upon all true believers. During Ramadan, when Moslems must fast from sunrise to sunset, Aramco continues to pay for a regular eight-hour day even though theoretically they expect no more than six hours work from their employees and actually they are likely to get far less.

Saudi Arabia is divided, economically and otherwise, into two chief parts. The eastern half, where the desert tribes of the Nejd make their home, has been traditionally the seat of the most conservative, even fanatical, Moslem thought. Unable except in a few spots to support anything but nomad life, it has been poor, backward and isolated, its people hardy, independent and proud. The western half, including the Hejaz, is less barren with a larger area on which crops have been produced. Mecca and Medina have, since the time of the Prophet, been the object of Moslem veneration and the annual pilgrimage provides income which was, until this decade, the main source of income in Saudi Arabia. The pilgrimage also kept the Hejazi in touch with the outside world, making them more sophisticated and liberal in their views to the contempt of the strait-laced tribes of the Nejd. The ironical fact now is that the Hejaz, which has been more worldly and less anti-foreign, continues to live on the pilgrimage traffic, while the Nejd, home of the Wahhabis, where distrust of foreign influence is most strong, has grown rich recause of the activities of foreign unbelievers. Today, knowledge is spreading through the Nejd in concentric circles from Dhahran and from other centers of Western influence such as the Al-Kharj project. Close by these centers the Arabs know that, surprising as it may seem, you can drill holes through the sand and reach pure drinking water. They know that mosquitoes bring malaria and that flies have all sorts of unwanted companions in the form of disease.

The oil concession which is chiefly responsible for these developments came into effect in July 1933 and was to run for sixty-six years. Drilling started in 1935 but it was not until the seventh well, drilled in October 1938, that the company struck oil in commercial quantities. Later, by drilling deeper, five out of the first six wells were also made economically worth operating. The first commercial shipment by Aramco from Saudi Arabia was in May 1939. Ibn Saud made this the occasion of his first visit to company headquarters in Dhahran. Up to that time he had received no revenue from the eastern half of his kingdom and there was no industry or commercial enterprise in the area. (In 1935 there was only one car in the whole region of Dhahran; now there are thousands.)

Aramco made plans for rapid expansion, including the building of a twenty-five thousand barrel refinery at Ras Tanura, but the war interrupted these plans. Most of the four hundred Americans employed by Aramco in 1940 had to be sent home. The staff was pared down to the point at which it could do no more than carry on essential maintenance. Geological exploration and construction had to be stopped. All but four of the twenty or thirty wells then drilled were shut down. At that time Aramco's exports amounted to only twelve or thirteen thousand barrels of oil a day, which were carried mainly by barge to the Bahrein refinery. In 1943 this was increased to twenty-five thousand barrels a day. Early in 1945 construction of an underwater pipe line to Bahrein was finished and exports went up to forty-five thousand barrels a day. This figure was not increased until the winter of 1945-46, when the refinery at Ras Tanura was completed. By November of 1948 output for export had reached a figure of 500,000 barrels of oil a day. By 1952 Aramco officials estimate that their production will average a million barrels per day.

In spite of the interruption caused by war, the development of the Saudi Arabian fields has been the fastest ever seen anywhere in the world. While the war created such uncertainty about future prospects that no major steps could be taken, the impetus already gained carried things along remarkably fast. When the army in 1944 requested that the refinery at Ras Tanura be built, that operation alone took all the resources of Aramco. Only after it was completed could Aramco begin to plan a long-range, over-all program including housing. Since then it has moved as fast as shipping and supply have permitted. Over the next five years the company plans to spend $330,000,000 on capital investments, as distinct from operating expenses, in Saudi Arabia. Additional huge sums will be spent elsewhere, on the pipe line, on bunkering, refining, ships and so forth. In terms of revenue to the Saudi Arabian government, this program should mean that in five years the present cash income of twenty million dollars received from Aramco will be at least doubled. That may not sound like a great deal to Americans who have watched the astronomical figures of our own national budget. To a country like Saudi Arabia it is an awful lot of money. How much may be gathered from the fact that in 1934-35 the first official Saudi Arabian budget gave estimated expenses at fourteen million riyals or about four and a half million dollars. The total revenues of the state were estimated at the same figure. Those revenues were derived chiefly from the pilgrimage traffic which, although interrupted by the war, is now in full swing again. Aramco had not yet started paying royalties. Now Aramco alone pays the Saudi Arab government almost five times the total national income less than fifteen years ago.

The king, needless to say, is not at all displeased by this development. It was only after careful study of the statements of Woodrow Wilson

and of American history, ibn Saud tells visitors, that he determined that
he must have an American company to develop his oil. These studies
convinced him that the United States had never tried to run other countries (Aramco and the United States have reason to feel grateful that the
king's studies apparently did not include the history of American relations with Mexico). He feels that his judgment in getting an American
company has been vindicated. When asked if he is pleased with his
choice he says, "Yes! The Americans work hard. They get the oil out
and they don't get into politics."

The company does not get into politics, it is true, but it does do many
things that one would not expect an oil company, under normal circumstances, to be doing. These activities are chiefly in the fields of public
health, public education and economic development, whose connection
with the oil industry might seem at first glance tenuous. But the activities are dictated by shrewd appreciation of what the company's long-
range interests are. In normal conditions oil and public health, oil and
public education, might not be closely related. In Saudi Arabia they are
and the company has been smart enough to recognize the fact. And what
they have done may remind us, if we have forgotten, that American
private enterprise has been a revolutionary force in the past, and can
readily become one again.

The Arab employees of Aramco get free medical attention and hos-
pitalization for themselves and their families. Aramco doctors also take
care of any other Arab who comes in for medical attention. The Arab
hospital in Dhahran handled sixty-six thousand outpatients a year and
Aramco doctors, etymologists and sanitary engineers do a great deal of
work for the Saudi Arab government. The company actually has one
full-time etymologist and one full-time sanitary engineer regularly on
call for the King. Whenever a health project is undertaken on behalf
of the company, it is explained to Saudi Arab officials, who are asked
if they would not like something of the same sort done in other areas of
the country as well.

One important project has been the antimosquito campaign. Malaria
has been a serious problem in Saudi Arabia and it was one of the first
to which company doctors turned their attention. The sand-colored Arab
towns, with their narrow alleys, covered markets, and the usual dominating palace-fortress, narrow slitted for the defending rifles, appar-

ently conceal numerous breeding places for mosquitoes, in spite of the perennial lack of water. To cut down the possibilities of water standing long enough for mosquito larvae to hatch, the doctors recommended that no water be distributed during one day of each week. This innovation, which also conserves the scant water supply for agriculture, has been markedly successful.

DDT has also been used extensively. One spraying of DDT leaves a residual film which will remain effective for at least three or four months. When I first arrived in Dhahran from Syria, I felt vaguely that something was missing. There were so many things in Dhahran life formerly unfamiliar to the region—air-conditioned houses, American children playing in the street, ice cream and coca-cola in abundance— that I could not put my finger on what was bothering me. Then one day a fly buzzed by my head, and I realized it was the *first* fly I'd encountered in Dhahran. Moreover, people apologized for its presence! The last DDT spraying had been almost five months earlier, they explained; its effects were beginning to wear off, and a new spraying was overdue. No one who has not battled, cursed and hated with consuming hatred the various Middle Eastern flies can fully appreciate what their absence can mean. The elimination of the fly from any Middle East country could be the most profoundly revolutionary event in its history!

Aside from malaria, the major public-health problems are: First of all the prevalence of all intestinal-borne diseases. These are extremely common because there is almost no proper sewage-disposal system in any of the native towns. Secondly, typhoid is prevalent and there is a high tuberculosis rate because of the diet, the veils worn by women, and the extent to which the people live in darkness, seeking to avoid the sun. There is, however, less leprosy in Saudi Arabia than in the United States. Thirdly, trachoma, syphilis and other infectious diseases of a similar sort are quite widespread. Aramco, which wants a healthy country for business reasons entirely aside from any humanitarian concern, treats the people who come to them until they are noninfectious. Then the company makes it a condition of employment that they continue to receive treatment until they are certified as cured.

For similar reasons and with possibly even more far-reaching results, Aramco is concerning itself with public education. From the beginning it has been understood between the king and the company that eventually only Arabs and Americans are to be employed. At the moment the Aramco pay roll is a small United Nations with Somalis, Sudanese, all the Middle East countries, India and Italy represented on the staff. This has been necessary because there have been any number of jobs which Aramco could not afford to have done by Americans. Transportation costs, housing and other problems would make that impossible. They could not be done either, for the moment, by the then untrained Saudi Arabs; it was necessary to hire anyone near by who could do the work. But Aramco's policy has always been to bring in Americans to train Arabs, rather than to employ, at a cheaper rate, Italians or Indians. Already the Arabs have made tremendous strides. For example, Arab foremen and crews can now put up a derrick without any supervision at all. Aramco has undertaken not only on-the-job training but also intends to provide a complete education. The students range in age from seven to about twenty. They get paid enough to enable them to support themselves, but many of them attend school on a part-time basis and work part time also for the company. (They have to be fourteen before the company will employ them.) The principal studies are Arabic, English and mathematics. The boys learn to read and write, to add, subtract, multiply and divide so that they can do a better job for Aramco as they grow up, and, incidentally, make better citizens for Saudi Arabia.

At the time I was there, there were only about eighty or ninety students in the school at Dhahran, although there have been as many as 190. At that particular moment Aramco was short on instructors and also on available space. There was one full-time American instructor, one Arab, and the rest were Indians. A teacher-training program was underway and as a result students received half their instruction in regular classes and half in classes conducted by trainees. Aramco has found it much better to have teachers come from the community rather than from outside. Naturally the chief concern is with long-term training programs. The schools do not yet give full academic training but prepare chiefly for work with the company. It is hoped, however, that soon it will be possible to give a full six years of elementary education before training for commercial or trade purposes is begun.

The abilities of the students, of course, vary greatly. The teachers say that, like U.S. youngsters, some of them are bright, some average, and some less than average. They have, however, something that is occasionally lacking in American classes—a thirst for knowledge so avid that they soak up learning like a dry sponge. I remember one, Ahmed, a little fellow of fourteen—I would have taken him for eleven or twelve —who fired questions at me like a hidden-microphone radio reporter. He wore the usual white *galabeah,* which is like a man's shirt above the waist and a nightgown below. On his head was an embroidered skullcap; this is generally worn under the headcloth (*keffiyeh* or *gutra*) or the turban, but many Moslems wear the skullcap alone when more substantial head covering is not required. This boy, who spoke quite good English, told me that he had another brother already in school, a still younger one who would come soon, and two sisters. Ahmed's father, an Aramco employee, had been injured a year before when heavy machinery fell on his leg. He was still in the hospital at Ras Tanura, and might not ever get the use of his leg back. "I'll know better than to let a thing like that happen to me," observed Ahmed dispassionately.

Ahmed and his fellows learn English more quickly than Americans can learn Arabic—but that may be simply because of the comparative difficulty of the two languages. The Arab students lack background, of course, which makes it more difficult for them to adjust to many of the mechanical aspects of their new life. On the whole they are very adaptable and quick to learn.

Aside from the regular schools Aramco also carries on adult education programs. In Dhahran and Ras Tanura (where the refinery is) they already have classes of two or three hundred. The biggest program of all is on-the-job training. In this field Aramco expects to cope with ten or twelve thousand trainees a year. The company runs foreman conferences and other employee-participation projects. Trade schools are underway in Ras Tanura and Dhahran.

In the field of education, unlike the field of public health, the Saudi Arab government has not yet asked for any assistance from Aramco. There is an obvious explanation for this—national and religious pride would not permit the education of the country to be under the direction of foreign unbelievers. On the western side of the country, in the Hejaz, there are a number of schools which have been established for long periods of time. In the eastern half, where the oil company is, the Saudi Arabian government is as yet taking no steps to develop its own schools. Rightly or wrongly, this is the result of deliberate policy, a hard choice, forced, so the government feels, by its relative poverty. The king told me that since the money available to his country is limited, and the tasks to be undertaken practically unlimited, he thinks he must concentrate on getting capital goods, such as tractors, agricultural machinery, and railroads, relying on the hope that on-the-job training will enable his subjects to cope with this new machinery. He feels that this is a more effective way to improve the lot of his people than to spend the money on teachers and schools. When we were discussing the matter and I was urging the importance of education, he said, rather impatiently, that of course he had never had any formal education at all. "Now look at me," he said. "I am doing a pretty good job of running this country, aren't I?"

I said quickly that of course he was. However, I continued, not many men were granted his tremendous abilities, which was just as fortunate for him. Saudi Arabia would be a hard country to govern if all of its inhabitants were leaders, rather than led.

The king, laughing heartily, agreed. But he seemed unconvinced when I suggested that in return for their allowing themselves to be led, he should make it possible for his subjects to have benefits which he had not needed. In my opinion, the failure of the government to provide educational opportunities in the Nejd is all the more dangerous because of the contrast with what the oil company is doing. There is no likelihood of trouble during ibn Saud's lifetime, but after his death, if there is occasion for dissatisfaction, critics of the government may seize upon the contrast between the do-nothing policy of the government and the vigorous action being pursued by the company. Neither will benefit from this comparison, which could seriously complicate relations between them. No government likes to be told that it is not doing as much as outsiders are for its own people. Moreover in times of trouble the educational program of the oil company is likely to occasion much distrust among the religious fanatics and the xenophobes.

This is one example of the kind of trouble which the oil company may face for reasons quite the reverse of the usual ones. The cause would not be that the company was doing too little for the people but, perhaps, that it was doing too much. Aramco is doing a lot of things which abstractly the government ought to do but, for various reasons, cannot. The oil company, on the other hand, can. The government has to pick and choose, to decide whether educated men are more important than increased food production. The oil company also has to pick and choose, but it has different objectives, which may lead it to choose different courses of action. For the time being, at least, the government has decided that technical advance is more important than educational advance. The oil company finds that for its purposes education of Saudi Arabs is extremely important. Some company officials are unhappily aware of the danger that in the course of time people may become impatient and angry with the oil company, for having made their government lose "face" by comparison.

In line with the emphasis upon technical advance, many Arabs feel that the most valuable contribution Aramco has made is in the encouragement of local initiative and industry. As I have indicated elsewhere, Aramco's activities in Saudi Arabia have not been limited to those connected with oil. The Al-Kharj project in central Arabia, where American agricultural experts experiment, give training in irrigation methods, and develop crops new to the country, has been given considerable assistance by Aramco. The king has also asked Aramco to help him find funds for a railroad from Dammam, the port near Dhahran, to Riyadh. It is estimated that thirty-two and a half million dollars will be needed, including the funds necessary for building Dammam's port facilities plus those required for the initial units for the railroad such as Diesel engines and cars. Aramco acts also as a general handyman, helping out with the repair of motor vehicles, the drilling of water wells, the carrying out of aerial surveys of the country where needed, and also in the many problems connected with the haulage of food. Saudi Arabia has to import almost all its basic foods as well as the textiles it requires. These are mostly carried by truck from the east coast to Riyadh, the capital. This is a long, tough haul over extremely bad sand and its record of successes is a real tribute to the ingenuity and mechanical skills of the engineers.

Aramco is also looking into other industries which American capital might develop in the area—especially those which need cheap fuel or which can employ the waste or by-products of oil operations. Company officials realize that the introduction of additional industry will help them by bringing additional prosperity. They also would like others to share the inevitable headaches that operating in a foreign country must bring. Thus they have explored possibilities of production of carbon black (used in auto tires, aluminum and so forth). Ethyl is another by-product of oil operations which could be produced. Cement also might be manufactured on the spot. But from the Arab point of view, so far at least, the most important aspect of this work has been the encouragement given to local business. Aramco established a special branch for this purpose—The Arab Industrial Development—which has done its work well. From only two local contractors, when the department was set up in 1944, the total working for Aramco had grown by September 1947 to 107, who in turn employ close to five thousand workers themselves.

Aramco makes a point of using as many Arab contractors in its work as possible. Any Arab with the necessary skills can get a contract from the company, but many of them are, of course, ex-company employees. One field in which contractors play an important part is housing. The brick factory in Dhahran is operated by Arabs on a piece-work labor contract, though it is run by a ceramics engineer for the company. However one Arab has already set up his own lime kiln and further developments along this line are expected. Arabs are also particularly active in the field of transportation. A number of light trucks and some heavy equipment were purchased by Arabs from American Army surplus. With these they haul fill, in connection with building projects; as well as doing much work for the company, they also haul for Arab stores and other concessions. About 70 per cent of the material coming into the country for Aramco is handled by these contractors. Arab contractors also work for the company garages. All the flat tires are repaired by them. The contractor in Dhahran had twenty-five men working on the day shift and twenty on the night shift—which gives you some idea of what the desert sand can do to tires. Contractors also do the greasing and lubrication work.

They have built up some pretty impressive records. In four months of actively operating thirty-six company trucks, they averaged 2.7 accidents for every hundred thousand miles. This is an extremely good rate in any country. One great American oil company, for instance, averaged 4.5 accidents per hundred thousand miles.

Saudi Arabia is not by any means typical of the Middle East. Ibn Saud's type of monarchy would not be appropriate or desirable in other circumstances. But for his country and for his time, he is just what the doctor ordered. And so is Aramco. There is of course the danger that a disproportionate amount of the oil royalties will be diverted from the public benefit to be spent for the benefit of a few—the princes, or the wealthy merchants of Jidda. The Saudi Arab government, and Aramco too, will have to keep a vigilant eye against that danger.

It is a well-known lesson of history that you don't get popular by helping people. The way to get popular is to help them to help themselves. Judging by this standard, Aramco is going to be very popular indeed. Arabians are proud, independent people. They do not want charity. They want to learn. Help in learning is help they appreciate—and the oil enables them to pay for it. You can understand what one reporter meant when he said "Aramco is half oil company and half Arabian American friendship society!" The Russians snarl about dollar imperialism and oil in the same breath. This may be one reason why the Russians have made no dent in Saudi Arabia, for the Saudi Arabs say "If this is dollar imperialism, we're for it. We'd like more of it." We Americans, all of us, have an asset here. What we need to do is to understand it—and to see that as many others understand it as possible.

P. S. ON THE ARABIAN PENINSULA

Apart from Saudi Arabia, the Arabian peninsula is as little known as any part of the world today. The only sizable (and clearly defined) political unit is the Yemen, an independent kingdom of about seventy-five thousand square miles with a population of three and a half million. Of the numerous sheikhdoms and principalities which run along the coast of the Persian Gulf and the Arabian Sea to the Gulf of Aden, two —Kuwait and Bahrein—are important for their oil. Others, particularly Qatar and the Trucial Oman, may prove to be so. Otherwise, they attract world interest chiefly from naval men, who are always interested in coastal areas. The waters surrounding Arabia have concerned European navies—British, French, Portuguese, Dutch, Russian and German—for centuries and, for almost as long, the Persian Gulf has been a British lake. It is no longer wholly so. The United States Navy has made its appearance. A brisk, occasionally bitter, competition is developing for supremacy of influence in sheikhdoms where Britain's supremacy of influence has not been questioned for generations. American ships look just as impressive as do British ships; American cigarettes and Coca-Cola are most acceptable; the American dollar has advantages over the British pound. The representatives on the spot always want to be top dog, and attach more importance to their position than their governments, thousands of miles away, are likely to do. So it happens that Britishers and Americans in the Gulf occasionally forget that this is, after all, a cousinly quarrel not to be carried to the point where it will benefit only those outside the family.

A few miles in from the coast, even the boundaries of these "countries" become vague. It would hardly be worth while to make them otherwise, for they end up, indeterminately and without hope, in the great Empty Quarter—the Rub al Khali—which is the absolute, lifeless desert of the horror story-book type. Western maps do not always agree on their names. The important ones, south of Yemen and Saudi Arabia are: Aden and the Aden protectorate, including the Hadhramaut, the sultanate of Oman and Muscat, and the Trucial sheikhdoms.

Aden is the only territory in the area technically a British colony. The territories around Aden are administered as a British protectorate, and the colony itself consists only of the port and a small area surrounding it. A London publication, *The Middle East,* says simply: "The Colony of Aden consists of extinct volcanic craters forming rocky peninsulas, joined by a flat, sandy shore." That makes Aden sound just about as attractive as it is.

The port is, and has been for thousands of years, strategically important. It is the link between the Arabian interior and the outside world. Since ancient times it has been a center of trade, and since ancient times it has been commonly under foreign rule. The Abyssinians, the Persians and the early caliphs of Islam held Aden. In the sixteenth century it was captured by the Turks, who abandoned it when they evacuated Yemen in 1630. The island of Perim in the Gulf of Aden, now part of the colony, was occupied by the French in the early eighteenth century. Later the British took over Perim too. Aden was the first territory added to the British Empire after the accession of Queen Victoria. As one British publication solemnly remarks, it "proved a most useful acquisition of the British government on account of its strategic position as a short route to India."

The governor of the colony is also governor of the protectorate, but the British do not administer the latter directly. British political officers with headquarters at Aden give "advice" to the local rulers who have bound themselves by treaty to accept advice in the improvement of their administrations. The local rulers exercise the direct control, however, over their own people. Tribal guards are in many cases under the joint control of their chiefs and the British agent. The interior has had little contact with the Western world. The few travelers who have been there naturally incline to write books about the experience; particularly to be recommended for the general reader are Freya Stark's books, *The Southern Gates of Arabia* and *Seen in the Hadhramaut*.

The sultanate of Oman and Muscat, famous in older days for its grapes and raisins, is nominally independent, has an area of about eighty-two thousand square miles and a population estimated in 1937 as half a million—mainly Arabs with a strong infusion of Negro blood. The Trucial sheikhdoms, including eight small Arab states, total forty-one thousand square miles and their population is about 120,000. The sheikhs have all signed treaties on behalf of themselves, their heirs and successors, promising never to enter into agreement or correspondence with any foreign power other than Great Britain. There are Americans who, in the British expression, take a dim view of this. But not many. The rest of us don't give a damn.

Yemen is another matter altogether. The United States has taken quite an interest in Yemen, and in the past few years American diplomatic missions have twice made their way laboriously up the mountains to the ancient walled city of Sanaa where the Imam, ruler of Yemen, makes his capital. Here they endured the tortuous, involved negotiations preceding a treaty of friendship and a loan, and admired what are among the oldest skyscrapers in the world. For Yemen, like other cities of the peninsula, was walled for protection against bandit attack. It was fortunate in having good stone, and a solid foundation on which to build. So as the city grew, it grew upward. A father would build a couple of extra stories on top of his own dwelling so that his son and his family might live there. Later, perhaps, a new generation would need more room; it was easier, and safer, to go up than to go outside the walls. And the masonry, particularly of the lower floors, was sturdy enough to survive for centuries.

The old Imam, Yahya, who received these missions, had for years jealously preserved the isolation of his fertile, mountainous and incredibly backward country from any outside contact. His rule was marked by informality (he kept important state papers tucked under the royal mattress) and rigid observance of the customs built by time. This conditioned his reaction to what little he saw or heard of the outside world. For instance when Queen Wilhelmina of Holland politely invited him to attend her daughter's wedding, the Imam was livid with fury. Why, he raged, should he be insulted by this invitation from a woman to attend a purely female function? Didn't the Dutch know he was a *man*?

Eventually the Imam was impressed by reports of how Saudi Arabia was flourishing on the proceeds of some slimy unattractive stuff which the strange Westerners got from underground and seemed to value excessively. Perhaps he was missing out on a good thing. Tentative approaches were made, and responded to. Meanwhile Yemen had become a member of the Arab League and, subsequently, of the United Nations. One of the Imam's sons, Prince Seif al Islam Abdullah, traveled to the United States, and then called at London to discuss the possibility of establishing diplomatic relations with Britain and getting some British technical advisers.

While Prince Seif was in England (in February 1948) the old Imam and three of his other sons were murdered, and the power was seized by a relative, the wealthy tradesman El Sayid Abdullah ibn Ahmed el Wazir. Wazir did not last long. He was captured and either hanged or poisoned. The former crown prince, Ahmed, is (at this writing) Imam, though peace has not been restored. Ahmed controls the major port, Hodeida, but has been unable to enter Sanaa and is making his capital at Taizz in the south. In spite of the disturbances which continue, there are some signs that the new government will not return to isolationism. It has been purchasing planes from Egypt and Sweden, and hiring pilots from those two countries to fly and to train Yemeni pilots. The field at Sanaa, used before the last war by the Italians, has already been restored to service. Other fields at Hodeida and Taizz are also being used. The air age is coming to Yemen, and the West must come along with it.

XVII

Palestine: House of Strife

*Better a dry morsel, and quietness therewith, than
an house full of sacrifices with strife.*

PALESTINE is a tiny country (about the size of Vermont). Much
of it is sandy waste or stony hillside. It has no great physical wealth
to offer. Yet it has been fought over since the dawn of civilization. Its
history is unique in a number of ways. Its ground is holy to three of the
world's great religions. It has seen the members of one of those religions
—Islam—occupying the land, forced to arbitrate and keep peace between the rival Christian churches. It has seen members of the third
great religion—Judaism—maintain during an absence of two thousand
years such immediate and passionately yearning sentiments for the land
that they still look to it as home.

Most remarkable, most significant and (in some ways) most terrifying of its unique features are the events which have led a majority in
the United Nations to approve the claim to part of that land of a people
long removed from it in time and space, over the claim of people who
have inhabited it for fifty generations. These events include some contradictory but powerful promises, a migration of awesome vision and
exaltation, the inhuman Nazi persecutions and attempts to destroy the
Jews, the ironic fact that Palestine, for the last generation, has enjoyed
comparative peace only during a world war, and a propaganda campaign which, for skill and scope, has been unequaled in history.

The Zionist case for Palestine has exercised a strong compulsion upon
the minds of Western men and, in a different way, upon the fourteen
semi-Oriental minds of the Politburo. On the other hand, it has failed
to win any appreciable support from the Near, Middle or Far East. The

reasons for its success and failure alike will bear analysis. First, let us examine the case for Zionism.

The historical, religious and emotional ties which bind Jews to Palestine have never been severed. Zionists say that not once have they surrendered their right to the possession of Palestine and that, aside from that right, they alone have the energy, money, skill and devotion to make the land fruitful. It is their manifest destiny to do this.

These rights, moreover, Zionists point out, have received international recognition on the highest level. In 1917 the British government approved the famous Balfour Declaration, which stated:

His Majesty's Government view with favor the establishment in Palestine of a national home for the Jewish people, and will use their best endeavors to facilitate the achievement of this object, it being clearly understood that nothing shall be done which may prejudice the civil and religious rights of existing non-Jewish communities in Palestine or the rights and political status enjoyed by Jews in any other country.

Subsequently the League of Nations assigned Great Britain the mandate for Palestine to carry out this declaration. The mandate employs in key passages the identical language of the declaration.

Tracts could be written analyzing the words chosen, and the reasons behind the choice, for almost every phrase of the Balfour Declaration. Since the poetical obscurity of the Delphic oracle, there has been no statement of historical importance which could match it in deliberate ambiguity. The Zionists, however, are not to blame for that; if they have misunderstood it (and who is to be judge of that?), so have others. The Anglo-American Committee of Inquiry (1946), which included such ardent supporters of Zionism as Bartley Crum and James G. MacDonald, stated in its unanimous report: "It should be noted that the demand for a Jewish state goes beyond the obligations of either the Balfour Declaration or the mandate, and was expressly disowned by the chairman of the Jewish Agency as late as 1932." Yet the Zionist argument that a national home *must* mean a political state has been supported by some of the statesmen most closely connected with the drafting of the declaration and the mandate. (Others have as strenuously denied the claim.)

In any case, the right of the Jews to a sovereign political state in

Palestine was expressly approved by a majority of the United Nations Special Committee on Palestine which visited the country in 1947. The partition of Palestine for that purpose was recommended by the UN General Assembly by a vote of 33 to 13. And the existence of Israel is now an unmistakable fact.

In bringing about that fact the strongest force was probably neither the historical or the legal arguments on the Zionist side. The most compelling argument was humanitarian. The horrible sufferings of the Jews of Europe under Nazi terror appalled the conscience of the world. The West in particular had (for the most part unconscious and almost always unexpressed) a sense of guilt. For the 1930's and 1940's were not the first decades, nor was Germany the first country, to see persecution of Jewry in Christian Europe. To our shame, anti-Semitism in one degree or another has been a distinctive feature of Occidental cultures from Russia to America, from the Pax Romana to the cold war. Violence has been epidemic. During the Crusades, massacres of Jews occurred all over Europe, they were expelled from England, their properties were confiscated in France, the Inquisition hunted them out in Spain. Pogroms were common in Russia and eastern Europe generally right up to the First World War. Inevitably, they made Zionists in Russia and eastern Europe, and supporters for Zionism throughout Christendom.

Anti-Semitism, even in recent years, has not been limited to eastern Europe. The Dreyfus case in France made Zionists of many western European Jews, who might otherwise have been content to back the cause with money and sympathy, but no sense of personal involvement. In England men like Sir Oswald Mosley and in America individuals like Gerald L. K. Smith have had somewhat the same effect. On the whole, however, here and in western Europe, Jewish people have supported Zionism from intellectual or emotional conviction, or from concern for their co-religionists in other lands, rather than from any acute fear for their own futures. While there is very real reason for describing the Jews of Cental Europe as a homeless people, the same phrase can hardly apply to British or French Jews. In the United States it has even less application: except for the Indians, we have all come to America comparatively recently from one land or another, and many Americans have so many national strains in their blood that they couldn't look back to *one* ancestral home even if they wanted to. For instance, I have Dutch, French, English, Scottish and Irish ancestry that I know of off-hand, and doubtless others as well. Yet I would resent being called homeless. The United States is my home, as it is the home of any other American.

It should be noted that the Zionist description of the Jews as a homeless people is resented by many Jews in this country, England, France and elsewhere. In the Arab countries especially, the word resentment is altogether inadequate to describe the feelings of Jews who, having made their home for centuries in Baghdad, Aleppo, or Cairo, are now being regarded as aliens—enemy aliens—because of the claims of political Zionism. In England there have been anti-Zionist Jewish organizations since before the Balfour Declaration. In the United States the American Council for Judaism strongly rejects the argument that the Jews consti-tute a homeless people or a national entity. Its members affirm that Jews have in common their religion and its great heritage, but that they do not constitute a nation or a race. Like Catholics or Protestants, they are nationals of their respective countries. The Council for Judaism be-lieves that equality will be gained and anti-Semitism ended by integra-tion of Jews, along with other religious groups, into the national cul-tures of the lands they live in, not by segregation of the Jews from non-Jewish life. And they argue that Zionism, with its insistence upon the homelessness of the Jewish people, plays right into the hands of anti-Semites who brand Jews as foreigners, not to be trusted as citizens because their loyalty to the Jewish "nation" transcends their loyalty to the state in which they live.

On many points, the arguments of the Council for Judaism are in-disputable. Anthropologists and historians agree that there is no such thing as *a* Jewish race. There are, to take obvious examples, black Jews in Ethiopia and yellow, almond-eyed Jews in China. What they have in common with each other and with Jews in Europe and America is their religion. Only a very stubborn and short-sighted visitor to Tel Aviv can cling to the theory of a Jewish race, for he will see on the streets and in the cafés a rich variety of racial types—all calling themselves Jewish. The visitor to Tel Aviv will learn another thing: the religion which the Jews of Addis Ababa, Warsaw, Baghdad and New York have in common is not held in common by all Palestine Jews. Judaism is by no means a dominant force in Israel, though it is the core of Zionism in many places outside Israel.

It might seem that the argument over the existence of Jewish nationalism has been made meaningless by the creation of Israel. Actually, the reverse is true. The creation of Israel gives new point to the argument. The fact is, certainly, that a new nationalism has come into being. Yet American Jews, or any Jews outside Israel, can quite properly object to describing it as *Jewish* nationalism and deny that it has any claim to their loyalty, whatever claim it may make to their sympathy. They cannot deny its existence. Zionist nationalism, or better, Israeli nationalism, demanded a sovereign state of its own, and has succeeded in obtaining it. So those who have opposed political Zionism on theoretical grounds have lost out. That makes it all the more important that their case be understood. It is now more than ever essential that there be no confusion of political with religious loyalty, that inevitable divergences of interest between Israel and other nations not be made the occasion for anti-Semitism, and that no one—Israelis or citizens of other states—assume that adherence to Judaism necessarily involves adherence to the political goals of Israel.

There are difficult times ahead for the new state. It is true that Zionist ideas, and sympathy for Jewish victims of persecution, have triumphed in the West. And triumph in the West, together with courage, determination and guns in Israel, was enough to bring about the creation of Israel. That will not, alone, be enough to insure its prosperity, security, or even its bare existence, in the future. To do that, Israel must come to terms with the Orient.

One of the dangerously mistaken ideas about the Palestine problem is that "world opinion" approved partition. It overlooks the inconvenient but indisputable fact that more than half the world's population lives in the Orient. The thirty-three nations which voted for partition represent a bit more than a quarter of the two billion two hundred million people in the world. The thirteen countries voting against it represent a little less than a quarter, while the ten which abstained account, like those favoring it, for something more than a quarter of the world's population. The remaining quarter is not represented in UN. Three quarters of the human race either was not represented, or its representatives opposed partition. The Arab case is not without its supporters.

It is, essentially, a very simple case. It rests on the assumption that those who have been living in a land have the strongest possible claim to that land. The population of Palestine has, for thirteen hundred years, been overwhelmingly Arab; even after more than a quarter of a century of immigration backed by arms, Arabs still outnumbered the Jews in Palestine by two to one.

Next to the question of who is to rule the land, the major problem is immigration. It would seem that Americans, who have recently shown themselves far from liberal in their own immigration policy, would particularly understand the Arab opposition to a mass immigration of foreigners imposed upon them by outside powers. Whatever the historical and sentimental attachment of the Jews to Palestine may have been and may be today, the fact remains that the Zionist immigrants are alien to the other inhabitants of Palestine in language, culture, religion, and way of life.

Moreover, the Zionists do not enter Palestine with the intention of being assimilated into the existing culture and state. This is quite natural; they regard the land as theirs, and themselves as the superior of the Arab inhabitants. But it does emphasize the difference between immigrants to Palestine who are coming with the idea of establishing their own political domination over the land, and immigrants to a country such as the United States, who come with the idea of becoming loyal subjects of an already existing state. Heavy Jewish immigration to Palestine is feared not only by Palestinian Arabs, but by their neighbors. Arabs fear that whatever foothold Zionists can gain by UN support will serve only as a springboard for further expansion. As Count Bernadotte reported: "They harbor grave fears that a Jewish State in Palestine will not stay within its defined boundaries, and through population pressure from unlimited immigration, encouragement and support from World Jewry, and burgeoning nationalism, a threat will be posed not only to Palestine but to the entire Arab Near East."

It is worth emphasizing again that Arabs point, plaintively and in growing despair, to certain principles which, they say, are basic in democratic political morality. One is majority rule. Another is the self-determination of peoples.

All over the world, Arabs declare, the United States has urged the right of the majority in a country to determine the future of that country in free elections. But to the inhabitants of Palestine, we have denied that right. The democratic way to have settled the future of Palestine would have been by a plebiscite conducted, if necessary, under international inspection and control.

To this, Zionists reply that the Jewish people are entitled to the right of self-determination too. The question is, does this right entitle people outside a land to have a dominant voice in determining the future of that land? The Arabs say no, unless a land is invaded in which case its neighbors have a right to come to its defense. The Zionists say that Jews have a special relationship to Palestine which gives them special rights —rights which could not normally be possessed by peoples other than the inhabitants.

Another answer to the Arab argument has been advanced chiefly by the Soviet Union. According to it, a minority which cannot get along with the majority in a country has a right to break away and set up its own independent state. The motives behind Russian support of this theory will be discussed later. Its application in Palestine is clear: Whatever the rights or wrongs of Zionist immigration, thousands of Jews are now in Palestine; they cannot get along with the Arabs; therefore they should have a state of their own.

Now it is an unfortunate fact that, despite all reports to the contrary, the Zionists in Palestine have *not* got along with the Arabs. This is particularly sad because it is also true that the Zionists have done much in Palestine that is wholly admirable. In the fields of education, medicine, agriculture, and in the introduction of other Western technical skills, they have made important contributions to the well-being of Palestine and, potentially, to the advancement of the whole Middle East area. The Hebrew University, the Technical College, the Agricultural Research Station and the Daniel Sieff Research Institute at Rehovoth, as well as the Economic Research Institute of the Jewish Agency would be outstanding institutions in any country. Jewish hospitals such as the Hadassah hospital in Jerusalem are among the finest in the world. Already Jewish talents in the sciences, and in the arts as well, have achieved great things in Palestine, and the promise is even greater.

Particularly spectacular have been their achievements in the field of agriculture. Earlier, I quoted Arab descriptions of some Zionist agricultural projects as "propaganda" farming. It would be very unfair to

give the impression that all of their farm settlements could be dismissed
as such. They have developed methods of farming which have proved
successful where other methods have failed. They have taught their
Arab neighbors much of their own skills. The men and women of these
settlements are, by and large, a truly remarkable group—sincere, hard
working, idealistic, filled with a most impressive sense of dedication.
Visits to their settlements, whether on the shores of Lake Tiberias, in
the coastal plain near Tel Aviv, or in the barren, bitterly disputed
Negev, invariably inspire respect and admiration. I have met, too, in the
communal farms a better understanding of the Arabs than is found elsewhere among the Jews in Palestine. Most farms have made a determined
effort to win the friendship of their Arab neighbors. If it had not been
for the basic political issue—the question, whose Palestine?—they might
well have succeeded. It is a world tragedy as well as a Middle Eastern
tragedy that Zionism has not been able to take a peaceful role in the
development of Palestine and of the Middle East.

It is sometimes argued that the Zionists have done so much for Palestine that the Arabs have no right to deny them further immigration. In
rebuttal, the Arabs offer a simple analogy.

Suppose, they say, that you and your family live in a house on a small
plot of land. The house is old and, perhaps, rather shabby. The land is
poor, parts of it are rocky and overgrown with weeds. But it is your
home. Your family have lived in it for generations and you love it.

One day some cousins of yours come down the road and knock at the
door. They are in desperate plight, the world has treated them cruelly,
and they seek refuge. (At this point the Arabs remind the listener of
their tradition of hospitality. "We have an expression," they say, "which
means in effect: My house is your house. We say this to our guests. But
we do not expect it to be taken absolutely literally!") So you receive these
refugees. They are industrious people. They pay for their board. They
paint the woodwork in the spare room, fix a leaky faucet in the bathroom and prop up the corner of the front porch which had begun to
sag. In a corner of the plot where nothing has grown for years they manage to raise some cucumbers.

But meanwhile, more and more of them are coming. Your neighbors
begin to worry that their own properties may be endangered, and your
own way of life has been upset. Your family has no privacy any more.

When you want to shave in the morning, you have to stand in line to get into the bathroom. So you say you are sorry, but enough is enough. You can take in no more guests, paying or otherwise.

Howls of protest greet your remark. You are assailed for ingratitude; look at all that has been done for you, the woodwork, the leaky faucet, the sagging porch—and the cucumbers. You have no right to refuse to take in more guests. And, from far off, these protests receive powerful backing. Your home is no longer your own.

That, conclude the Arabs bitterly, is a hell of a price to pay for cucumbers!

The dispassionate outsider may reject the position presented in the above story as being in many points based on illusion. The theme of hospitality, for instance, does not belong. Although Feisal agreed, subject to conditions never met, that he at least would welcome Jewish settlers to Palestine, the Arabs have not received Zionist immigrants as guests but as unwanted intruders forced upon them. But whatever our personal views may be, we must recognize at least the existence of such a view among most Arabs. We must go further, I think, and admit that such a view is not without foundation in fact and in democratic morality—just as even those who deny that the Balfour Declaration promised support to a Jewish State must admit that Zionists, who believe that it did, have been given grounds for the belief by responsible British and League of Nations (not to mention American) statesmen.

Much of our failure on Palestine can be attributed to failure to admit the vitality if not the validity of opinions contrary to the particular one we as individuals may hold. We argue passionately from the past. We expend our energies and our time and our fury on the MacMahon correspondence, the masterful ambiguities of the Balfour Declaration, the matter-of-fact cynicism of the Sykes-Picot agreement, the Feisal-Weizmann pact, the White Paper of 1939 or the Biltmore Program. The documents are indeed important. They are happy hunting grounds for the historian, and some excellent doctoral dissertations will be written upon them. But neither the documents nor anything written upon them can change what has been, not on paper, but in people's minds and hearts.

Many Jews have felt, deeply, that Palestine belongs to them, has been promised to them by God and by man. With that conviction they moved to Palestine, built homes and farms and factories, and fought.

The Arabs have felt, deeply, that by right of habitation Palestine is theirs, and that no one—British government, League of Nations or American president—has the right to promise their land to someone else against their will.

And the British felt, with a growing sense of frustration and anger, that they were committed to assist in the establishment of a Jewish national home in Palestine, and at the same time to the protection of the "civil and religious rights" of the existing non-Jewish population. Some also recognized a commitment to help the Arabs gain their independence.

The Jewish and Arab views were incompatible with each other; the British view was not only incompatible with them, but incompatible within itself. But all were strongly and sincerely held, so that no one— Jew, Arab or British—could really understand why *everyone* did not agree with them. This inevitably leads to the conviction that one is being persecuted—a conviction which pervades Palestine. Not only the British in Palestine, but the British government and much of the public at home, felt that their motives were being deliberately misunderstood and that they were being vilified for doing what was their plain, inescapable duty. Arabs believe that justice is so obviously on their side that anyone who is not 100 per cent for them must be an enemy, bought by the Zionists, insincere in his protestation of neutrality, deviously seeking to do the Arabs all the harm he can. A foreigner taking a photograph is doing so to make Zionist propaganda. A newspaper correspondent visiting a Jewish collective farm in an effort to see all sides, may become, in Arab eyes, an implacable enemy. That is one reason why a number of correspondents—actually unprejudiced, trying to get the whole picture—never did get a chance to see much of the Arabs. For the Arabs shrugged their shoulders and said, "It's hopeless. They are already against us."

The most extreme feeling of persecution was to be found among the Jews. This has obvious and tragic reasons. For all too many, persecution was not an imagined thing but had been, not long ago, something felt, tasted, and suffered. Everyone had been against them then; it was difficult to realize that things might have changed. Whatever happened they saw as the result of an intricate and devilish scheme against them. Fitzhugh Turner, who was Palestine correspondent for the *New York Herald Tribune*, wrote that the Sternists practically never accepted events at their face value. "Their own crazy thinking perceived an answering lunatic brilliance in the minds of British politicians, so that the most innocent act of the mandate government assumed, by devious reasoning, the aspect of a complicated British plot." In less extreme form, this kind of thinking had won the minds of countless Jews who were not terrorists. Thus Count Bernadotte, the United Nations mediator, was regarded as a secret British agent because, occasionally, he found the Jews at fault. Bernadotte, a sincere, upright man if ever there has been one, was singlehearted in his desire to bring peace and do justice to all. But to many Zionists it was inconceivable that a man could be fair-minded and not entirely on their side. Bernadotte was bitterly criticized—and killed for his pains.

A consul in Jerusalem once told me: "My grandmother, toward the end of her life, made life miserable for everyone around her because she got the idea that if you didn't do or give her just what she wanted, you must hate her. If she wanted three tickets in the sixth row center and the man at the box office said he didn't have them, it was just to spite her. If she called a man at his office and the secretary said he was out, she didn't believe it for one second. The secretary just didn't want her to speak to him. Or her boss had said he was always out to her. The result was that every time she picked up the telephone you could be sure there'd be the most godawful row. A lot of these Zionists remind me of my grandmother."

This consul, who was neither British nor American, was the only foreigner I met who seemed to enjoy his assignment in Jerusalem. Others got satisfaction, perhaps, from working hard at a difficult job, but the tragedy, the endless strain and conflict wore them down. But this man got a sardonic pleasure from what he regarded as the essential futility of it all. "It's a hopeless mess," he used to say. "All you can get out of it is hatred. If you try to be fair, you'll get hatred from both sides. If you back one, the other will hate you—and the one you've backed will make ever-increasing demands on you, and hate you if you don't do everything they ask.

"You watch. America will do everything and more, more than her our national interests should allow, to help the Zionists. But the day will come when she'll have to say no. And then it will be as if she hadn't done a thing. Just like the British. Without them, the present hopes of the Zionists would have been impossible. And the hatred felt for them is unbelievable." He smiled a cold, satanic smile. The charitable explanation of the smile is that he had broken under the strain—perhaps the combination of life with his grandmother and a long assignment in Jerusalem. The urgent hope is that his predictions will be proved utterly wrong.

The problem of Palestine is many sided. To the Western world, its most important aspects seem to be Jewish. It is offered as a possible solution to the plights of Europe's displaced Jews. Support of Zionism is claimed as reparation for the crimes of anti-Semitism. Politicians maneuver for the legendary "Jewish" vote (which, in the United States at least, has not been proven to exist except in campaign managers' dreams. Americans of Jewish faith do not vote as a bloc any more than those of Protestant or Catholic faith do). Liberals, sincerely anxious to help a suffering people, and reactionaries, looking to the day when they can cry "Send them back where they belong!" worked for the creation of a Jewish state. Some Jews glow with pride because now they, like the Irish, the Swedes or the Germans, can point to a "homeland," while other Jews wait uneasily for Gentile reaction to the creation of a "Jewish" nationalism which they as Jews reject. Alone in the West, foreign policy experts, generals, missionaries, educators and a few businessmen ponder the effect upon the Middle East outside Palestine. For all the rest the problem is, more than anything else, one that relates to and affects the Jews.

In the Orient at large, the Palestine issue is seen as a test of justice to small, undeveloped nations; as a struggle between Islam with a host of smaller religious communities against the alliance of Christianity and Judaism which dominates the world; or as an extension of Western imperialism backed by powers which have proclaimed that imperialism is dead.

But seen from the Middle East, which is the province of this book, Palestine appears as essentially an Arab problem. The rest of the world may worry about European or Asiatic refugees; Palestine has given the Arabs their own refugees, over half a million of them, who present not only a human tragedy and a public-health threat, but a very real political problem to the shaky Arab governments. (Trouble flows out from Palestine as the troubled flow in.) You see a different set of statistics from the Old City in Jerusalem, from Nazareth, Damascus or Baghdad, different from the statistics you see from Tel Aviv, Maidanek, Paris or New York. Both sets of figures stand for lives, hopes, sufferings and deaths, but not for the same ones.

There is nothing in the Middle East to match in horror the figures that stand for Hitler's victims. But where we see DP's in Europe the Arabs see an equal number of DP's in and from Palestine, refugees from the fighting which followed partition. Instead of approximately twelve million Jews in the world at large, they see thirty-five or forty million Arabs in the Middle East. In terms of these and other figures, Palestine becomes a problem which concerns more Arabs, and concerns them more, than anyone else. That may not be the whole picture, but in the Middle East it is the part of the picture held right before your eyes. What you might overlook elsewhere cannot be overlooked there.

Take, for example, the population figures for Palestine for three representative years:

	1919	1936	1946 (est.)
Arab Moslem	515,000	900,000	1,100,000
Christian	62,500	100,000	140,000
Jew	65,300	400,000	600,000

It should be noted that most of the Christians in Palestine are Arabs. In 1919 the Jews constituted about a tenth of the population, by 1936 somewhat more than a quarter, and by 1946 about a third. Since 1919 the Arab population (Moslem and Christian) has more than doubled itself; the Jewish population has increased by ten times. The Arab birth rate is higher than the Jewish—not only in Palestine, but in neighboring countries. Barring genocide on a fantastic scale, Palestine is and will be primarily an Arab problem in terms of the numbers of people affected.

The creation of Israel does not change this situation. For Zionists above all, it is vital that the Arab problem be faced squarely and honestly. As an English Jew has written:

The cardinal problem of the Palestinian issue can be summed up in a single sentence that we Jews had to build our National Home in a country in which another people is living. From this root all other difficulties have ultimately sprung, and although many outside influences—economic, political and religious—have affected the issue, the Jewish-Arab problem has remained the core of the matter. The solution of this problem was, therefore, the paramount task. But, instead of concentrating on this task all our efforts and creative energies, we have treated the Arab question, when it was remembered at all, as if it were of secondary importance.*

Speaking of the claim that Arab opposition to Zionism was the result of British, Fascist, or other outside propaganda, this same writer went on to say:

In a world where from Algiers to Java the nations are yearning for independence, we made ourselves believe that in Palestine alone the indigenous population had no interest in national self-determination and self-government. And this in spite of the fact that the Palestinian Arabs have not only to face a *static* foreign rule, as had the Indians or Syrians, but a most *dynamic* change of their situation by the continuous flood of Jewish immigration into the country.

That is the point that remote observers, and even Zionists on the spot, have missed. All the United Nations support which the establishment of a Jewish state received was from people far from the scene. Palestine's neighbors, from Greece and Turkey through the Arab states to the furthest members of the community, Pakistan and India, all were united in their opposition.

This is part of the Palestine picture because it is part of Palestine's future. If ever there was a time when a small strip of land could cut itself off from its surroundings to live in a protected isolation like an incubator baby for all its life, that time is past and gone. Small Israel will be unable to do on a large scale what larger Turkey has found it almost impossible to do on a smaller scale—maintain in constant readiness a standing army against the possibility of attack, or military pressure, from a neighbor. The extent to which Zionism has depended upon outside assistance can hardly be exaggerated. Without British backing, it could today have been no more than a scattering of settlers, cultural and religious organizations providing in Palestine a focus for Jewish cultural, religious and sentimental regard throughout the world. (In this role it is quite possible that the Zionists would have been welcomed by the Arabs.) American financial, political and moral support has been

* Walter Zander, *Is this the Way?* Victor Gollancz, London, 1948.

almost equally necessary. Soviet backing also was necessary in the United Nations. Now, unfortunately, developments have been such that Israel can count on no special help from Britain. That leaves the United States and Russia. But can Israel be satisfied to become the colony of a big power? An independent country cannot survive indefinitely upon foreign aid. It might seem that, since the U.S. and U.S.S.R. are on opposite sides of the fence, Israel could sit in the middle and play each against the other. This is more difficult than it sounds. For one thing, it is not as if Israel were the only child of divorced parents who are trying to buy her favor. Israel is one member of a large family. Any favor done her is going to be bitterly resented by the others, and neither parent is going to bid for Israel's support with the necessary abandon until that parent is sure that it has irretrievably lost the love of the other children.

Aside from political or military worries, Israel cannot survive economically if the hatred of all her neighbors makes trade with them impossible. Partly because it is trying to cope with large numbers of immigrants in a poor land, the Jewish economy in Palestine is one of the most artificial the world has ever seen. Without constant infusions of dollars and pounds (but especially dollars) from outside, it would long ago have withered away. In spite of its spectacular accomplishments, Zionist agriculture is not on a sound footing. In 1947 Zionist spokesmen informed UNSCOP that their agricultural developments as a whole were unable to meet the interest on their loans, and that they produced only a third of the food consumed by Palestine Jews. Another third was produced by Palestine Arabs, and the remainder had to be imported. American experts, notably Walter Lowdermilk and Robert Nathan, have stated that Palestine could support a much larger population through development projects such as a Jordan Valley Authority along the lines of our own Tennessee Valley Authority. This is probably true. If sufficient capital is available, almost any land can be made to support an increased population, if that land is at peace. The soil of Iraq, for instance, could be easily and rapidly enriched by irrigation projects—if the necessary skills and capital were available. Israel undoubtedly can get the skill and the capital. But can she win the peace without which they will be of no avail?

Agriculture will be needed if Israel is to supply her essential food

requirements. Industry is required if she is to be prosperous. And industry needs markets. The new Jewish state could not hope to compete
on any large scale in the markets of Europe or the United States or Latin
America, where the great industrial powers have markets already well
established. Israel, to prosper, must trade with her neighbors. For some
time at least, this will present difficulties. Arab hostility will be economic as well as political. The Arabs fear that the Zionists dream not
only of expanding their state but of establishing a semicolonial Arab
hinterland from which they would draw raw materials and to which they
would export their goods. Naturally, the Arabs would not relish such
a prospect, the more so as they are presently engaged in developing their
own industries. For this no less than for other reasons, their good will
and confidence must be won.

Even though it seems certain that Israel can count upon generous
financial assistance from American Zionists for some years to come, she
cannot count on it forever. Sooner or later—militarily, politically, and
economically—Israel is going to have to stand on her own feet. The
Jews of Palestine are going to have to get along with their neighbors,
just the way everyone else in the world has to do.

This will require a fundamental change of attitude from Zionists.
The report of the Anglo-American Committee of Inquiry on Palestine
observed: "It is not unfair to say that the Jewish community in Palestine has never, as a community, faced the problem of co-operation with
the Arabs. It is significant that in the Jewish Agency's proposal for a
Jewish state, the problem of handling a million and a quarter Arabs is
dealt with in the vaguest generalities." If military success encourages
Zionists to continue to ignore the Arabs, the end result can only be disaster. To quote Walter Zander again: "Initial successes for us Jews may
even ultimately share the fate of Napoleon's and Hitler's campaigns
against Russia. At best, military successes will bring only temporary
respite; and until we succeed to secure the good will of the Arabs a dark
and portentous shadow remains over the National Home." All friends
of Zionism should unite in urging that truth upon the new state. As
Count Bernadotte wrote shortly before his assassination: "Above all, the
Jewish state needs peace. A new organism of limited resources, its hope
for development must very largely depend in the long run on the cultivation of peaceful and mutually trusting relations with the neighboring

Arab states whose overwhelming numbers dwarf into insignificance any population total to which the Jewish state may aspire."

Of course it takes two to have peaceful relations. I believe it is up to Israel, and to her advantage, to take the initiative. The Jews, notwithstanding their ancient connection with the land, are now the newcomers. Moreover the Arabs can get along better without them than they can get along without the Arabs, though both could gain incalculably from friendly co-operation. Provided Israel will make the effort, what are the chances that the Arabs will respond favorably?

Obviously no categorical answer can be given. Arab feeling against Israel is unbelievably bitter and is likely to continue so for some time. Many Arabs, no matter what happens, will hope and plan for the day when they will be strong enough to destroy the new state. (Just as some Jews, no matter what happens, will hope and plan for the day when they will be strong enough to seize all of Palestine and Transjordan as well.) If, however, it is clear that Israel is strong enough to defend herself, or that the big powers will guarantee her borders against attack, most Arabs will have to accept, tacitly at least, the *status quo*. Tacit acceptance may grow into permanent peace. That was the late Count Bernadotte's hope, and it is the only hope there is.

The prospects for at least temporary peace depend to a great extent on the fate of one man, the notorious mufti of Jerusalem, Haj Amin el Husseini. At the time of the partition resolution of the UN General Assembly, in the month following November 1947, it appeared that Haj Amin would be an important national leader, in spite of his distinctly unsavory record. Much of that record which appears especially unsavory to us, to be sure, notably his relations with the Axis during the last war, does not necessarily condemn him in Arab eyes. If he were a sincere patriot and an effective leader, few Arabs would have held his association with the Nazis against him. And on the surface he did have qualifications for leadership. He had been and still was, the top religious and political figure among Palestine's Arabs. As mufti of Jerusalem, he is their highest authority on religious law. As president of the Supreme Moslem Council he presided over what was the nearest Arab equivalent of the Jewish Agency for Palestine. And he still held the office of president of the Arab Higher Committee. He has, moreover, an obvious singlemindedness which is fanatical in intensity. Arabs set great store by oratory, and Haj Amin is a man who can set fire to other men's hearts. He has, in other words, the reckless quality which may inspire devotion to a desperate cause.

But as a leader, even the leader of a desperate cause, he has his faults too. Opponents say, pointing to his many spectacular escapes from the British, the French and others who were trying to catch him, that he enjoys playing cops and robbers so much that he is no good for serious politics any more. He has intrigued for so long that he may love intrigue for its own sake. And he trusts no one. He is, too, a bad judge of men. He will tolerate no opposition, no questioning of his authority. The most serious thing against him, in Arab eyes, has been his treatment of those Arabs whom he thought to be his opponents. There is, for example, the case of Sami Taha.

Sami Taha was head of one of the two big Arab trade-union groups in Haifa—the anti-Communist one. Like all Arab leftists, he was an intense nationalist. Even the mufti could not complain that Taha was lukewarm in his opposition to Zionist immigration. I saw Taha in the summer of 1947 when I last visited Haifa, and remember him as a shy man with much book learning. His manner was in sharp contrast to that of his Communist rival—a glib individual of great personal charm. In August of 1947, Taha's Palestine Arab Workers Federation had a conference and passed a number of resolutions. One warmly supported the mufti's Arab Higher Committee. But another praised the Land Development Scheme sponsored by Musa Alami, and the work being done by Alami's Arab Offices.

Musa Alami is an honest, able Arab patriot. He is generally admitted to be without political ambitions, but the mufti is suspicious of anyone who might rival his position. He turned against Alami. Therefore, in his view, all loyal Arabs must instantly repudiate Alami and all his works. Sami Taha didn't see it that way. So the mufti's papers let him have it. Taha was, they informed their readers, a despicable traitor and more. He deserved to be shot like a dog. By no coincidence, he was, a few nights later, shot in cold blood near his home, without a chance of escape. The murder remains unsolved.

There is, of course, no evidence to show that the mufti or one of his lieutenants drew a particular man aside and said, "You are chosen to knock off Sami Taha. Do it neatly." Maybe all that happened was that someone took what he read in the papers literally.

But that kind of thing does discourage opposition. It is the kind of thing that has made the mufti hated among his own people. Many a young Arab progressive, who has had for lack of anything else to accept the mufti's leadership, has done so with grave misgivings and regret. Given any reasonable alternative they would turn elsewhere for leadership.

Moreover the mufti was badly discredited by the failure of his assistants—whom he has always chosen poorly—in the fighting which followed partition. The Husseini party failed to come across, from the Arab point of view, when the chips were down. The volunteer forces under Fawzi Kawukji were a total flop—largely, perhaps, because Fawzi had delusions of grandeur as a result of his German training and thought he could fight a real war instead of a strictly guerrilla-type war, which was his only chance.

Only a great leader, and preferably a noble one, can survive failure and keep his backing and his own confidence. The mufti is neither great nor noble. Once he began slipping his record started to catch up with him. Other Arab leaders saw no reason to stomach his perpetual plotting against them. Stories of his ruthlessness, ambition and lack of scruple, stories which many had known but few dared tell, began to get wide circulation and belief. It was recalled that Haj Amin had no consistent record even in his supposed patriotism.

One story, for example, relates that during the municipal election of 1927 Haj Amin was most anxious that Raghib Bey Nashashibi be defeated as mayor of Jerusalem. The long family rivalry between the Husseinis and the Nashashibis was so important to him that he was willing to make a deal with the Zionists if necessary to assure a Nashashibi defeat. Therefore he requested a meeting with the late Colonel Kisch, then head of the political section of the Jewish Agency. The home of Justice Gad Frumkin was agreed upon as the meeting place and the mufti went there twice to keep appointments which he thought had been confirmed. But at the last moment each time, Colonel Kisch had decided not to attend. The explanation is current that he was piqued because, a few years earlier, when he had first come to Jerusalem, Colonel Kisch called and left his card in proper diplomatic fashion, upon the mufti. But the mufti had never returned the call. This breach of etiquette may have made Raghib Bey mayor of Jerusalem and Haj Amin a Nazi guest. If only Colonel Kisch had met with Haj Amin and had obtained proof of his intentions, the mufti would have been compromised beyond hope of recovery and a dangerous career would have been cut short. (Colonel Kisch, unfortunately, was killed fighting in the British Army in North Africa.)

In spite of the revulsion of feeling against Haj Amin in many quarters it was by no means easy to fill the place of the mufti as leader of the Palestinian Arabs. To many King Abdullah of Transjordan seemed the only possible alternative. But to many others Abdullah, with his vanity, his instability and his overweening ambition, and particularly because of his dependence on the British, was even more unacceptable than Haj Amin. Still Abdullah had his adherents both in Palestine and without. If Abdullah had been able to satisfy the Arab League of his honorable intentions, he might have won the day without further opposition, particularly since Count Bernadotte in his recommendations submitted to UN just before his death, suggested that Arab Palestine be placed under the rule of Transjordan. However, the Arab League was divided. In spite of their strong lack of enthusiasm for the mufti, Egypt and Iraq (even though it too is a Hashemite kingdom!) were the first to announce their support of the mufti-dominated government-in-exile. At the date of this writing the issue remains in doubt.

There are many disadvantages in turning over Arab Palestine to Transjordan. Neither can be economically self-supporting, both are in need of help and not in a position to give help. Abdullah is hardly the ruler one would choose for the delicate and patience-consuming job of setting the new country and its distraught inhabitants upon their feet. On the other hand, aside from the fact that there is no more promising solution in sight, there are definite advantages to the arrangement. At least it might eliminate Haj Amin from the picture and unless he is eliminated the trouble he has made in the past will seem as nothing to the trouble he can make in the future. That is a reason which appeals to many a Palestinian Arab who has no love for Abdullah, but who realizes that Haj Amin could bring nothing but strife and more strife as his contribution to Palestine. His presence and the undeclared war he would undoubtedly foster would provide Israel with every excuse for a defensive invasion of Arab Palestine. Many Arabs would like to continue fighting. Many others are convinced that they do not have the necessary strength to win and they would prefer peace to inconclusive but weakening war, or even worse, to defeat. Chances for peace seem better under Abdullah than under any other arrangement.

Informed Arabs realize that Arab Palestine could not survive on its own. They realize that it is only the British subsidy which keeps Transjordan going. They see a danger that the new state might become simply a larger British puppet. To stave off this fate they rely on the support of the other Arab states and outside powers. Also, they feel confident that the Israelis would not welcome the British as neighbors. Over the years—perhaps the death of Abdullah would provide the occasion— they believe that the Palestinian Arabs could be the strongest and most persuasive advocates of a republican Greater Syria. More fully than anyone else the Palestine Arabs can recognize the disastrous results of disunity. Better educated than their fellows of Transjordan and deprived by circumstances from an attachment to a political entity as a "homeland," they may have the ability and the desire to translate a much-discussed dream into an actuality.

That does not mean that Arabs will necessarily give up their claim to all of Palestine. But, in the view of a few far-sighted Arabs it offers a peaceful, constructive way out. Just as they are convinced Arab Palestine cannot stand alone, so are they certain that Israel cannot survive in isolation either. Time will show that. What they want now is a guarantee that Israel will not expand by force of arms. If she cannot survive as is, and cannot expand by force, she will have to merge herself, to a greater or lesser extent, with her neighbors.

If and when that time comes, the terms she can obtain will depend on what she has then to offer—and on what she has done or can do to convince her neighbors of their identity of interests and of her own recognition of that identity.

Earlier I remarked that almost everyone in Palestine feels persecuted. Fear also is present everywhere, in the lands around Palestine as well as in Palestine itself. Arabs fear that the Zionists will not for long be content with what the United Nations has voted them. They see not only the terrorists and other Israeli political groups, but Zionists in America as well, demanding that Israel be given more and more Arab land—all of Palestine, Transjordan, part of Lebanon, Syria, Egypt, Iraq; the boundaries are ever expanding. Peace will be impossible as long as such fears are encouraged by Zionist words and acts. In Israel too, there is fear—fear that the Arabs are waiting only until they feel strong enough to crush the new state. As long as that fear persists, peace will come only after complete military victory by one side or the other. The United Nations has ruled that the conflict may not be settled by fighting; therefore it must be resolved by the removal of fear.

In the removal of fear, the United States can do more than any other power. We will, of course, take our part in guaranteeing both sides against aggression from the other. But we should go further than that. Israel depends for her very existence upon support, financial and otherwise, from this country. So far we have given without asking for return. In fact, Americans have encouraged Israel to increase her demands. Now we should say flatly that we are not going to contribute, or allow any more American resources to be contributed, to a country or groups within a country which endanger peace. The Irgun Zvai Leumi has received most of its financial backing from this country, though its arms have come from behind the Iron Curtain. American contributions to that and other trouble-making bodies should be halted immediately. American influence in Israel, which is very strong indeed, should be brought to bear *for peace*.

We are also in a position to exercise considerable influence with the Arabs and this, it goes without saying, should be used to the same end. Our influence with the Arabs can, however, only be effective if it is clear that the American government is not acting, to put it bluntly, as a "stooge" for Israel. It may seem ridiculous to us that Arabs believe that American policy on Palestine is determined by American Zionist pressure, which in turn is directed from Israel. Nonetheless that is what many Arabs believe. And their belief has been given some degree of plausibility by the timing of American moves on Palestine, and by the remarkable failure of the United States, alone among important nations, to give any explicit recognition to Arab rights, even though we may regard Jewish rights as predominant. We cannot expect to be regarded as reasonably impartial, by the Arabs or anyone else, until we have performed this act of elementary justice. Until then, our influence for peace will be less than it should be.

This book is concerned with Palestine as a Middle Eastern problem, even where it concerns countries outside of the Middle East. It has, of course, many important ramifications which have little if any connection with its geographical surroundings. In concluding this chapter I would like to express my opinion on one of these points.

I do not believe that political Zionism in Palestine is going to solve the Jewish dilemma in the world. On the contrary, I fear that it will make it—certainly in Moslem countries and probably elsewhere—even more difficult. The arguments of the Zionists constantly provide ammunition for the anti-Semite. The emotions and fears aroused over Palestine may be turned by unscrupulous men against Jews everywhere.

Yet this should be recognized: While one may disagree with Zionist arguments, it is the actions of Gentiles, many of them self-styled Christians, which give the Zionist arguments weight. Many Jews, who rejected Zionism and who believed that integration in the countries of their adoption was the only lasting solution of anti-Semitism, were profoundly shaken in their faith by events of the last twenty years. Most of the Jews of Germany, for instance, had made every effort so to integrate themselves, and thought that they had succeeded. Yet evil times and evil leaders came, and they were the chief sufferers. You cannot blame Jews for deciding that they must learn from that bitter lesson.

I believe myself that integration *must* be the solution for Jewish and other minority problems. But the Jews cannot do the job alone. And for the tragedy of Palestine, it should not be forgotten that Christians bear the heaviest responsibility.

⚶ XVIII ⚶

Iran: Tribesmen, Soldiers and Intrigue

NOW we turn to what might be called the "fringe lands" of the Middle East, lands that are not Arab but Moslem, lands that border directly upon the Soviet Union. Russia, her ambitions, intentions and strength, have come to be day-to-day concerns of Americans only recently. To Iranians, Turks and Afghani they have been matters of life and death for centuries.

In modern Iran—the country used to be called Persia—there are three dominant problems: The conflict between East and West, which finds Iran caught in the middle; the corruption and inefficiency of the Iranian government; and the divisive power of the tribes. No one of these is any novelty to Iran, nor does any one of them seem likely to be solved in this generation.

For the last hundred and fifty years the land has been the scene of the most severe and continuous clashes of interest between Britain and Russia. This rivalry temporarily ceased when in 1907 the British and Russians reached agreement over Persia, but the Soviet revolution resulted in an immediate conflict in Persia between British and Russian forces. Later the Soviet Union disclaimed any interest in Iran and it was not until the last war that Soviet Russia assumed an aggressive role there again. Iranians, like the inhabitants of many small nations, consider that it is only the rivalry between big powers that gives them any hope of survival. As one Persian poet put it long ago: "When the British lion and the Russian bear move together, the fate of Iran will be sealed."

Many Iranians have, however, looked to others than the British for support against the Russians. German influence has been strong in Iran, particularly among the tribes in the south, where the famous Dr. Wass-mus, the German Lawrence of Arabia of the First World War, was able to plague and elude the British with the help of the tribes for years. Although the late Shah Reza Khan, the modernizer of Iran, seems to have had Russian assistance in taking over the crown of Persia, once he was established he continued the old game of playing the British and the Russians off against each other. More and more when he wanted as-sistance he turned to the Germans and it was during his rule that their influence became most strong. Commercial travelers and technicians from Germany entered Iran in large numbers, took advantage of the popular Iranian fear of Russia and hatred of Britain. Their power in Iran became so threatening that it was necessary for the Allies to invade Iran and depose the shah in 1941, when Iran assumed tremendous im-portance as a southern supply route to the Soviet Union.

The United States' interest in Iran, as in the rest of the Middle East, is comparatively modern. The first American advisers to Iran, however, came at the request of the Iranian government as early as 1911, when W. Morgan Shuster headed a group of five experts to reorganize the administrative and financial agencies of the Persian government. Rus-sian and British pressure combined to force the Persians to send Shuster and his men back to the United States. Thirteen years later, before Reza Shah's dependence upon the Germans had become as complete as it later did, another American mission, headed by Arthur C. Millspaugh, came to Persia where it stayed five years and achieved some success in reorganizing Iranian finances. During the last war Millspaugh again headed an American economic and financial mission to aid the Iranian government and held the office of administrator general of Finance in the government of Shah Mohammed Reza Pahlevi, son of the old shah. There was also an American military mission, headed by Major General Clarence S. Ridley and a gendarmerie mission under Colonel H. Nor-man Schwartzkopf. Other American experts supervised food distribu-tion and agricultural and transportation matters. Some served as munic-ipal policy advisers and in many cases actually ran Persian towns. I remember during the war encountering one American in charge of a large Iranian town whose mother was head of the WCTU in one of the midwestern states. I was urgently requested not to explain to his mother, if I should ever encounter her, just what the man's duties involved—

because among them was the administration of a government owned and operated opium factory! Many of these American missions have been continued after the war at the request of the Iranian government, but the opium factory has been shut down.

During a large part of 1946 Iran was the hot spot of the world. It was the first place where the democracies had stood up to Soviet Russia; so far it is the only place from which Soviet Russia has retreated. Iranians who can look back on an exceptionally grand and violent history felt that their country was getting again the attention it deserved.

Their boastful proverbs had come to sound a nostalgic note: "When Shiraz was Shiraz, Cairo was one of its suburbs," the Shirazi say, admitting that Shiraz is no more than a shadow of its former self. But in 1946 Azerbaijan was more talked of than Paris. For a time the words of Iranian delegate to UN Ala were listened to more closely than those of any man except the big three leaders. Since then attention has shifted without, the Iranians think, really adequate reason. Certainly Turkey and Greece were menaced; but they are not as important strategically, do not offer as rich a prize to the Russians as does Iran. Iranians charged that the Truman policy of aid to Greece and Turkey increased the chances of Russian aggression against them by warning the Soviet Union that attack on certain countries would mean war with the U.S.—and then leaving Iran off the list. They do feel confident that when Russia's action makes Iran's plight evident, the United States will come to her aid. The question in their minds is, will that be time enough?

The complementary question in American minds is, will the Iranians ever give up their complete reliance on outside aid and begin to help themselves? The Iranians expect trouble and have been expecting it for some time. You might suppose, then, that they would be making every effort to prepare for it. You would suppose wrong. For even fear of Russia has not succeeded in uniting the Iranian nation or in making a corrupt government and equally corrupt army efficient in the cause of national safety. *Some* progress is, of course, being made. But the country is divided into different factions, which, while they talk about the Russians and about improving Iran, seem more interested in doing each other in than anything else.

Governments come and governments go, but the four main elements in Iran's political setup remain the same. They are: the young shah himself, the army, the civilian politicians, and the tribes. The political dance is marked by frequent changes of partners but no music yet written has been able to bring the army and the tribes together. Few tunes suit the taste of both the shah and the civilian politicians. The shah and the army, on the other hand, have found that their steps go very well together.

It is hard to estimate the strength of the different factions. No one politician, not even the old fox (and frequent prime minister) Qavam, is very strong in himself. But the civilian politicians are a tightly knit federation and can put up a stiff fight against any outsider trying to break their hold upon the government.

Recently the shah has enjoyed great popular support, largely because of the firm manner in which he has stood up to the Russians. He appears to have the army well under control. On the other hand the history of modern Persia shows how easily shahs and their governments may be overthrown.

The army, except in alliance with the shah, does not appear to have any soundly based strength politically. It certainly has none militarily. Its officers are corrupt, its discipline poor, its equipment inadequate, and its morale almost nonexistent. It has been pushed around with disdainful ease by the big tribes whenever it has tried to assert itself.

The present strength of the tribes is plain. They are vigorous, rich, well armed and determined. For the first time they have turned to Parliamentary methods as a possible way to achieve their goals and they have the most powerful single cohesive bloc—35 out of 136—of representatives in the Majlis. That is a small bloc, to be sure, but if it can fly in the face of Persian tradition and retain its unity, it could exert influence out of all proportion to its size. Strong central government, if it can be established, is bound to limit the independence of the tribes. But where is the source of strong central government in Iran to be found? At the moment there is no one to be seen on the horizon who is likely to be able to curb the power of the tribes. Depending on the way that power is used, Iran may continue as a united state or may break up into fragments—the northern ones falling under Russian domination, the southern ones subject to American and British influence.

So it was with particular interest that, during my last trip to Iran, I accepted an invitation to visit in the south. Even though the distances are long, and our time was short, the chance was too good to be missed.

My wife and I sat gratefully back and relaxed in the restful room. An impression of coolness was given by the sound of running water—it splashed from a fountain at the head of the room and ran, through a sunken channel in the tile floor, out into the garden at the other end. The sight of green grass and trees through windows on each side was soothing to the eye. We had just finished one of the roughest and certainly the hottest airplane trips I've ever made—from Teheran to Abadan, where the plane sat in the boiling sun until it was like a steam bath inside, to Shiraz. The other passengers had been mostly young mothers with their children escaping from Abadan to the relative cool of Shiraz; they were all, without exception, air sick. It was nice to be drinking ice-cold American beer on a brocaded couch instead of passing paper bags around in a lurching, sweltering airplane.

When we felt strong enough, and when the heat of day had broken, we could walk in the garden, admire what is reputed to be the tallest cyprus tree in the world, and inspect the roses and zinnias and sweet williams that grew in profusion beside the marble pools. We could look upon the colorful mosaics and carvings which decorated the outer walls of the palace. The sculptured lions, walking like proud kings upon their hind feet, would remind us of our ancient history books picturing the reigns of the Persians Cyrus and Darius thousands of years ago. Now we were only a few miles from the ruins of their imperial capital, Persepolis, which is still one of the most impressive and beautiful sights in the world. Its pillars stand straight and mighty above the sand, and bas reliefs show the emperors locked in mortal combat with lions or with queer one-horned beasts (perhaps the fabulous unicorn?), or receiving the tribute of conquered kings from Greece to Ethiopia to Cathay.

Shiraz is also a city of poetry. Two of the greatest poets of Islam, Sa'di and Hafiz, were inhabitants of Shiraz and spread its fame with their verses. Their pride of city sometimes involved them in trouble, as when Hafiz, writing of his Shirazi sweetheart, said "I would give Bukhara and Samarkand for the mole upon her cheek." Tamerlane, the great Mongol warrior then engaged in conquering half the world, called those cities home. When he seized Shiraz, Hafiz was dragged before him.

Tamerlane, not renowned for gentleness, was known on occasion to carry on the venerable Mongol custom of making pyramids out of the skulls of conquered peoples. He looked sternly at Hafiz and thundered, "Miserable wretch, I subjugate continents to adorn Bukhara and Samarkand, and you would sell them for the mole of a Shirazi wench."

Hafiz, who had been living in poverty, looked pointedly at Tamerlane's gorgeous garments and then at his own rags. "Sire," he replied, "it is through such rash spending that I have fallen on these evil days!" The story goes that Tamerlane was so pleased by this answer that, instead of punishing Hafiz, he rewarded him liberally.

Shiraz is still a city known for its pleasant life, for fine silver, wine, roses and wit. It is known, and important in Iran, for other reasons as well—and that was why we were there.

Our host was a stocky, smiling young man in a double-breasted suit who looked like a college boy, a football player. He offered us more beer. My wife said,

"No thank you, Khosro Khan."

He smiled broadly. "Is this a good introduction to nomadic, tribal life? Would you think this was the headquarters of the Qashqais?"

The answer was clearly no. When we think of nomads, we think of black tents, of humped camels stretched along a desert sky, of flocks of goats and sheep ever moving in the search for grass. We think also of a way of life that is close to vanishing, as the red Indians and the buffalo have practically vanished in this country. But that picture is not entirely correct. The number of nomads is constantly decreasing, it is true, and more and more of them are being settled on the land or given steady employment—for instance in the great oil fields of Iraq, Iran or Saudi Arabia. Governments are making a steady effort to absorb the tribes into a stable national life. Improved agricultural methods and ambitious irrigation projects are being advanced, so that lands whose sparse yield forced a wandering life upon their inhabitants may now support a settled population.

These efforts are made not only because the governments wish to improve the lot of their citizens. They are also anxious to maintain law and order, to have the authority of the state accepted without challenge. The nomadic tribes, who look with contempt upon the sedentary townsman or villagers, take the law into their own hands. Traditionally they have lived off the land; not only the grass and the flocks, but whatever else was at hand they have raided and plundered. His rifle has been the tribesman's dearest possession. It is difficult to overcome the habits of centuries—particularly in areas where it has so far proved impossible to substitute any other life for the nomadic one. In the Sahara, in the Arabian and Syrian deserts, and in the mountains of Iran, there are still many and powerful nomadic tribes.

Perhaps the most powerful of all these is the Qashqai tribe, or rather the Qashqai federation of tribes. They are not, it is true, entirely or absolutely nomadic. The 400,000 people owing loyalty to the Qashqai chiefs or khans make a sizable private kingdom, a state within a state. About half of these are Qashqai tribesmen; the others include forty small tribes, villagers who have found it desirable or expedient to place themselves under Qashqai rule and protection. The villagers stay put, wresting their living from the land in crops of barley, wheat and rice. The "elite" of the Qashqai—the strongest, bravest, proudest—move with their flocks twice a year, in spring and fall, from the hot coastal areas where they winter to the mountains where melting snows make grassland through the summer. It is the nomads, with their rifles, their bravery, and the wealth of their livestock, who make the Qashqai a power to be reckoned with. The nomads—and the four Qashqai brothers who rule over this private kingdom.

Reza Pahlevi, the "old shah" as he is respectfully but not affectionately referred to in Iran today, made determined efforts to crush the strength of the tribes, especially the Qashqai. He tried to get their rifles away, to settle them in villages. He enticed their leaders to his capital in Teheran and held them hostage there. To some extent, and with some tribes, he succeeded in his aim. The Bakhtiari, for instance, have not recovered from his attentions. But Reza Shah was deposed for his German sympathies by the British and Russians in 1941. The tribes, benefiting from the presence of foreign armies and the confusions of distant war, accumulated more rifles than they had ever had before. And the Qashqai brothers played a shrewd game indeed. The result is that the nomadic tribes, far from being a vanishing way of life, have regained much of the strength they lost under Reza Shah.

Any ideas I might have had that nomadic chiefs were necessarily simple souls, country bumpkins in competition with big city politicians, had been dissipated long before my visit to Khosro Khan in Shiraz. I had heard of these four brothers before. Nasser Khan, the eldest, has the reputation in Teheran of being a very astute politician indeed. The youngest, our host Khosro Khan, is the military leader of the tribes and had distinguished himself the previous October by soundly defeating the Iranian army sent against the Qashqai to take their rifles away from them. As it turned out, the army did not diminish but rather increased the Qashqai arsenal, for Khosro Khan captured two thousand rifles from the defeated army. His loot also included some light artillery and tanks. Since the tribesmen lacked training in such weapons, Khosro Khan disdainfully returned them to the government. There were some very redfaced generals in Teheran when the news got out.

The in-between brothers are named Mohammed Hosayn Khan and Malik Mansour Khan. (Khan is a title, meaning lord or ruler.) It was because of them that I first heard of the Qashqais—and realized that they were a pretty smart crew. That was during the war, in connection with a particularly neat trick the two young men had pulled upon the Nazis.

When the war began Mohammed Hosayn and Malik Mansour were studying in Berlin. A Persian working for the Nazis approached Malik Mansour and urged him to support a movement in Iran against Reza Shah—this in spite of the shah's German sympathies. Malik Mansour, who wanted to get home, pretended to be eager to help and proposed to enlist the powerful support of his brother, Nasser Khan. He convinced the Abwehr that Nasser Khan, if supplied with money and arms, could do the Allies great harm and aid the Axis most effectively.

For this purpose the Abwehr organized a secret mission to Iran consisting of five Germans and a Persian liaison officer named Farsad. The latter had been hand picked by Malik Mansour, and carried, in addition to the official messages given the group, secret—and quite contrary—messages to Nasser Khan. The mission took also, in addition to arms and explosives, $100,000 in U.S. bills. It promised to be a fat prize for the Qashqais.

Dropping by parachute into southern Iran, the Germans landed some distance from their destination, but they managed to reach the Qashqai tribe. Here—except for Farsad—they received an unpleasant surprise. Far from welcoming them, Nasser Khan confiscated all their weapons and equipment, including the $100,000. He then informed the British consul in Shiraz of their arrival and capture, saying that he would hold them as a guarantee for the safety of his brothers. Meanwhile Malik Mansour had persuaded the Germans to allow him to go to Istanbul to serve as a "forward base" to keep in touch with the mission. From there he was able to make his way to Iran. The German agents, with the exception of their leader, who committed suicide to avoid capture, were turned over to the British. Everyone except the Germans had turned a good profit on the deal.

The money and arms helped re-establish Qashqai fortunes—tribal and fraternal—after the beating they had taken from Reza Shah. The tribes and the brothers who rule them are strong again, and growing stronger. Their strength is no subtle thing, but obvious. It is made up of money, rifles and muscle.

Tribal life is hard, but healthy if you can survive it. The average Qashqai nomad is strong and wiry; unlike many Persians he is rarely addicted to opium and is free from venereal disease. He is an independently minded fellow, courageous, loyal and—though Moslem—monogamous. He has a strong family feeling which extends to cousins so far removed on the family tree that the average American would hardly recognize them as relations. He dresses, like most Persian tribesmen, in floppy trousers and a wide-sleeved cloak with a tightly sashed waist, his distinctive garment being a round brimless felt hat with unusual flaps which can be pulled down to protect the ears or face.

The women do most of the everyday tasks. They are on the go continuously from the hour before dawn until about nine in the evening. They milk the flocks and prepare the various milk products (curdled milk and cheese, particularly) which form the important part of the nomad's diet. The women also put up and take down the black goatskin tents, sew and weave cloth from wool and goat or camel hair, bake the thick loaves of bread, cook the meals and rear the children. When the tribe is not on the move the men sit around most of the day, talking and smoking the communal water pipe. Every few days they do something very active, like hunting or raiding some other tribe to steal horses or cattle or anything else movable. Raiding is dying out, but slowly, putting up a stubborn fight for life. It has been an integral part of nomad life for so long that it is hard to eliminate. And it is hard to get tribesmen to regard stealing as evil; they look upon it as a perfectly natural part of the competitive life, respecting the skillful thief, despising the careless owner.

A friend of mine stayed with another nomad tribe in Iran and suggested playfully one evening that it looked like a good night for horse thieves. (He comes from Texas, where horse thieves are not highly regarded.) To his consternation, the tribesmen took his suggestion seriously. But, they pointed out, it would be far more sporting to try to steal some rifles—which would be more closely guarded. My friend developed a very severe cramp in his left leg and the expedition had to be called off.

Aside from those elements of the tribe which stay put in one section of the land—those who, for example, have rice paddies and must stay through the summer heat and court malaria in the low coastal regions —the life of the tribe revolves around the seasonal migrations. During the winter the "garmsir" or hot district of southern Iran is green from the rains, but with spring it dries up. Then the tribes take their flocks of goats and fat-tailed sheep and move north, through an intermediate zone of wooded hills and pleasant valleys. But the sun moves with them, parching the land as it goes, so the tribes keep on the march. They know that only in the mountains of the great central plateau will they find secure summer pasturage. Melting snows keep the grass fresh and plentiful. But though these are ideal summer quarters, the weather is fit for nomads in tents only from mid-May to September. There are few trees, and therefore little fuel; in winter the Qashqai would freeze. In summer, however, the rich meadows make possible a close gathering of the clans. It is not unusual to see, in one small valley, as many as several thousand tents, while the plain is dotted with goats and sheep. (The sheep are best when their tails are fattest; while not esthetically appealing, these appendages contain valuable fat, and reach a weight, in good season, of twenty pounds.)

Tribesmen who own land in the summer grazing areas plant crops as well. The first crop is planted in autumn, just before they leave. It lies fallow, under two or more feet of snow until spring, when it sprouts and is ready for harvest in late June. The second crop is planted on the tribes' arrival in mid-May. It is irrigated by ditches from the streams of mountain snow, and is harvested in late August or September. Maize is the most common crop. But in spite of such plantings, wealth among the Qashqai is figured primarily in terms of fat-tailed sheep, worth $12 or $15 apiece. Horses, camels, cattle and rifles are the other most important "capital investments" of the tribes.

What is the connection between the black tents and the fine palace in Shiraz? Why do these hardy independent-minded tribesmen support a luxurious establishment in Teheran, which only one in ten thousand of them is ever likely to see? The contrast in life could hardly be more startling. The tribesmen at times make long marches with their flocks at night, to avoid the unbearable heat of day. At other times they climb barefooted through snowy mountain passes, and swim ice-cold rivers leading and encouraging their animals (all except the goats, who cross together with the women and children on crude rafts made from inflated skins). The Qashqai khans, on the other hand, have more protection from the elements. If the daylights hours are too hot, the sumptuous receptions they give can start after dusk—and end before dawn. They can escape the heat in Switzerland, or in an air-conditioned suite at the Waldorf in New York.

Although the khans do in point of fact spend a good part of their time in the headquarters of the tribes, such contrasts can be made, and could be resented. If the tribesmen were not satisfied that they were getting full value for their contributions to the khans' scale of living, there would indeed be resentment. Nasser and Khosro and the others would have to change their ways—quickly. But the tribesmen are satisfied. They feel they are getting their money's worth.

We don't question the need of our governors or presidents for official residences far grander than our own, for entertainment allowances, and so forth. Nasser Khan is the governor, or president, of the Qashqai state within a state; his brothers are his cabinet and Khosro Khan is in addition general of the armies. The parties they give so lavishly are for purposes of state. Attending one you can hardly fail to notice that. The parties provide occasions to talk on friendly terms with, say, the American ambassador, not only for the effect it may have on him but for the impression it makes upon rivals of the Qashqai—such as the shah's chief of staff—to see how intimate they are with the world's great.

Until recent years, the job of the tribal khans was mainly that of providing protection for the tribes, judging intra-tribal disputes, and directing such tribal activities as required over-all direction—particularly the twice yearly migrations. Those duties, of course, still remain. But others have been added to them. Now the Qashqais have many problems developing out of their relations with the Iranian central government, which is trying everything in its power to restrict the independent power of the tribes. And the tribes combat this effort with everything in *their* power. This includes resistance by force, of course, such as that led by Khosro Khan less than two years ago. But more and more the khans are recognizing that force is a last resort and that it can often be avoided by political maneuvering in advance.

Thus the tribes carry on their own "foreign affairs" with the big powers. In the past, the Qashqai relied frequently upon the Germans to oppose Russian influence in Iran and to assist them in resisting control of the Iranian government. Now the Qashqai place their hopes on America. Although American representatives have made it plain that they have no intention of assisting the Qashqais against their own Shah, that does not prevent the wily khans from seizing every possible excuse to magnify the friendly personal relations which exist.

Last summer, for instance, a member of our embassy in Teheran ran into one of the brothers and asked, casually, his opinion of a new cabinet member. A few hours later the Qashqais were boasting all over Teheran that the Americans placed so much reliance upon them that they asked their advice on the attitude the United States should take to cabinet changes! The shah, needless to say, was furious, even though he realizes that the boast was entirely untrue.

The tribes have recently been working through constitutional means —by ballots as well as bullets. In the last elections they entered a full slate of candidates in the areas where their strength made victory possible. The army, their bitterest enemy, sought to block them by pressure and intimidation, but the Qashqai formed an alliance with the prime minister, who also hated the army. The alliance was victorious; the four Qashqai brothers were all elected, plus another twenty or so of their friends and allies—enough to make a very powerful bloc in the Iranian Parliament.

When we were visiting Khosro Khan in Shiraz, some elections were still in progress, and the atmosphere of the house was a mixture of GHQ during a big push and party headquarters on election eve. Servants, soldiers and political henchmen were continually scurrying into the room with slips of paper which they thrust on Khosro. While he was reading the notes, they stood by impassively waiting for orders, but the minute he had given his instructions they were off like nervous jack-rabbits with a hound close on their tail.

These practical aspects of the khans' job, together with the educational, public-health and other programs they are also advancing, will take on greater and greater importance as compared with the military services which used to be paramount. The latter, however, are still the source of spectacular stories. Just as we were leaving I remembered one of these, and asked Khosro about it.

The story runs that during the October 1946 fighting between the tribes and the Iranian Army, the U.S. assistant military attaché was instructed to survey the scene of fighting and report to Washington. The Iranian Army and the Qashqais, both anxious to make good impressions, gave him passes and, in a jeep with a U.S. flag painted on it, he took off for the front. The army let him through without difficulty, but in the no man's zone men of a tribe allied with the Qashqai fired upon him and pursued his jeep. (Our attaché fired back, killing, he believes, one horse and discouraging pursuit, whereupon Reuter's reported that American forces had wiped out close to a score of tribesmen in a pitched battle!) Later, this discourteous behaviour to his American friends was reported to Khosro Khan who expressed his displeasure by riding over to the village of the offending tribe and shooting their head man dead.

When I asked Khosro Khan if this were true he smiled and shrugged his shoulders but made no direct reply. Holding open the car door for us to enter, he said he was sure that we would have a pleasant, and peaceful, drive to Isfahan. He was quite right.

When you see the independence of the tribes and their contempt for the central government, you can sympathize with the problems of the shah, who argues very reasonably that it is impossible to have a stable, effective administration while there are armed groups within the state which are almost independent states themselves. However, it is also possible to see the point of view of the tribes as well.

Their argument is as follows. First, the government is corrupt and inefficient. With this charge it is impossible to disagree. Almost everyone in Iran will concede that. Tribal leaders such as Khosro Khan point to unashamed graft, exploitation and almost open plundering by officials. They say that there has been a "closed shop" of about one thousand men who have had control since the days of the old shah and who, out of community of interest, back up each other. They do not even pretend to help the country or to know its problems—or even its geography. In Shiraz they tell of an occasion when the city of Lar requested of the central government that an official be assigned them to do a particular job. Teheran replied naming an official in Shiraz, saying that he should go to Lar every morning and return to Shiraz each night. The distance from Shiraz to Lar being about 350 kilometers over bad roads, the trip would take at least one day each way. If he had tried to obey his instructions, the official would soon have worn a deep and unproductive rut in the desert midway between the two cities, never getting closer than fifty miles to either.

Once Khosro Khan was talking about Persian history and he told me of a rather picturesque, old-fashioned way of raising money. At the courts of the eighteenth-century shahs the custom was to allow princes and other wealthy members of the court the "privilege" of purchasing for high prices the fleas which had been gathered from the royal garments. The idea was that the opportunity of killing a flea which had dared to attack the heavenly majesty of the shah was so obviously priceless that the lucky individual offered the chance would pay very handsomely for it. If he were so blind as to be unable to recognize the privilege and its worth, so much the worse for him. "Sometimes," said Khosro Khan reflectively, "I think it would not be a bad idea if we returned to the old-fashioned system! That is no more unfair or inefficient than some of the ways money is raised now."

Of course the tribes' great enemy is the army, which they charge is the most corrupt of all branches of the government. That is partly due to the poor pay. Nominally a conscript in the army receives seven and a half riyals per month, which is about fifteen cents. Even this is not usually paid to him. Of course he does get food for himself and a uniform, plus whatever he can pick up in the way of extras. These are not great for a private soldier, but increase with rank. A colonel's pay is equal to about $120 a month. Obviously officers could not live very well on their pay alone. Yet one army officer, now a general, who started in with nothing, is said to have accumulated a fortune of over a million dollars. It is clear that he must have engaged in extracurricular activities to do so. A starving man, engaging in somewhat similar activities, who steals a little grain from a wealthy man, will be sentenced to ten or fifteen years in prison.

The generals are accused not only of capitalizing on troubles to establish "temporary" military rule over an area and thus lining their pockets, but of instigating or inventing troubles for the same purpose.

Of course it must be remembered that these and other charges are leveled against the army by people who are, from circumstance, bitter enemies of the army. Nonetheless, while individual stories may prove to be untrue or highly exaggerated, most competent foreign observers agree that there is real substance behind the charges.

One must also remember that almost any Persian can talk a good reform program. This is particularly true when they are criticizing their opponents. Tribal leaders, for instance, ask rhetorically what it is that Iran needs. They answer their own question in a very liberal manner. Public-health measures, they say, schools, and a fairer distribution of land. If the shah is sincere why does he not give away some of his lands? Or spend what he spends for a B-17 on a program to combat trachoma? If Iran is to withstand the Communist challenge she must have some degree of socialism, perhaps, or at least drastic social reforms.

There is general agreement on the last point. Shortly before I visited Shiraz the shah had told me much the same thing. Although his training had been largely military, he had become convinced, he said, that in Iran the most important front was the civilian front. As long as the Iranian people were ill-fed, ill-clothed, ill-educated and just plain ill there could be no real security against outside aggression. An army could be defeated, a people could not. But the people must be strong, united, and convinced in their cause. Therefore, he continued, the course Iran should follow is evident. The government must institute a program of free public education, free hospitals and clinics and of economic improvements; particularly important are irrigation and agricultural methods which will provide the Iranian with his basic necessities in food and clothing. Later the head of the National Bank outlined to me a seven-year program by which the government hoped to effect the major aims of this policy.

Critics of the government have seen such plans before and are not impressed by new plans. There has been too much talk and paper work, they say, and not enough action. How is action to be obtained? Only by cleaning out the present government and the governing class root and branch, is their reply.

"And how," I asked, "could that be done?"

One young man gave me a simple answer.

"First," he said, "you might buy the present ruling clique of a thousand out." But he could not see where the money to do this would be obtained.

Secondly, you might make an example of five or fifteen or some appropriate number of the ruling clique by trying them for crimes and by hanging them. This, he thought, would scare off the others. But who in the present government would have the determination to do that? Therefore, the remaining answer was: revolution.

This left one fourth question, to my mind. Revolution by whom? I could see no group in Iran which combined the incentive, the strength, the program and the persistence to make a successful revolution—without foreign support. Soviet observers may well have reached the same conclusion.

✵ XIX ✵

Turkey and Afghanistan: Gray Wolf,
Black Lamb

ONE day in the spring of 1947 I listened to Senator Brewster (R., Maine) describe his plan for a forthcoming investigating trip he and a few members of his committee were planning to take.

"We'll spend two days in Greece," he said, "and then go to Turkey for a couple of days. We should be in Jerusalem for Easter, and in Cairo for two days immediately following. Another two days in Saudi Arabia should finish us up."

"What's so magical about the two-day formula, senator?" I asked.

The senator pulled at his cigar reflectively. "Well, young man, it's like this. I don't think one day is enough to really give you the hang of a country. And if you spend much more than a day or two there, you're likely to become a prejudiced native. But two days is just about right to make you a real expert."

By Senator Brewster's standard, I am an expert on Turkey. It is with reluctance, and an acute awareness of my limitations, however, that I write about that country. Obviously I could not be happy as a senatorial investigator.

Turkey is not entirely of the Middle East. Part of her land (Thrace) is part of the European continent. Her most noble city—Istanbul (Constantinople)—is in Europe, though her capital, Ankara, is in Asia Minor, and the Turks choose to regard themselves as a Balkan nation. Turkish relations with Yugoslavia and Rumania have been particularly good until those countries were pulled in behind the Iron Curtain. Turkey has no desire to suffer a like fate. Of the old Balkan Entente of 1934 only Greece remains as a possible friend to Turkey. This entente, which included in addition to Greece and Turkey, Rumania and Yugoslavia, represented the great hope of Turks who had looked eventually to the creation of a Balkan federation. At the moment this is obviously impossible. As a result the Turks may participate much more directly and actively in the affairs of the Middle East than they have since the end of the First World War. (The Greeks for similar reasons are showing a similar tendency.) The poor showing made by the Arab states in Palestine, however, has distinctly chilled Turkish interest in working more closely with them. In any case, whether the Turks regard themselves as more of a Balkan than a Middle Eastern country, from a strategic and military point of view they are inextricably part of the Middle East.

Like Iran, Egypt and other Middle East countries, Turkey has a triumphant past to look back to—only the glory is not as far back as it is in the case of the other countries. The old Ottoman (Turkish) Empire reached its peak in the sixteenth century under Sultan Suleiman the Magnificent, when its rule extended in Europe to central Hungary and in Asia and Africa included Egypt, Syria, Palestine, most of the Arabian peninsula, Tripolitania, Tunis and Algiers. One of the few dates that we are likely to remember from our history lessons is 1453, when Constantinople fell to the Turks; many students date the European Renaissance from the fall of Constantinople because of the impetus given to Western learning by the Greek scholars who fled to Italy from Constantinople to escape the Turks. For the next two centuries the danger that the Turks would overrun Central Europe was ever present. Twice their armies "thundered at the gates" of Vienna itself.

In addition to a triumphant history, Turkey has one of the great romantic cities of the world—and one of the few which fully lives up to its reputation. The blue Bosphorus, the ship-packed Golden Horn, the massive majesty of Sancta Sophia are as beautiful as they are reported to be. You leave the quiet splendor of the mosques, dodge busses through the modern business section, take a small boat whose oarsman directs you skillfully through the crowded waters to a landing up the Golden Horn, whence you walk through narrow, paved streets thronging with Oriental sights and sounds and smells until you come to a little restaurant, where you lunch succulently on lobster, chicken pilaf—or roast beef with Yorkshire pudding.

Probably most of us know Istanbul more through spy stories than through any other source. The sewage system of Istanbul has been more written of than any other system, with the possible exception of the Paris sewers. I remember reading a book years ago—I think it was called *The Eunuch of Istanbul*—in which practically every time you turned the page the hero or heroine was being dumped into some underground conduit which invariably brought them, struggling but still alive, up in the middle of the Bosphorus. These stories which picture Istanbul as one of the espionage centers of the world were not wholly divorced from fact. Istanbul has been of interest to the great powers, to Russia, Germany, England, France, for many centuries. Reporting to foreign agents seems to have become second nature to most of the inhabitants of the city. Moreover the sultans had an extensive secret police of their own. Their spies were everywhere and behaved, so it appears, in the best story-book tradition. In the last war, of course, Turkey was a center of Allied and Axis activity and even today it has probably not lost its standing in the community of spies. Crowded with refugees from everywhere, refugees who are full of information and rumor, eager for revenge or money or just for a sense of importance, the city is bound to attract practitioners of the ancient art of espionage. Visiting foreigners are likely to be shadowed regularly by the secret police, who are generally so clumsy that you are certain to spot them. If there is the slightest possible excuse, it is assumed that you are an intelligence agent and no denials that you can make will be accepted. Information will be pressed upon you and you will be pumped in the most suspiciously innocent manner. At first sight Istanbul is like something straight out of Eric Ambler, but once you check the dates you find it is actually the other way around—that Ambler is something straight out of Istanbul.

Aside from the flamboyant and faintly unbelievable aspects of Turkey's international role, there is a solid, matter-of-fact toughness about the Turks and about the situation they find themselves in. Turkey's problem—which is Russia—is no new one for her, nor is assistance from the West in holding off Russia new to Turkey either.

The main attraction is, and has been through modern history, the Dardanelles. Russian governments, czarist and Communist alike, have consistently agreed that control of the Dardanelles by another nation throttles Russia, because it threatens to block her free passage in and out of the Black Sea. At present, use of the Dardanelles is governed by the Montreux Convention (1936), which allows Turkey the right of fortifying the straits but specifies that the merchant ships of all nations shall have free passage at all times. During peace the warships of Black Sea powers also have the right of free passage, and other countries have the same right for warships up to thirty thousand tons. During war no belligerent vessels are to be allowed through at all.

This is only the latest of many efforts to settle the Dardanelles issue. Other European powers have long been agreed that Russia herself cannot be allowed to occupy the straits. Through much of the nineteenth century the crumbling Ottoman Empire, which was not finally demolished until after the First World War, was known to statesmen and readers of *Punch* as "The Sick Man of Europe," and on occasions everyone had to pitch in to keep the patient from succumbing entirely to the drastic surgery periodically attempted by czarist Russia. One of these occasions—the Crimean War—has been immortalized by Tennyson's "Charge of the Light Brigade," the work of Florence Nightingale and, on the Russian side, the writings of Tolstoy. The Truman policy of aid to Turkey has not yet been so signalized. But, in its less colorful way, it is following the same path.

The new Turkish republic is much more vigorous and healthy than the old Ottoman Empire of the nineteenth century. It is largely the creation of one man—The Gray Wolf, Kemal Ataturk, or as he used to be known, Mustapha Kemal. He is the outstanding figure of the modern Middle East. Ataturk earned his military reputation during the First World War fighting the British, and afterward fighting the Greeks. Because of the spirit instilled by him and because of the sickly nature of the empire with which she had started the war, Turkey, though defeated, emerged from the war a far healthier country than she had been before it (this was a situation which gave even the victors much occasion for envy). Under the empire the national energy had had to be expended in holding together peoples of many nationalities and religions under an outmoded and unwieldy government which no one wanted or liked.

In the early part of the century the Young Turks had made a revolutionary attempt to modernize and liberalize the empire, and to create a strong sense of Ottoman nationalism. This proved impossible; gradually the Young Turks found themselves pushing for a Turkish nationalism which could not be expected to appeal to the Arabs or other subject peoples of the empire not of Turkish stock. The defeat in the war removed from Turkey her non-Turkish subject peoples. Turkey still does have minorities, although 90 per cent of her population is Turkish speaking, and 98 per cent of it Moslem. The Turkish treatment of minorities—Jews, Armenians, Greeks, Kurds, and so forth—is notoriously harsh, though it has become civilized to the extent that it now relies on discriminatory taxes instead of the sword.

After the war, Turkey not only lost her empire, but threw out her imperial government. A republic was established with Kemal Ataturk serving as first president. He continued to serve until his death in 1938. Ataturk was out to make the break with the past as complete and thorough as possible. He abolished the caliphate and the power that Islam had had in the Turkish government, making the new republic a strictly secular state. To emphasize this, he forbade the wearing of the fez which had been sanctioned by religious custom. (By Islamic practice the head must be covered—the sun requires this even if religion should not—but there must be no brim to come between the head and the ground when the head is lowered in the posture of prayer.) Ataturk encouraged the abandonment of old Turkish costumes in favor of Western dress and in 1928 he made the new Turkish alphabet based upon Roman letters universally compulsory. He even went so far as to make Sunday the weekly rest day instead of the Friday as provided by Islam. His Republican Peoples' Party proclaimed six principles of faith: Turkey is republican, nationalist, populist, *étatiste*, secular and revolutionary.

Taken as a whole Ataturk's program must be judged to have been remarkably effective. His successor, Ismet Inonu, has sought to follow in the same line but in recent years the process of reform has been slowed, if not virtually halted. This has been due not so much to events in Turkey as to pressure from the outside. Ataturk had made a determined effort to establish peaceful relations with neighboring states and with the big powers. In the early years of the Soviet republic the Russians were so occupied with internal concerns that their relations with their neighbors were comparatively friendly. Turkey was able to relax her military precautions. Since 1939, however, the reverse has been the case. And this has had an inevitable effect, not on the desire for reform but on the ability to carry out progressive programs after they have been approved. For instance, there is the land reform bill of 1946, the purpose of which was to provide every Turkish peasant with sufficient land to support himself and his family. It was also intended to settle the nomad tribes in the eastern provinces and to grant land to other Turks coming back from Balkan lands to Turkey and to transfer as well a large number of landless peasants from the overpopulated parts of Turkey to the sparsely inhabited eastern provinces. This program obviously takes considerable money to carry out and it has been drastically slowed up because of the continuing military tension.

Turkey has a standing army of 600,000, which is really much larger than a country with a population of twenty million can afford. But this army has to keep standing practically all the time because of the Russian menace to the Dardanelles and to Turkey's eastern provinces. Periodically the Russians issue a stiff note demanding concessions, periodically they hold "maneuvers" close to the Turkish frontiers, while the Soviet press and radio fulminate against the Turkish government. So far the Turks have stood up firmly to this war of nerves, as they did to German pressure. During the last war they stayed neutral until the very end. They did quite well out of the war, what with preclusive buying by the Allies (in which we and the British paid large prices for Turkish chrome, hides, wool and mohair to keep them from going to Germany) and Lend Lease aid. Now Turkey is getting cold war lend lease. Her independence, together with that of Greece, from Russian domination has been declared by President Truman essential to American security. What this means in effect is that we are subsidizing the Turkish economy to make it possible for Turkey to support an army much larger than it could normally support.

That army is made up of tough, willing fighters. The Anatolian peasants have proved their courage and determination many times in the past. They could make it difficult for an invader in the jagged mountainous areas of Turkey. In addition, we have strengthened the Turkish Navy with some American submarines and the Turkish Air Force is getting American planes as well as American pilot training. Even so, Turkish military strength, when stacked up against Russian capabilities, is obviously insignificant. The Turks lack planes, tanks, artillery and even manpower. Without quick and effective outside assistance it is difficult to see how, in any serious war, the Turks could have more than a limited nuisance value. What the Turkish aid program does, however, is to make sure that Russia could not take Turkey without war, and that in the event of war, we would at least have a chance to aid Turkey and to make use of Turkish bases. Under the circumstances, the Turkish army seems like a pretty good investment.

Armies are not uncommon in this discombobulated world. Turkey does have one thing that is very rare indeed: an opposition party created by a dictator who hoped to make democracy by decree. The Democratic party was established by instructions from President Inonu, who is head of the Republican Peoples' Party, in 1946. Judging from its platform, its major disagreement with the Republican Peoples' Party is that it would cut down the sphere of government activities, reduce the bureaucracy and relax the vigor of state activity and control, leaving a broader field to private enterprise. The opposition party, it appears, has shown a distressing quickness in learning how to oppose. There appear to have been moments when its creators have regretted their handiwork. After all, there are limits—and some things that a well-trained opposition simply should not do, such as threaten to win too many votes. Elections have occasionally required rather special attention. But such action is reported to occur in countries with considerably longer democratic traditions than Turkey. The important fact is that Turkey, with many of the aspects of a police state, thought it worth while to create an opposition party rather than to continue a single party system. The plan has succeeded, perhaps too well to please all of its originators. Anyhow, the Democratic party, in spite of some rather special attention from the government, won sixty-five seats in Parliament in the 1946 elections.

Turkey is not yet a democratic country. Democracy cannot be introduced overnight. With all their faults, however, the Turks have made progress. They might make much more progress if they didn't have to devote so much of their energy to maintaining an army. It would be completely unrealistic to think that American aid to Turkey will produce democracy in a hurry. Turkey may do that herself if and when the Russians are contained and their neighbors need no longer live in constant fear of attack. Meanwhile the American program of aid to Turkey is a purely defensive one. Even taking account of the road and port facilities developed with our help, the Truman program could be kept on for generations without doing much more than maintain the status quo. We are assisting the Turks to maintain an army which, without our help, they could maintain only by making drastic cuts in their civilian economy and by eliminating what few political liberties they have. To do the job alone, they would have to create in Turkey the same kind of totalitarian state that they are trying to resist.

One last point: I have called the Turkish Army a pretty good investment in the circumstances. That judgment should be qualified to this extent. The defense of Turkey, as of Greece, Iran and Afghanistan, is essential if the Middle East is to be preserved, as it must be, from Soviet domination. But obviously, there is no sense in pouring money and arms into Turkey if we are going to let the Arab countries—the heart of the Middle East—go by default.

Afghanistan

Afghanistan is a mountainous, independent, little-known country which forms the buffer between the Soviet Union and the rich subcontinent of India. Alexander the Great and the Persian conqueror Nadir Shah are only two of many who have led their armies through the passes of Afghanistan to fall upon India from the north. The first European interest in this remote land was shown in 1809. Napoleon had realized that the best way to strike at the British Empire was through the Middle East. His ambitious invasion attempt had stalled in Egypt, but the British in India were alarmed by his intrigues in Persia; they began to look to the defenses of Afghanistan. In a few years the French threat vanished, but its place was taken by a far more serious danger from Russia.

The first British conquest, in 1838, was inspired by the friendly reception given to a Russian envoy by the Afghan ruler. From then on until 1919, the Afghanis were either at war with or under the influence of the British. Periodically, the British would occupy the capital, Kabul, and periodically the hardy, independence-loving and foreigner-hating tribesmen would wipe out small British forces. In 1880 the British began to pay the Kabul government an annual subsidy of half a million dollars, in return for which they were given the direction of Afghanistan's foreign policy. Even that did not always keep the peace. However, during World War I the country did, in spite of strongly pro-Turkish sentiment, remain neutral. But immediately afterward Afghan forces suddenly attacked the British in the Northwest Frontier of India. This war was short but reasonably satisfactory; it was concluded by a treaty granting Afghanistan full independence.

Most of us know of Afghanistan chiefly as the scene of some of Kipling's stories and as the home of very superior black lambskins. The United States imports about three million Karakul (Afghan lamb) skins a year. Karakul means "little flower" and the skins are so named not in an effort to get the New York trade but because good specimens have, in the center of the shoulders, a swirl of hair resembling a blossom. Most prized in this country are the brilliant jet black skins with tightly curled fleece, but Karakul skins range in color from black to steel gray and golden brown. The latter are favored in Afghanistan. In some cases the Afghans perform a sort of Caesarean operation upon their ewes to get the lambs before their skins are coarsened by birth. Neither Kipling nor black lambskins give an adequate picture of Afghanistan.

The vital statistics are, briefly, as follows: The population is about twelve million, chiefly Pushtuns (Afghans) and Tajiks, though there are numerous other tribal strains as well. This is important because the tribes overlap the national boundaries. There are five million Pushtuns (Pathans) in the old Indian Northwest Frontier zone, now part of Pakestan, which Afghanistan would like to consider part of itself. A somewhat similar situation exists, as we shall see, to the north as well, only here it is not Afghanistan that dares to be covetous.

The predominant languages of the country are Pushtu and Persian, of which the former is the official one. The state religion is Islam, and the majority of the Afghans are Sunni, often known as Hanafi Moslems because they follow very strictly the law code of that name. There is a sizable Shia minority, and minute Hindu and Jewish minorities. The Afghans, incidentally, have through their ancestry a claim to Palestine, though they have not yet pressed it. They are said to be descended from the tribes taken captive by Nebuchadnezzar. As Colonel Ernest F. Fox reports in his informative and enjoyable *Travels in Afghanistan,* "They call themselves Ben-i-Israel, or 'Children of Israel' and claim descent from King Saul through a grandson named Afghana."

To conclude the vital statistics: The capital city, Kabul, is rather dreary looking from the outside; but behind the mud walls which line the streets are beautiful gardens with fountains and fine roses. The ruler, H. M. Mohammed Zahir Shah, came to the throne in 1933 after the assassination of his father through some local jealousy. His father's predecessor, Amanullah, in turn, had been deposed by a revolution in 1929, because he was extravagant, trying to modernize the country too rapidly (so he offended the mullahs) and neglectful of the army (he didn't pay them on time, which was most injudicious under the circumstances). Amanullah now lives in straitened circumstances in a suburb of Rome, where he has been in the real-estate business. Being a king in Afghanistan is no sinecure.

The Afghans have been understandably leary of foreigners. They want to remain independent. And they realize that for either of their big imperial neighbors to become suspicious of the other's activity in Afghanistan would be too bad—for Afghanistan. Thus ever since they gained complete freedom from England there has been an unwritten rule: There are to be no Russian consular offices in southern Afghanistan, and no British consular offices in the north. When the American Colonel Fox was carrying on mineral explorations for the Afghan government in 1937, and had cleared all his travels with officialdom in Kabul, he was surprised suddenly to find local officers blocking his passage to the northern borders. They did so, he was told, on orders from Kabul. Colonel Fox could not understand why. On his return to Kabul, he found that a rumor had spread identifying him as Colonel T. E. Lawrence (Lawrence of Arabia) in disguise. The government, even though he was working for them, would not risk letting him go too far north under the circumstances!

As part of the same system of precautions, no foreign diplomats are allowed to travel outside of Kabul without "interpreters" being assigned to them. These interpreters watch to see that nothing is done to excite the suspicion of either Russia or Britain.

Recently the Russians have been protesting that their suspicions *are* aroused—by the presence of a number of Americans in the country. There are no official U.S. missions in the country apart from the normal diplomatic staff. But there are prospects that agricultural and antimalarial missions will be sent out by our government, and the State Department has helped the Afghans to recruit American teachers and hospital assistants for its own employment. The Afghans have also employed an American city planner and mining engineer, and an American company is constructing irrigation projects and roads. The Russian radio and press, as might be anticipated, accuse Afghanistan of building hostile bases—for American use against the Soviet Union. So far the government of Afghanistan has refused to take the charges seriously or to show any worry over Soviet threats on that score.

Apart from any aggressive intentions the Soviet Union may have, she has other reasons for interest in Afghanistan. The latter borders upon three Soviet states, the Turkoman, Uzbek and Tajik republics. Right across the border these states are faced, respectively, by Afghan Turkomans, Uzbeks and Tajiks. Tribal and religious ties are strong, and it is doubtful that Communist indoctrination has completely broken them. The Russians keep harping upon minority problems in other countries —on, for example, the treatment of Negroes in the United States. But the Politburo cannot forget that it has its own acute minority problems, and that its southern borders particularly are very susceptible to penetration through minority groups, and to division by exploitation of minority grievances.

Someday the opponents of Soviet Russia may tire of doing nothing but replying to endlessly repeated attacks upon them. They may realize that you do not win even a propaganda war by staying on the defensive. If and when they do take the offensive, this southern border and its minorities offer the most promising target. Besides the Turkomans, Uzbeks and Tajiks there are Armenians, Kurds, Circassians and a host of others. Many Armenians, disappointed in the support they have received elsewhere toward their dream of an Armenian state, look to the Soviet Union as their best hope. But word filtering back from Middle East Armenians who have emigrated to Soviet Armenia has been most discouraging to them. The Union of Soviet Socialist Republics has Achilles' heels—ideologically and practically—in a profusion rivaled only by a centipede.

Our ability to exploit these weaknesses will depend directly on our ability to give these peoples—Turkomans, Kurds, Armenians and their neighbors—confidence in our intentions, our discretion and our power. The history of Afghanistan, like the history of countless small countries, is full of object lessons of what happens when two big powers start fighting over or through it.

PART THREE

The Big Powers

XX

Bit Players and Stars

AS ONE British official told me wryly, "If all the Blue Books and White Papers and other documents our government has published on Palestine and Middle East problems were laid end to end across the Atlantic—they'd all sink, and a jolly good thing too!" His remark represents more than fed-up frustration; it emphasizes the vital and continuing interest which one country thousands of miles away has felt toward the hot cross roads of the world.

Britain and Russia have been acutely aware of the importance of the Middle East for several centuries. For both, its significance was obvious. Russia, as soon as she felt her own strength, saw the Middle East as the most promising avenue to the warm-water outlet she needs to be properly great. For Britain, the fact that the Middle East lay between her and India was sufficient. In both cases, propinquity and the most elementary strategical considerations forced attention upon an area which, in any world struggle, is a vital key to victory or defeat.

Other imperial powers—the early empires of the Portuguese and Dutch, the French, and later Italy and Germany—likewise learned this lesson. The United States, however, had none of the obvious interests that led others to early appreciation of the Middle East's significance. We are far away; we have not been an imperial power. Even so, the last ten years have seen us dragged, protesting and uncertain of our lines, onto the stage to play a leading part. A partisan and divided audience has alternately applauded and booed, or stared in puzzled silence at a performance which, from time to time, resembles that of a comic juggler, a ventriloquist, a ventriloquist's dummy, a somnambulist, or a real-life missionary who suddenly finds himself plunked down before Broadway footlights playing opposite Tallulah Bankhead in *Rain*.

Throughout preceding chapters there have been references to the special interests and policies of the big powers in the Middle East. The strategic significance of the area, the special attributes which inevitably attract world attention, have been indicated: communications, oil, and religion raise issues in which the big powers inevitably become involved. We have seen, here and there, signs of the tug of war between the Soviet Union and the Western democracies. These signs have appeared as incidental to the main story—the story of the lands and peoples over whom the tug of war takes place. In this concluding section I shall try to put together the bits and pieces into a coherent picture.

What, to the world at large, is the relation between an opposition leader in Baghdad, an anti-British riot in Cairo, an antimalarial campaign of American doctors in Saudi Arabia, a Kurdish Communist in Syria, and an American-educated dentist in Amman? Or, for that matter, what is the significance of a Swedish pilot landing on an air strip outside a walled city of Yemen, an Italian who combines the jobs of bodyguard and procurer for a king, a French nun teaching little girls in Beirut, or a German archeologist digging among the massive ruins of Persepolis? We know *why* outside powers are interested, must be interested, in the Middle East. What remains is to summarize the form their different interests take, the methods they employ to advance them, and the success which has been achieved or may be expected from those methods.

Foreign countries have, of course, a complex of cultural, commercial, political and security interests in the area which vary greatly in intensity. Individuals and religious groups of many countries, for instance, have property or representatives in Palestine. These include American Jews, Chinese Moslems, Russian Orthodox and Coptic Catholic Christians, Persian Baha'is—representatives of most Christian, Moslem and Jewish sects of the world.

To take another example, the Suez Canal, which is owned chiefly by British, French and Dutch interests, is used for shipping by many other nations. The Canal Company is French, although the British government holds nearly half the shares, and it will revert to the Egyptian government in 1968, when the concession expires. Shareholders include citizens of several other countries, and the canal performs a valuable service for all the Mediterranean, Middle East and Indian Ocean countries, not to mention those as far away as Australia, Norway and the United States.

Before the last war, there were several powers with concrete political, or even imperial, footholds in the area. Italy had Libya and Eritrea as well as Italian Somaliland and Ethiopia. France had the mandate over Syria and Lebanon. Great Britain had the mandate for Palestine, plus rather special relationships with Egypt and the Anglo-Egyptian Sudan, Iraq, Transjordan, and the sheikhdoms of the Persian Gulf. Germans had particular influence in, and ambitions for, Iran. Dutch, French, British and American interests held important oil concessions. Soviet Russia, though showing unmistakable signs of her intentions toward Iran and Turkey, held no concessions or other major assets in the area. Her Middle East policy was, of course, already established in its essentials; its aims had not changed since czarist days. But details were still unsettled, and opportunity for vigorous pursuit of her ancient aims was not yet open.

Since the war, France and Italy have lost their territorial footholds (and even if Italy recovers some part of hers, she can no longer be an important power in the area). Great Britain too has had to abandon most important positions, but remains a force which, particularly in alliance with the United States, could play the decisive role in the area. Soviet Russia failed in her one attempt to extend physical domination into a part of the Middle East, but she is now pursuing a vigorous and, on the whole, extremely effective policy. And the United States has seen its political and economic interests suddenly assume major importance. Cultural interests of which most Americans had been wholly unaware became, overnight, important assets in the maintenance of our own physical security. Since the war, powers interested in the Middle East can be divided into two categories, the first consisting of Britain, Russia and the United States, the second consisting of all others.

The second category can be disposed of briefly. I do not mean that countries in this class may not look to the Middle East with acute concern for their own safety. As a matter of fact the French, who have North Africa on their mind as well, probably have a far clearer idea than we do of the way their national future is tied up in developments in the Middle East. The difference is that where they can do little about it, the British, the Russians and ourselves can do a lot. French cultural influence is dominant (among the intellectuals) in many of the Arab countries and in Iran. But how many divisions does cultural influence command? Italians are influential in Abdin Palace in Cairo, but the object of their influence is not strong and in any case they have nothing behind them but chicken cacciatore, Chianti and Capri. Swedes are being hired as technical advisers by some Middle Eastern governments, precisely because their land is far away and without strength in the area. Some of the Balkan and Central European countries, such as Yugoslavia with its own Moslem population, have a natural link with the Middle East. But except for Greece, what activities they undertake there are chiefly to serve Soviet interests.

There is much that is colorful, and often much that is constructive, in the Middle Eastern role of the small powers. The real story today, however, is the story of Russian, British and American activity.

⚕ XXI ⚕

Soviet Union: How to Move One Way
in Opposite Directions

RUSSIA, the only one of the major powers with a common border touching the Middle East, has been nibbling away at Persia and Turkey for three centuries. Peter the Great was following a well-defined path when he captured Baku from Persia in 1723 and partitioned Persia by treaty with Turkey in the following year. Although the Persians soon regained most of their losses, the story has been repeated with minor variations many times since. Czarist Russia also intervened in the Arab countries, mostly to make trouble for the Ottoman Turks, and insisted upon her right to assume the role of protector of Orthodox Christians within the Ottoman Empire. However, it was not until after the last war that Russia's strength and ambitions made her a threat to the territorial integrity of Middle Eastern countries other than Iran and Turkey.

As the German documents published by the Department of State in 1948 show, Russian ambitions in this direction were well understood by the Nazis during the period of the Nazi-Soviet pact. Ribbentrop wrote: "The focal point in the territorial aspirations of the Soviet Union would presumably be centered south of the territory of the Soviet Union in the direction of the Indian Ocean." His judgment was, for once, sound. It was in this direction that the Soviet Union turned immediately after the war was over. In 1940 Russia was willing to join the Axis if she could be given the Dardanelles and a foothold in the Middle East. It has been reported, but never proved, that as late as 1943 the Soviet Union was willing to sign a separate peace with Germany to attain these same ends. Whenever the chance is favorable or her strength sufficiently great it is certain that the Soviet Union will try again.

Although Russian objectives in the Middle East are different from our own, the prizes which draw them are substantially the same— strategic location and oil. Russia's need for Middle East oil is acute. Her own production of oil should not, theoretically, have been hard hit by the Nazis, who overran only 15 per cent of the Soviet oil wells. Nonetheless the damage must have been severe, for the planned goal of Soviet oil production for 1950 has been set at only 35.4 million metric tons, which is one sixth of U.S. production and far below the goal set for Soviet production for 1937 (44.3) or 1942 (48.5 million metric tons). Russia has within her own boundaries rich oil fields. We know they are rich although, needless to say, the Russians have not made available information by which we could judge their full extent. The Russian oil industry is certainly old fashioned and inefficient. Its 1950 goal would be considered extremely modest by American standards. Even so, there is considerable doubt that it will be met—which means that, for an immense and powerful country, the Soviet Union will be extremely short of oil. Oil adds an attraction to those which have drawn Russian eyes to the Middle East for centuries.

Parenthetically it should be remarked that what constitutes a crippling oil shortage for the United States would not be nearly so serious to the Soviet Union. In case of war it would be extremely difficult for the United States to devote its oil production 100 per cent to war purposes unless our danger were so acute that every Congressman and every consumer of oil could perceive it unmistakably. Russia, however, would use her oil exactly as the Politburo or the High Command wanted, without a peep from anyone. Moreover, the Russians would live off occupied areas far more thoroughly than we would ever do. Finally, their society is not geared to consume as much oil as is ours. Apart from military requirements, a "shortage" crippling to American industry and civilian life would be a normal supply for the Russian state.

Russia's Middle East strategy must be viewed not in isolation but as part of a world strategy. The Soviet leaders do not believe in unlimited commitments on every possible front. Neither they, nor anyone else, have the resources for that. The Russians have, it is true, great maneuverability, for they are on the inside of the semicircle which stretches from Manchuria to Finland; it is easier for them than it is for us to apply and to shift pressures in accordance with the strengths or weaknesses of the forces assembled against them. Thus when opposition grows too strong, they can transfer their main efforts from Iran or Greece or Turkey to Germany or Italy or China—and vice versa.

Recently, in the Middle East, Russian strategy has been largely *destructive*. That is, the Soviet Union has been less concerned with strengthening her own position or with winning friends than with weakening the position of her opponents. Winning friends usually means making commitments, but stirring up trouble for the opposition *may not*. For example, in determining her policy in the UN on Palestine, Russia had the chance, if she chose to support the Arabs, of winning roughly forty million friends. Many observers expected her to seize that chance. But there were risks, and heavy commitments, involved. For one thing, it would have meant that in an open conflict over which Russia could have small control she would be firmly aligned on one side; her only allies would have been the Moslem world, unpredictable, none too strong. Even if she kept out of the fighting herself, in the face of determined Anglo-American opposition, the help she might be obliged to give to those allies would be a drain and an embarrassment. The cost of gaining forty million friends might be more than they were worth. In eastern Europe and China, Russia already has more in the way of friends and dependents than she can properly look after.

As Walter Lippmann warned Americans recently, "the earth is much too large, and its troubles and disorders much too extensive, for us to regard ourselves as the ultimate fixers of everything everywhere." We must exercise practical judgment, which consists in "choosing to what ends the available limited means shall be applied." The Russian leaders, at any rate, are strong in that kind of practical judgment. And they discovered that they could get a large part of what they wanted without making any new commitments at all.

The point is that in the Middle East, as in France and Italy and India, chaos fights on the side of Communism. To win their objectives the Russians do not, in the beginning at least, have to win friends at all. It is, to be sure, nice to do so; but it is a luxury which they can for the moment do without. Arab Communist parties are not strong, and the Russians have not expended the money and efforts to make them strong that they have expended, for instance, in Greece, or France, or the United States, or even Iran. (Iran provides a good comparison, for the Russians made their chief efforts there at a time when they were pursuing a *positive* policy and hoped to take over at least the northern part of the country.) It is important for the Russians to have a nucleus of trained and tested people upon whom they can rely. But it is not important to them, with their present objectives, for Communism as a doctrine to be widely propagandized, or even for the Soviet Union to have many friends among the populace. This explains the nature of the local Communist effort in the different Arab countries.

In penetrating these countries the Russians have relied largely upon exploitation of four groups: their own Soviet Moslems; minority groups in the Middle East, particularly those groups that have close relations with their fellows living under Soviet rule; middle-class intellectuals; and the Orthodox churches.

Pilgrims from the Soviet Union have made, whenever possible, the pilgrimage to Mecca. For the pilgrimages offer not only a unique opportunity to find out what Moslems are thinking but also the chance to inject desired ideas into the stream of Moslem thought. The Communists have also assigned Soviet Moslems to diplomatic posts in the Middle East when that is feasible. Sultanov, whose post was Egypt, but who was used as a sort of roving ambassador, made a point of attending with appropriate ostentation services at the most prominent local mosque wherever he was.

The Russians have made adroit use of minorities generally. Particularly in Iran, Syria and Lebanon they employed for some time large numbers of Armenians as their main agents. Many Armenians are emotionally attached to Soviet Armenia and the Russians have had considerable success with a campaign designed to attract Armenians from the Middle East generally to settle in Soviet Armenia. The Soviet Union has had to modify to a great extent its use of Armenians because this device was too obvious. However, a number of the leading Communists in Lebanon, Syria and Iran, and possibly in Egypt as well, are still Armenians. The party in Lebanon, for instance, had a central committee of the Armenian section headed by Ohannes Aghbashian, who has visited Soviet Armenia on several occasions.

The Communists also make a strong appeal to Kurds whose nationalist aspirations they encourage; the Kurds have, as do the Armenians, an ingrained hatred and fear of the Turks upon which the Russians can play to good effect. The head of the Syrian Communist party, Khalid Bakdash, one of the most able and popular Communists in the Middle East, is Kurdish. Bakdash polled nearly enough votes to get into Parliament during the Syrian election in 1947. This represents quite an achievement, even if he did accomplish it largely by trading votes with candidates of other parties. This is a very useful device for Communists, who can guarantee to deliver to anyone those few votes that they do have. Bakdash had, perhaps, two thousand voters in his pocket. He could count on them to split their votes without making an error. Therefore he could go to some candidate who badly needed two thousand additional votes, but who could in turn deliver a fair number of votes which he himself could rely on. Sufficient deals of this sort account for the eleven thousand votes which Bakdash gained. Bakdash has studied in Moscow and is one of the top Russian agents for the whole area. He is careful not to call attention to the fact of his Kurdish origin but identifies himself, instead, with Arab nationalism, so far as possible.

Although Communism has made some inroads in the ranks of the slowly growing labor movements in Arab countries (notably in Lebanon and Palestine) the most active workers for the cause, even in the labor movements, do not come from the proletarian or peasant class. The most active and effective Communists are mainly from the middle class or even higher. A leading Egyptian Communist, for instance, is Henry Curiel, who comes from a well-to-do Jewish family. In Palestine there is Emil Touma, whose father, a Christian, was a banker in Haifa. Touma was educated at Oxford and is a very smooth article indeed. In Lebanon the local chapter of the Friends of the Soviet Union was able to attract a number of intellectuals into the Communist net. Prominent among them is Emily Faris, the French-educated daughter of a celebrated artist, who is herself a well-known intellectual. The head of the Communist party in Tripoli is a doctor, a member of a very influential Tripoli family, who is wealthy in his own right. Another is a well-known architect. One of the key organizers of the party in Lebanon, Raif Khoury, was for a time professor of Arabic literature at the American University of Beirut. Qadri Qalaji, now one of the top Communist propagandists, started off his career as a student at the American University, where he was the leader of a fairly sizable Communist movement among the students. Among the Palestinian leaders is Dr. Khalil

Budairy, who studied medicine in England and Geneva and who is a nephew of the grand mufti.

I have already mentioned the role of czarist Russia as protector of Christians of Orthodox faith throughout the Turkish Empire. There is thus a background of friendliness for Russia, which the Soviet Union has not been slow to exploit. A number of Lebanese Communists, including the party's president, Nicola Shawi, were brought up in the Greek Orthodox faith. This is also the case in Syria, where Greek Orthodox are the dominant Christian group. During the last war, apparently as a gesture of good will toward the Allies, Stalin reinstated the Orthodox Patriarchate of Moscow and All the Russias. This resulted in a visit to Moscow by Alexandros III, patriarch of the Greek Orthodox whose seat is in Damascus. In 1945 this visit was repaid by Alexei, patriarch of Moscow, who traveled extensively in the Middle East and was seen constantly in the company of the Soviet minister to Lebanon. The Soviet Union has also been pressing for the return to them of Russian Orthodox properties and holdings in Palestine. It is not to be expected that the Orthodox churches are going to make propaganda for Communism. That is not the Soviet intention, nor would it be possible for them to achieve that aim even if they had it. But they will gladly make use of anyone motivated by any kind of religious, historical, or racial feeling for Russia, even though that may not involve approval of Communism. As a matter of fact, as we shall see, a surprisingly large proportion of Communists in the Middle East are not required or expected to advocate Communist principles at all.

In Egypt, which is fairly remote from the Soviet Union, Communism is outlawed and there is no open Communist party. In many respects, however, Egypt seems to offer the most promising field for Communism of any country in the Middle East. For one thing, Egypt is the most industrialized of the Arab countries. There are large numbers of very poorly paid industrial workers. Many are unemployed, although labor unionism has been growing in strength. The unions have, since 1945, carried out a number of successful strikes. Even where the strikes are not successful, they cause trouble, violence, bloodshed and social unrest. It goes without saying that this plays into Communist hands. There is also, surprisingly since all Arab countries claim that they lack technically trained personnel, an appreciable number of university graduates and white-collar personnel who are unemployed. There is growing discontent and radicalism among university students (the Soviet Union has even sought to enroll students from Russia in the religious University of al-Azhar to take advantage of this situation). It is clear that Egypt's major problems—overpopulation, extreme poverty and widespread disease, already discussed in an earlier chapter—make fertile ground for Communist seed, although they also mean that likely converts to Communism may be too weak and feeble to do anything active on its behalf, even if they are converted.

In spite of stringent government measures against Communism, the large Soviet diplomatic mission in Cairo finds plenty to keep it busy. Nothing that the government can do, short of correcting conditions, can prevent Soviet agents from utilizing the inevitable hatred of the many million poor for the few hundred rich. The rabidly anti-British feeling which is prevalent also serves Soviet purposes. Communists do not make the mistake of dwelling on Marx or Lenin, or of crying down religion as the opiate of the people. They are content to agitate against imperialism, and for the removal of foreign troops; they call for the improvement of public-health measures and working conditions; they decry corruption in high places; they are, like Mr. Coolidge's minister, against sin. This kind of talk doesn't involve the Russians in any burdensome obligations. Also, since they keep well under cover, it doesn't make many friends for them. But it does make enemies for their enemies, and that will do for the time being.

A report on Communism in the Near East, prepared by a subcommittee of the House Committee on Foreign Affairs, summed up the situation in Egypt as follows: "Neither repressive measures by the Government, nor repercussions of the U.S.S.R. vote on partition, have seriously hampered the development of the Egyptian Communist party, which is believed to number at present some five thousand active members organized in several hundred cells imbedded in government bureaus, the universities, police, army, even the reactionary Moslem Brethren and the great theological university of the Azhar." The strongest opposition party, the Nationalist Wafd, has also been penetrated to an important extent.

Egypt, with its comparatively large urban proletariat population, is the most promising goal for Communist ideology. Iran and Turkey have been the traditional targets of Russian expansionism. Lebanon and Syria may have the best-organized Communist parties. Yet it is in Iraq that the Soviet threat seems to me the most immediately dangerous. Iraq is rich in oil. From the point of view of grand strategy, occupation of Iran has more immediate prizes to offer, giving direct access to Pakistan and the Arabian Sea and almost completing the encirclement of Afghanistan. But if the Soviet Union could establish a sympathetic puppet government in Iraq, she would threaten the whole Allied position in the Middle East. Further resistance on the part of Iran would be almost impossible. The democracies would be lucky if they could hold, speaking politically and not militarily, along the line of the Suez Canal, the Red Sea and the southernmost area of the Arabian peninsula. Geographically the penetration of Iraq offers a somewhat more difficult problem than the penetration of Iran, since the Soviet Union has no common border with Iraq. However, that need not cause insuperable obstacles and politically Iraq could prove to be a very easy conquest. Any government formed under the present Regent, Abdul Ilah, is likely to be fundamentally pro-British. However, the governing class in Iraq is extremely shaky and almost universally hated in the country. This hatred springs chiefly from the rather obvious way in which the ruling class is dominated by the British. Russian prospects in Iraq are thus double edged. In case the present ruling class is overthrown, their successors are very likely to turn to the Russians for lack of anywhere else to turn; also, as noted earlier, they have been labeled Communists so long that they are beginning to wonder whether they are not, perhaps, in fact Communists. The second prospect for Russia is that the present ruling class become sufficiently desperate to turn to Russian support for lack of any other possibility of saving its own skin. And, whether the problem is to fill it or save it, their skin has always been the chief concern of most Iraqi politicians.

It is true that any Arab League government, with the exception of the Saudi Arabian and Yemen's, might fall at any time because of the Palestine debacle. Of them all, the Iraqi and the Egyptian governments are fundamentally the weakest and Iraq is more susceptible to Soviet pressure. Once at least, already, Iraq has trembled in the balance. In May and June of 1948, when the Security Council was considering the Palestine problem, the Soviet Union sponsored a resolution imposing sanctions against the Arab states. It is easy enough to see why the Soviet Union backed such a resolution. Why it received backing, as well, from the United States is another question. In any case, the resolution was defeated. But, as columnist Stewart Alsop reported from London: "For some days we were on the edge of an abyss." Sanctions would have thrown the whole of the Middle East into turmoil and political, as well as economic, chaos. The effects upon American and British interests would have been literally catastrophic. Nowhere would castastrophe have struck more swiftly and with more obvious advantage to the Soviet Union than in Iraq. Iraq is always on the thin edge of starvation. The stoppage of imports and other assistance from the West would immediately push her over the edge. But the Soviet Union had already made preparations to step in. This step was to be in the form of an immediate gold loan to Iraq from the Soviet Union. It had already been discussed with pro-Soviet Iraqi and was to be made subject to certain conditions which would have assured Soviet control of Iraq. Although these conditions might have been rebelled against later, at the time they would almost surely have been accepted. This incident offers a good example of Soviet techniques. On the one hand, the Soviet Union proposes in the Security Council sanctions against the Arab states. On the other, she makes preparations for an immediate violation of those sanctions to her own advantage. In this particular case we can only be thankful that the support which the United States gave the Soviet Union did not prove sufficiently effective to put the resolution across.

Iraq has large minorities of Kurds and Armenians who, as we have seen, are particularly susceptible to Soviet propaganda. In addition to dissident groups which may accept Soviet gold, there has been a Communist underground. These Communists, though not particularly successful, have been active. Railroad, dock and oil workers, university students, rural schoolteachers, and the lower ranks of the army have been the particular targets of Communist proselytizing. Early in 1947 the Iraq police executed several very successful raids upon Communist groups. They captured most of the Communist leaders, together with the printing presses which had been used for preparation of the illegal Communist sheets. Some of these leaders including Yusuf Salman Yusuf, known as Fahad, the Leopard, were later sentenced to death. The sentences were commuted to terms of imprisonment calculated not to make martyrs of the men but at the same time to prove that the government was determined in its efforts to wipe out Communism. Police confidence that they were succeeding in this aim was somewhat shaken when the illegal Communist publication which the Leopard had edited appeared again for the first time on the day that his condemnation to death was announced. It is clear that the Iraqi Communists have not been completely liquidated and that they maintain effective liaison with the Lebanese and Syrian Communists, as well as with Soviet officials in Teheran and other neighboring capitals. But the main strength of the Soviet Union lies not in any Communist organization or in the popularity of the U.S.S.R.; it lies in the spreading (if still inactive) opposition to the present governing clique and in the explosive possibilities presented by the Palestine situation.

In Iran, too, the Soviet Union must rely more upon internal weaknesses and stresses in Iran than upon Soviet strength there. Here, as elsewhere, the Russians have played upon minority and tribal grievances, have sought to penetrate the army and win over the dissatisfied intellectuals. The Russians have been immensely aided, of course, by the fact that during the latter part of the war Soviet troops occupied northern Iran. Since there was more political freedom in Iran than in Iraq the Russians had their own party—the Tudeh, or "Peoples' Party"—whose following stretched far beyond the Russian zone of occupation. (Isfahan, with its large rug-weaving industry, was a Tudeh stronghold.) Later the Tudeh spearheaded the attempt to set up "independent" (Russian satellite) Azerbaijani and Kurdish states in northern Iran.

Soviet preparations for this scheme were well made. Back in 1936, a number of "refugees" from the Soviet secret police burst into northern Iran begging for asylum. Among them was included Jafar Pishevari, who later emerged as the leader of Tudeh and of the Soviet cause in Iran generally. In spite of the well-founded suspicions of Iranian security officials, these self-styled refugees were admitted. They later formed the nucleus, not only of an intelligence network, but of the whole Tudeh organization. Supported by masses of agents brought in by the Red Army during the latter years of the war, Tudeh succeeded in establishing its rule, temporarily at least, in the Azerbaijani Peoples' Republic (of which Pishevari became president) and, a few months later, in a Kurdish Peoples' Republic. Backed by the Soviet Union, these two self-styled republics demanded their independence from Teheran. The United States, however, led a vigorous campaign in the United Nations which resulted in strong backing for the Iranian government. The Shah and Prime Minister, Qavam, for once united, acted with unexpected firmness and the uprising was put down. The speedy and utter collapse of the movement indicated that although the Soviet puppets may have been able to arouse initial popular enthusiasm for their project, the people were very soon disillusioned. Soviet support in Iran fell away almost entirely with the collapse of the Azerbaijani and Kurdish puppet states. In addition the Russians did themselves much harm throughout the Middle East by abandoning the "leaders" of the short-lived states to the mercy of the Iranian government—which strung them up in short order—instead of carting them off in safety to Russia. Left to their own resources, the Russians would have taken years to gain another following in Iran.

But they have had assistance from the Iranian government in general and the army in particular. Army rule in Azerbaijan was brutal, corrupt and ineffective. The effort of standing up to the Russians seems to have worn out the government, which has lapsed into its old bribe-taking, do-nothing ways. Moreover the Tudeh has proved most difficult to destroy, entirely apart from its Russian backing. It seemed on the surface to fill a need which badly needed filling. In Iran no less than in other Middle Eastern countries, there are no adequate, progressive labor movements. Tudeh does not fill the lack, but neither does any other party. And at least Tudeh has given much impetus to the drive for labor unionization. However, it is certain that under Tudeh domination the unions would do much more harm than good. For Tudeh is motivated more by the political aims of an outside power than by any genuine desire to improve conditions in Iran. This, of course, has made Tudeh infiltration of the Anglo-Iranian Oil Company (AIOC) particularly dangerous. In July 1946, Tudeh inspired a strike in Abadan, which led to much violence and a rather costly Tudeh failure. The British recognized that the strike was politically motivated and therefore the strike was politically fought. The British government sent troops to Basra, just across the border in Iraq, and started organizing a pro-British tribal league in Khuzistan, location of the richest Iranian oil deposits. Faced by unexpectedly firm opposition, Tudeh leaders in Teheran backed down. In spite of this defeat,

Tudeh is not broken. As long as there are grievances the unions will want to strike (AIOC estimates that 95 per cent of its native employees are members of the unions, still Tudeh dominated). And grievances are bound to continue. Even if they wanted to, the oil company could give substantial wage raises only at the expense of disrupting the economy of the country at large. For other wage payers would not be able to keep up with too rapid an increase, prices would be further inflated, and everyone not working for the oil company would starve. This might suit the Russians very well, but it wouldn't help Iran, nor would it help the oil companies.

Lebanon and Syria, being the most democratic of the Arab countries, naturally have what are openly the strongest and best-organized Communist parties. In both countries, until the spring of 1948, the Communist party was recognized by law and thus its organization and recruitment program was made easy. In Lebanon particularly the party made considerable headway among labor organizations and boasts of a goodly number of intellectuals. Communist leaders gained respectability by working with other parties against the French mandate and have been loud in their support of the Arab cause in Palestine. (After the Russian vote for partition, they trooped up into the mountains of Lebanon to assure Haj Amin al Husseini, mufti of Jerusalem, that the Soviet action had not changed their attitude in the least.) In fact Lebanese and Syrian Communists do not talk like Communists at all, but rather like good nationalists with a reforming streak. Their professed aim is the end of foreign imperialist domination; to secure the freedom of *all* Arabs they will fight whomever stands in the way—even in the unlikely event (they say) that it should be the Russians. The Syrians and Lebanese Communists are most unlikely to convert their countries to Communism—they don't even seem to be trying to do so at this time. But they are useful to the Soviet Union in other ways. Their leaders are exceptionally prepossessing, articulate and well trained. They make a good showing for Arab Communists in the international party conferences. Also, they make Communism respectable in the Arab world, and show that good Communists, with the blessing of Moscow, can be vigorous in the defense of Arab Palestine. Finally, and probably most important, the Syrian and Lebanese Communist parties provide a nucleus of well-disciplined and well-trained men, who are also said to be well armed, for service to the Soviet Union in whatever capacity may be required.

In Palestine, the Arab Communist organization conforms to much the same pattern as that established in Syria and Lebanon. Its main stronghold is among the laborers of Haifa and it has an impressive array of intellectuals. On the whole it has supported the mufti and his various organizations without serious reservations. Palestinian Arab Communists will, of course, oppose any effort to give the Arab portion of Palestine to Abdullah of Transjordan because the Soviet Union, together with most Arabs, regards Abdullah as purely a British puppet.

There was at one time an effort, dictated from Moscow, to bring the Arab and Jewish Communist parties together; all they could agree on, so far as the future of Palestine was concerned, was that the British should get out, and this did not prove a sufficiently firm basis for partnership. It is hard to avoid the suspicion that the Palestinian Arab Communist groups are intended more as show pieces than as serious working bodies. If they can direct Arab resentment against Britain and America, and away from the Soviet Union, they will have served their purpose.

Israeli government leaders such as Ben Gurion, Shertok, *et al.* are strongly and sincerely anti-Communist—as are their followers. However, it is still true that the main Russian hope of gaining a foothold in the Middle East by way of Palestine is, for the moment at least, through the Jews rather than the Arabs. This is natural from every point of view. It does not mean that Communism as such makes an appeal to Palestinian Jewry. Even though intellectually it is a European product and could be expected to appeal more easily to people brought up in Vienna, Frankfurt or Warsaw than to those who have lived in Nazareth or Nablus all their lives, Communism as such cannot make much of an appeal to most of Palestine's Jews, because it is inherently the antithesis of Zionism, an intensely nationalistic movement. The House Foreign Affairs Committee report on Communism in the Near East states:

> Most of the Jewish Communists in Palestine were such before they came there. All the others realize that Soviet control or domination would shatter their dream of an independent state. Therefore, in spite of some contrary indications, possibly in an attempt to secure arms and other assistance, the overwhelming majority of the Palestine Jews and members of the Jewish Agency are spiritually and materially committed to the United States.

This kind of commitment has not prevented Palestinian and even American Zionists from threatening that if the United States fails to give complete and unlimited support to Zionism there is a danger that Israel will turn to the Soviet Union. Moreover, there has been for some time a strong group in Irael which has felt that Zionism should look to eastern Europe rather than to the United States and Britain for support of its national aspirations. As among the Arabs, Jewish Communist groups are presently insignificant. They do not, however reflect the full extent of Soviet influence. The Stern Gang, once a Fascist organization, found the extreme right too crowded for comfort (the Irgun was taking the play away from it). It is now a Fascist Leftist organization, armed and financed from the Soviet Union. Even the Irgun Zvai Leumi, largely financed from the United States, has been getting most of its weapons from behind the Iron Curtain, as, indeed, has the Israeli Army. American correspondents report that the basic weapon of Israel's armed forces are new Czechoslovakian rifles which would never have become available to them without Russian approval. Kenneth Bilby, writing from Tel Aviv on August 7, reported on the effect that this had had in a dispatch to the *New York Herald Tribune*. Recognizing the existence of strong sentiment toward America, he wrote:

Sentiment however cannot wash away de facto attachment to Russia. The Soviet has much more powerful support here than the tiny Jewish Communist party, which makes far more noise than its size warrants.

Russian sympathizers in and out of the government comprise a formidable strain of completely unrelated political factions. Most important is the United Labor Party or Mapam, a fusion of left wing labor groups which ran second in the last election.

Mapam has adopted an almost straight Communist line. Its newspaper, for example, was critical of Marshal Tito when the Yugoslav leader was denounced by the Cominform.

It is true that of the refugees who have recently entered Palestine large numbers have fled to escape anti-Semitism in Soviet-dominated central and eastern Europe and they must be bitterly anti-Soviet. Included among the shipments, particularly those coming from behind the Iron Curtain, there must inevitably be an appreciable number of Soviet agents and hand-picked Communists. It is perfectly certain that the Jewish Agency, and later the state of Israel, made every effort to sift the immigrants and eliminate Soviet agents. Nevertheless the whole pattern of illegal immigration to Palestine has offered an ideal opportunity for penetration by Soviet agents, even when shipments came from the West. Until the spring of 1948 the bulk of refugee traffic had been from Soviet occupation zones to British or Americans zones and thence, via France or Italy, to Palestine. In the last year or so many immigrants came direct from behind the Iron Curtain to Palestine. Only a very dull-headed intelligence service would let slip such a perfect occasion for planting its agents, and the odds against spotting them all would be impossibly high. We have seen the use that the Soviet Union made of refugees in Iran in 1936. It is too much to hope that they would let slip an even bigger opportunity in 1945 and since.

An analysis for the reasons behind the Soviet Union's support of partition of Palestine is revealing of Soviet strategy in the Middle East. For many years the Russians have vigorously opposed Zionism, both within their own borders and without. Within, the Communists branded Zionism as a nationalistic movement, support of which necessarily reflected upon the individual's loyalty to the Soviet Union. This is still Soviet policy. There are no Zionists, or at least no professed Zionists, within the borders of the Soviet Union.

As long as Great Britain was backing Zionism, Soviet external policy was consistent with internal policy. In 1930 the Executive Committee of the Comintern declared: "Zionism is the exponent of the exploiting, big power, imperialist oppressive strivings of the Hebrew bourgeoisie which uses the oppressed position of the Hebrew minority in eastern Europe for imperialist policy and for the securing of their domination. To realize this purpose, Zionism was linked by the mandate and the Balfour Declaration with British imperialism, Zionism was converted into a weapon of British imperialism in order to suppress the national liberation movement of the Arab masses at the same time that it converted into its own weapon the Hebrew population of Palestine down to the semi-proletarian and proletarian layers." While the average non-Communist reader may have difficulty in understanding the above quotation we can at least gather that it is distinctly unfriendly in tone.

The British White Paper on Palestine of 1939, which set a limit on further Jewish immigration without Arab approval and also restricted the sale of land to Jews, immediately aroused Zionist hostility against

Great Britain and drew the attention of the Soviet Union to the Zionists as possible allies. Soon Communist parties outside the Soviet Union, notably in Great Britain and in the United States, began to support the establishment of a Jewish national homeland in Palestine. Official Soviet policy, however, did not change until Gromyko revealed Soviet support of partition before the United Nations in May of 1947.

In giving their support to partition the Russians appear to have been motivated by five reasons:

(1) They hoped to win new friends among the Zionists of the Western world as well as in Palestine.

(2) Russia wants to see British influence and, above all, British military power weakened in the Middle East in every possible way. Partition was as good a way as any other to end the mandate and bring about withdrawal of British forces.

(3) Russia wants to damage American influence and prestige wherever possible. The success of the Zionists is attributed by Arabs to American backing—financial as well as political. Arabs used to look on Zionism as British economic imperialism. Now they fear it may be the spearhead of American conquest by dollars. Soviet agents encourage this fear with every argument at their command.

(4) Soviet experts believed, as did British and Americans also, that partition was certain to bring chaos and violence to the Middle East. The correctness of that belief was tragically demonstrated immediately after the partition resolution was approved. Unlike Britain and America the Soviet Union, as suggested above, would benefit from that chaos. The House document on Communism in the Near East already quoted analyzes the Russian position as follows: "It was foreseen that a pro-partition vote would result in an intensification of anti-Russian sentiment throughout the Near East and the inevitable adoption of more stringent defensive measures, yet it was discounted for reasons of weight. A vote against partition, or even abstention, would surely have been followed by a wave of good will similar to that which followed the U.S.S.R.'s support of Egypt in the Security Council in the summer of 1947; it would have undercut Government measures against them and no doubt led to a spurt in local Communist membership. This would also have resulted in a general stabilization of the Near East, inasmuch as Zionist reaction to a negative UN vote would have been comparatively

weak and not serious, for without the moral advantage of a favorable decision they would lack both world-wide and, to an even greater degree, United States support. But stabilization of the Near East would have delayed indefinitely realization of Soviet aims there; i.e., elimination of British forces and influence and depriving western Europe of oil. This was a gain far outweighing Arab good will and the temporary strengthening of local Communist parties." Also, in spite of an inevitable loss of Arab good will, Russia stood an excellent chance of making positive gains as well as inflicting damage on her enemies. For one thing, she could hope to establish a military foothold herself in the area through international enforcement of partition. She could hope also, as the Iraqi incident already mentioned shows, to substitute herself for the democracies in relationships previously enjoyed by them.

(5) Finally, the Russians supported partition in Palestine because they hope to establish the *principle* of partition elsewhere. Their speeches in the UN emphasized that a minority which cannot live comfortably with the majority should be allowed to break away and establish its own state. The implications of this interpretation of the doctrine of self-determination, just for the crucial Persian Gulf–Eastern Mediterranean area, are tremendous. Iran, Iraq, Turkey and Greece could be carved to pieces, with Soviet instruments and surgical assistance, to form Azerbaijani, Kurdish, Armenian and Macedonian states. Then we could write off the so-called fringe lands of the Middle East as we have had to write off eastern Europe.

There is, of course, no reason to assume that the Soviet Union will continue to support Israel. At any time, if it should seem to serve her interests more effectively, she may switch to unequivocal support of the Arab position. Already contradictory indications of future Russian intentions have appeared. On the one hand, it has been reported that the Soviet is renewing its antireligious campaign with particular attention being devoted to Islam. This of course refers to Islam within its own borders, but nonetheless it would be bound to affect Soviet relations with Moslem countries. Taken by itself it would suggest that Russia has abandoned all idea of winning the Arabs and would propose instead to concentrate on minority groups within the Middle East, particularly non-Moslem minorities such as Jews and Armenians and Greek Orthodox. The purpose behind this new Russian move seems to be to make a clear and sharp break between the Moslems of Iran and Afghanistan and the Moslems inhabiting large portions of Russia's underbelly.

On the other hand, when Russia showed opposition to returning Italy's African colonies to her, many observers suspected that this might be the first move in the campaign by the Soviet Union to woo large-scale Arab support. The Russians are known to have offered to build a small-arms amunition factory in Syria immediately after the partition resolution. They have also been supplying arms and money to certain Arab groups such as the rabidly anti-Western Moslem Brotherhood.

In any case the Russians are sitting pretty on Palestine. They are uninhibited by concern for principle or even by "bourgeois" ideas of consistency. The United States cannot say, officially or unofficially, one thing at Lake Success and another in Damascus. Zionist charges that American officials have done just that are based on the fact that many State Department men have been, inevitably and obviously, more concerned over and sympathetic to the Arab states than have other Americans with no knowledge of the area. But aside from generalized expressions of good will, and exhortations to trust America, there was little they could do even if they had wanted to. They could not, like the Russians, make specific promises of gold and arms to be used against the cause which the United States was publicly backing. The Russians can do this with either side. Thus the official backing that the Soviet Union has given Zionism, and the substantial assistance which they have provided Israel through the clandestine arms shipments and so forth, have done them less harm than might be expected in the Arab world. This has enabled the Soviet Union to go even further in its support of Israel than the United States. The result, as we have already seen, is that there has been much criticism in Israel of the United States for pusillanimity. This puts Soviet representatives in the position of being able to say, happily, to both sides: See, the United States is betraying you!

It has not hurt the feelings of the Soviet Union that Arab propagandists have been arguing for some time that American support of Israel will force the Arabs into Soviet arms. The Arabs kept plugging away at that theme in spite of a disappointing lack of response from the United States. But the Communists were by no means displeased. They figured that if the Arabs went on saying it long enough, they might believe it. Now the Communists have further cause for content. For Zionists are using the same argument—that unless we give full support to Israel in the form of loans, arms and political backing, Israel will turn pro-Russian. Depending on the course of events, either the Arabs or the Zionists may prove right. What the Russians are hoping, of course, is that they will both prove right.

✣ XXII ✣

Britain and the United States: The Push-me-Pull-you Team

IN A broad sense, the objectives of the United States and Great Britain in the Middle East are identical. Both countries want to preserve free access to and passage through the area which, as the hub of three continents, is one important key to world communications and transport. Both countries want to preserve the right of free access to and development of the economic wealth of the area, in which they have secured for themselves an extremely fortunate role. And both countries want to see peace and stability assured to the area. They recognize that if an aggressive power should become dominant there, whether by conquest in time of war or by infiltration and revolution in what is technically a time of peace, the security of a far wider zone would be threatened. They know, as do the Russians too, that violence and chaos in the Middle East may spread, and endanger the peace of the whole world. The Americans and the British have in common the *desire* to follow a policy which could assure the political, social and economic advancement of the Middle Eastern peoples. The Anglo-American interest is the same; it is in the means of advancing it that differences develop, and that Washington and London find themselves, angrily, at cross-purposes.

The Soviet objective, of promoting violence and chaos, is obviously an easier one than the Anglo-American goal. It is easier to slice the "Mona Lisa" to pieces with an old razor than it is to paint a good picture. It requires less skill to crush a cyclotron with a sledgehammer than it does to make one. Human nature being what it is, you can spread dissension and hatred with less effort and imagination than is required to promote understanding and mutual respect among peoples.

On the other hand, the painter is a better man, and may even go further in the world, than the vandals who destroy his pictures. A civilization that concentrates more upon constructing scientific instruments is likely to progress further than one that specializes in destroying them. And Dale Carnegie, the person and the institution, stands forth as proof that it pays to win friends and influence people. It may be harder work, but you get better wages for it.

Of course, you have to do the work well. How well have the Anglo-Americans done in the Middle East, and what are the prospects of their doing as well or better in the near future? It is worth taking a look at the record.

The British record is a lot longer than ours. It differs in other respects too. Being longer, it has room for more black marks on it. These include, inevitably in the times and circumstances, some shoddy cynical intrigues and promises, of which the Sykes-Picot agreement is but one example. Some British officials in the region have been good, others evil; they have used their position to support, on occasions, the most worthy elements and, on many other occasions, the most corrupt and self-seeking groups within the different countries. Any American with experience in the Middle East knows of times when British representatives on the spot were, in defiance of London's instructions, doing all in their power to knife their American opposite numbers and make Anglo-American collaboration in the area a strictly one-way proposition. It is, unfortunately, equally true that there have been Americans on the scene whose every act was inspired by a desire to "do the British in." There is no future in endless recriminations over the past. The pressing need for collaboration now should bring an end to that. The past should be read with the present need in mind.

The British story in the Middle East begins, of course, with private adventures and commercial activities. From the earliest days of European penetration of the Middle East, it appears to have exerted a peculiar fascination for Britons. Soldiers of fortune fought with Arab and Persian armies, and, as private individuals, organized and trained many a local force. There was a Scottish convert to Islam named Thomas Keith—his Moslem name was Ibrahim Agha—at Mohammed Ali's court, who saved the life of Mohammed Ali's son Tusun when the Egyptian Army was defeated by the Wahhabis in Arabia in 1811. (Other British converts have included the novelist Marmaduke Pickthall and ibn Saud's trusted adviser St. John Philby.) A year later, when a Russian Army defeated the Persians the Persian infantry was commanded by a Briton, who was killed in the battle. The famous adventurer Bethune organized and commanded the forces of Mohammed Shah; later, when the shah had fallen under Russian influence, Persian resistance to him was organized by another Englishman, Lieutenant Pottinger, who made his way to Herat for the purpose in disguise. Although many experts deny that any Westerner has ever spoken Arabic so perfectly that he could pass among Arabs as an Arab, the claim is made on behalf of a number of Englishmen, including Lawrence of Arabia. (Arabs who have known both say that Glubb Pasha's Arabic is better than Lawrence's ever was.)

Whether they have succeeded in passing as Arabs or not, they have surely succeeded in passing themselves off among Arabs as Indians, Kurds, Turks, Persians or other Middle Eastern people. Richard Burton, translator of the *Arabian Nights*, made the forbidden pilgrimage to Mecca disguised as an Indian Moslem. Countless others, including Pickthall and Aubrey Herbert, are said to have been able to don native dress and vanish without trace into quarters which no foreigner could enter. Herbert, whose tragically early death was a great loss to his country, was one of the models from whom John Buchan drew the character of Sandy Arbuthnot in *Greenmantle* and other wonderful adventure novels.

Herbert was deeply loved and admired by the Turks. During the Gallipoli campaign, when there was a truce to bury the dead, Herbert was assigned to the British detail going into no man's land. When he came within sight of the Turkish lines, he was welcomed with cheers, and the Turks immediately gave him command of their own burial detail. (War is a grimmer business now. There were no such heart-warming incidents that I know of in World War II!) Later, Herbert was offered the crown of Albania, which he gratefully declined for family reasons. King Zog, the eventual choice, then asked (unsuccessfully) for the hand of Herbert's elder daughter in marriage, to insure a continuing Herbert representation in Albania! The affinity between

Britain and the Middle East has often been strengthened by such wholly personal contributions.

It has depended, too, of course, on much more official activities than those discussed above. As early as the first years of the seventeenth century, the British stepped out of the role of simple traders or adventurers to help the Persians fight off the Portuguese. The British were strong in the Persian Gulf even before they had established a position in the eastern Mediterranean. In fact for some time they saw their interests far more clearly in the vicinity of India than Egypt. The British government even turned down a chance to get in on the ground floor of the Suez Canal building, which it dismissed as visionary. Fortunately for the empire, Disraeli snatched the opportunity some years later to purchase a huge block of stock from the bankrupt Khedive of Egypt, but the operating company is still French. As late as the 1920's the British India Office was making much British policy for the Middle East, often quite at variance with British representatives in Cairo. The India Office, for instance, was backing ibn Saud when Cairo and Lawrence were placing all their bets on ibn Saud's enemy Sherif Hussein. British interest in the Middle East has for years been far more complicated, and important, than the simple explanation of "protecting the lifeline of empire" suggests. By empire was meant chiefly India; and India, while still at this writing a member of the commonwealth, is no longer part of the "empire." The independence granted to India, Pakistan and Burma has modified British interest but has not diminished it or changed its fundamental nature. For Britain still has far-flung commercial and strategic concerns. Her security depends upon vigilance to prevent the creation of a vacuum in the Middle East which might be filled by a potentially hostile power. Before the First World War, the power to be feared was czarist Russia and, for a short time, Germany. Between the Wars it was Italy. Now it is Soviet Russia.

In her weakened economic condition, Britain needs peace in the Middle East more than ever. Her oil holdings there are even more vital to the empire and commonwealth than American holdings are to the United States. As her need is greater, her strength is less. The British are face to face with the fact that, bled to a pasty gray if not to paper white by their recent struggle for survival, they are now dangerously weak. Their economic and military resources, as compared to their commitments, are at the lowest ebb reached in modern times. Russia may be weak too, but no one dares count on that. Britain's weaknesses are too well known to give her much chance to bluff.

How, in these dreary circumstances, do the British propose to safeguard their interests? First, by withdrawing wherever possible from commitments that cannot be met. Secondly, by carefully husbanding their resources, by putting them, sparingly, to the best use, and by utilizing to the fullest extent such intangible assets as experience, special skills, and prestige. And thirdly by working together with other nations whose interests coincide with theirs. This means, above all, the United States.

Frank and explicit recognition by a great nation that certain undertakings are beyond her power is indeed rare. The British are known to be a stubborn people. But, in the present crisis at least, they have not carried stubbornness to the point of stupidity. And their admission that they can no longer support the burden in Greece and Palestine does not show a craven resolve to abandon the field. It is a strategic withdrawal, not a concession of defeat.

Elsewhere, the British are hanging on with all they have. The loss of defense bases in Egypt and Palestine is a serious blow, but in spite of all the talk of withdrawal to an imperial defense base in East Africa they have no intention of abandoning the Middle East if they can possibly help it. They are trying to conclude defense agreements with Egypt, Saudi Arabia and other Arab countries, although Iraq's repudiation of a recently concluded treaty represents a serious and significant failure. The British troops taken from Palestine were for the most part redistributed in the area, a small force in Cyprus, another larger one in Cyrenaica, one in Eritrea and the Sudan and the remainder in Kenya. Cyprus is being built up as one important strong point in the Western defense against Russia, and this is being done with American collaboration. (Air base and radar establishments have been constructed, as well as radio monitoring units for the analysis of Soviet propaganda.) In addition there is still the RAF base in Iraq and the British-trained (and partially officered) Arab Legion in Transjordan. The British may or may not end up with a base in Palestine's Negeb. Counting their forces in Greece, the British now have more troops in the eastern Mediterranean area than they did before the outbreak of the recent war. And their position is further strengthened by the existence of American air bases at Mellaha (Libya) and Dhahran (Saudi Arabia).

Even so, some observers believe that, in the event of war with Russia, British-American military strength in the Middle East would be wholly inadequate. They concede only that the forces can play a political role by protecting British-American interests against any action short of total war. On the other hand it is argued that if the war may be won by rapid use of atomic bombs, the Middle East offers the best hope for quick victory. Next to the United Kingdom itself and the supply lines on which it must live, British strategists regard the Middle East as their most vital security zone. (More and more American strategists hold that the same is true for the United States as well.)

Although the British have in no sense been the foremost supporters of the new state of Israel, the conflict in Palestine has done much damage to Britain's position with the Arabs. In the first place, the Arabs can see perfectly well that while the British are not happy at the result, the Zionists would never have become strong enough to have created their own state if the British had not backed them for twenty years while they got started. The British, like the Arabs, gravely underestimated the military strength of the Jews, and took altogether too rosy a view of Arab strength. The Arabs are even less willing than the British to look their own weakness in the face; they prefer to blame their defeats upon American support of Zionism and British "betrayal" of them. The secretary general of the Arab League, Azzam Pasha, said officially that Britain's failure to honor promises and obligations to the Arabs during the fighting "was clear evidence that our treaties with Britain have no value unless they serve British interests alone. After this no sane person could accept a new alliance." So far no Arab country except Transjordan has—but the British position has survived what were apparently even worse setbacks than this. Already a number of prominent Egyptians have urged negotiation of a new alliance with Britain. The governments which have rejected British offers of alliance may not long survive themselves, and may well come to the conclusion that their only hope for survival is support from the West. But for the time being, British political strength is at a low ebb.

Financially, the British are also in poor plight. During the war they paid for many of the goods and services which they had to have by pounds sterling which were "blocked" or frozen in London. Egypt and Iraq, for examples, have sizable sterling balances which they would now like to use to replace worn-out agricultural or industrial machinery. Since they can't buy what they want with sterling, they would like to be able to convert the pounds they hold into dollars. The British, who are desperately short of dollars themselves, find it difficult to do just this. However the British have recently concluded an agreement with Egypt which goes some distance to satisfy Egyptian demands. It suggests that the British, in spite of some distinctly acrimonious exchanges, have not entirely given up hope of Egypt; they would surely not make such an expensive gesture in a lost cause.

Next to Palestine, Egypt has been giving Britain more trouble than any other Arab country. At the root of it is the thoroughly understandable Egyptian resentment at the fact that, although they have been theoretically free since the early twenties, they have in effect been pretty much of a British protectorate until the last three or four years. The British Ambassador, Lord Killearn, behaved like a small-time viceroy, making or breaking prime ministers with superb, if unbearable, arrogance. Now he has been replaced and British troops have withdrawn to the Canal Zone. But their continued presence there continues to cause headaches. An even more serious threat of trouble is the embittered question of the Anglo-Egyptian Sudan, in which Egyptian influence is now limited to a half-share in the name. Both matters were referred to the UN by the Egyptian government with, so far as it was concerned, unsatisfactory results. Palestine developments further inflamed opinion against Britain.

The fact is—and it cannot be emphasized too strongly—that there is now no stability, not even British stability, in Egypt. This is true to some extent of other Arab countries, whose weak foundations have been badly shaken by the Palestine imbroglio. But it is particularly true of Iraq and Egypt. Those two countries are trembling on the verge of political and economic chaos—of a power vacuity which is what Britain, with occasional assistance and occasional hindrance from the United States, has been trying to prevent and which the Soviet Union has been trying to bring about.

Egypt's King, the flashy Farouk, has enough sense to perceive his danger, but not enough imagination or courage (so far) to take the only possible saving action—to forestall a revolution by conducting one himself. I remember late one night watching one of the king's close relations by marriage swaying back and forth while the Scotch splashed in his glass to emphasize his words. "They hate us," he said thickly but earnestly. "They look on us as a bunch of rich no-good Albanians.* It won't be long now. Madame Nahas is already issuing invitations to visit her at Abdin Palace." (Madame Nahas is the young-ish ambitious wife of the ancient ambitious opposition leader.) As this none-too-inspiring representative of Egyptian royalty continued with his gloomy forecast, the bejeweled ladies around him tittered nervously and tried to pass it off as a joke. All except one, a handsome bold-faced woman in high spirits, who would never mind desperate times if they gave her enough of her kind of excitement. She snatched off a diamond brooch and flung it to the floor. "That's right!" she exclaimed. "If you don't give them something, they'll take it all away."

The distracted royalty put a heavy approving arm around her shoulder. "You've got it," he observed, pulling her closer, "and you've got to give it to keep it." The glance he gave her was not purely political.

I'm not sure that I interpreted this last remark the way it was intended. But I got the total effect all right—the scotch, the diamonds, the paté and roast pigeons, the scattering of English (with even a few Americans) among the carefully selected guests, the conscious (and rather enjoyed) atmosphere of "drink deep and throw the cup away . . ."

There have been, of course, strikes and violence in the working quarters. Censorship grows even tighter. Any kind of opposition to the government, on any grounds, is subject to severe punishment—the enforcement of which is increasingly desperate and inefficient. The giveaway is 'strikes among government employees, above all among the police. Foreign war and victory, the traditional escape, seemed to Farouk and his ministers the way out. Instead of victory there was defeat.

This is the country in which Britain is trying to maintain a position, a position traditionally based upon control, direct or indirect, of the ruling class. It is like courting a ghost or drinking with an invisible rabbit. You could almost say—at this writing—that there *is* no ruling

---

* The Egyptian royal house is descended from an Albanian adventurer in Turkish pay.

class in Egypt, for it is so shaky that it hardly dares to rule. You could not say, you could only guess, who the ruling class will be. But you can hazard this prediction: that the British, who have shown some pretty fancy footwork in the past, are going to have to come out fast and on their toes if they are going to win this round. Bevin has pointed the way with his famous statement that British policy would have to concern itself with people, not pashas, in the Middle East now. Along the same line, some American officials have talked of a Marshall plan for the Middle East. The situation in Egypt points up the need, the opportunity, and the difficulties in such a program.

The need is obvious. Unless Egypt, as one example, is given assistance, wisely and firmly, in straightening out her glaring inequalities and settling herself on a sound economic basis, the Russians win and we lose. The opportunity exists; the Anglo-American team, if it can work as a team, has the ability and the resources, and should have the incentive, to do the job. The difficulties are that more effort is required to deal with common people (even though God loves them) than with pashas, and that the rewards which justify effort are not as obvious or as quickly won as in the age of the pasha, when the diamonds knocked your eyes out and the scotch finished the job.

In Iraq the picture, different in detail, is substantially the same. British control over the economy and small ruling class of the country has been in recent years tighter than was possible in Egypt. But there too the British position is insecurely founded. As pointed out earlier, Iraq's economy and government are equally shaky. Regent Abdul Ilah is probably sincere in his friendship for Britain, and the distrustful hatred which he and his friends feel for Russia is undoubtedly genuine. But the regent is far from being a strong character. He has shown his quick reaction to popular pressure by the promptness with which he repudiated the defense treaty with Britain negotiated in January of 1948.

There have been increasing signs of a rift between Abdul Ilah and his uncle Abdullah of Transjordan. Since Abdullah has been getting strong British backing this could have indicated that Abdul Ilah is no longer following the instructions of the British advisers. It is just possible that the British-educated regent will turn to Moscow, as a last resort. Stranger things have happened—but not many. It is more than possible, however, that a number of those around him will throw in the British as a losing hand and try their luck with Soviet cards. If the regent is to stay in power, he must do one of two things: broaden the base of his government and win popular backing by effective public-health, education and agricultural-development programs; or develop a more efficient police state. Either step would require technical and financial assistance from outside. This much is clear: power has remained too long in the hands of a few dozen men who have done little to cope with the increasingly urgent economic and social problems of the country.

Perhaps Abdul Ilah has decided to be neither British nor Russian, but Arab. Certainly that is what the Iraqi people want. But it is rather late in the day for Abdul Ilah to change his spots, and Iraq has by no means proved her ability to be Arab all by herself, and be healthy in the process. This is another case where the Anglo-American doctor should step in and heal the patient, for diseased Arabs are just as contagious as anyone else.

In Transjordan the British position is for the time being far stronger. A backward country, with a population still largely nomadic, it can be ruled more easily by a few men who know the tribes and their problems. But opposition to King Abdullah is growing, and action against his government is being directed by a group of political exiles in Syria who already have considerable backing. They may get even more as the split between Transjordan and other Arab countries on Palestine grows wider. Moreover while Abdullah is a charming old gentleman, his age is not the only thing that makes him a weak reed on which to lean. At the moment it is easier and more effective to deal with the small time Transjordanian "pashas." Soon, there too, the people will intrude more and more upon the scene.

In Syria and Lebanon the British are perhaps more genuinely popular than in other Arab countries. The role that they, together with the United States, played in assisting the Syrians and Lebanese to obtain their independence from the French has gained them much gratitude. Their experience in Arab affairs and in the kind of problems the new governments must face also stands the British in good stead.

In Iran the identity of British and American interests, and the ability to work together in their defense, has been most obvious. Perhaps working together has been easier because Iran is a Moslem, but not an Arab, country; therefore the handicap of American Palestine policy has not been so heavy. Perhaps it is simply because the threat from Russia has been more direct. In any case the short-term results, considering local conditions, have been quite satisfactory.

At the moment the most valuable contribution the British have to make to Anglo-American joint effort is probably the fruit of their long and varied experience in the Arab world. We have Middle Eastern experts of our own—many of them the sons of missionaries born in Syria, Iraq or Iran—who are in their fields every bit as good as any of the British. Thus we would be able to evaluate the British contribution without having to accept it on blind faith. British experts can make as many mistakes, and disagree as much among themselves, as any other experts. But knowledge in Western minds of the Middle East conditions, problems and view points is altogether too rare to be lightly thrown away.

In discussion of Soviet objectives in the Middle East many of the possible threats to American security have been brought out. Recapitulation of British interests in the region has indicated much of the basic American interests as well. There is no need to repeat them. But a review of the American record reveals some special assets, as well as a few special disadvantages, which affect our advancement of our national concerns.

Unlike Britain and Russia, the United States is, officially, a newcomer to the Middle East. Until this last war the American government and the public as a whole took little note of that far-off region. It was strange, romantic, perhaps a good place for strong-stomached tourists to visit, but there did not seem any way in which it could become important to us as a people. But *some* Americans, even then, were helping to make the modern history of these ancient lands.

The first significant appearance of Americans in Middle East affairs was when American missionaries, who had appeared in Syria in 1820, moved their mission printing press a few years later from Malta to Beirut. This was one of the very first printing presses in the Arab world, and played a most important part in the Arab cultural and national awakening that soon began. This awakening will either be given fresh impetus or be practically stifled by the crisis over Palestine.

From this beginning developed that close association between American educators and the Arab renaissance which has so brilliantly been carried on by American schools and colleges in the region—particularly the universities at Beirut and Cairo, and Robert College in Istanbul. The American University at Beirut (AUB), for instance, has an influence extending far beyond the boundaries of small Lebanon. Of its 1,400 students, a tenth are there on scholarships provided by the Arab states, so that they may receive training for leadership in their own lands. There is no other foreign institution in Lebanon or near by comparable to it. Throughout the Middle East the percentage of national leaders in government, education, medicine or other professional fields, who have received their training at AUB or other American schools, is so high as to suggest the existence of a union—or at least an old school tie.

The good will these schools normally create for the United States is intangible, but of very real value. They represent American undertakings which, though private, serve the interests of the nation as a whole. In the long run the institutions thus developed and backed by American citizens could prove more effective bulwarks of national security than the imperialisms of Russia and Britain. Richard Crossman, Labor MP who was one of the umpteen official "investigators" to visit Palestine during the British mandate, wrote of the universities of Cairo and Beirut: "These two centers of learning, because they were completely disinterested, have done more to promote American interests in the Middle East than all the British diplomats and armies put together [have done for the British]."

During this phase, when American interests in the Middle East were largely private interests privately advanced, there were other relationships of long-range significance being established. An account of the activities of American oil companies has already been given. Other commercial and philanthropic activities of American citizens were such as to help win for the United States a unique regard and respect from the different peoples and religions—including, of course, the Jewish immigrants to Palestine. Americans of Jewish faith have given generous financial and moral support to Zionism for over a generation. Up to the last few years that support, it should be noted, was similar to other American activities in the Middle East in this vital respect: that it was offered for humanitarian rather than political ends, it was unofficial, its purpose was not the advancement of United States national interests. The disinterestedness of the American government was generally recognized, and only the highest motives were attributed to it.

In the course of World War II the position of the United States in the Middle East changed in two respects. First, America's economic and strategic stake there assumed obvious and increasing importance. A national Middle East policy became for the first time a recognizable necessity. Second, American support of Zionism grew more and more official in character, committing not merely groups of Americans citizens but the government as well. At the same time, the cause supported had come to be a political rather than a purely humanitarian one. These latter developments came to a climax in the aggressive support given by the United States government and private citizens at the United Nations General Assembly to the proposed partition of Palestine and the creation of a Jewish political state.

The simultaneous recognition of a national stake in the Middle East and support of political Zionism inevitably raise one question—a question which has proved exceptionally difficult to discuss without the generation of undue (almost unbearable) heat. That question must be asked about any government policy. Namely, to what extent does American official support of political Zionism support or endanger our own national interests?

I should like to make several observations about that question.

First, that American national interests are of several kinds. There are material and strategic considerations—matters of military support, oil, bases, essential scarce commodities and the like—which affect our own security. There are broader political and economic considerations, related to our conviction that a peaceful and prosperous world is essential to our own peace and prosperity. And there are ethical considerations, arising from the religious or at least moral conviction that human life can reach its noblest expression only in the creation of a world where law and justice shall prevail. All of these kinds of interests are to be considered in judging national policy, whether on Palestine or a minimum-wage law.

The second point is, we cannot expect to develop a policy on the Palestine issue, or any other, without free debate and public consideration. Any group which insists that there *is* no issue, and brands as anti-Semite anyone who says there is, does itself, its cause and its country a profound disservice. Such tactics are bound to backfire.

For a variety of reasons discussion in America of the Palestine issue has been heavily one sided. That is not because there is only one side. No matter which side he ultimately decides to support, any fair-minded student of the problem will admit that there is justice in the Zionist *and* in the Arab case. But the Arabs have lacked the ability and the resources to argue their own case effectively in this country. A handful of Americans not bound to silence because of official or business position, were yet interested and informed enough to present that side. But their voices were drowned out in the clamor of sincere, well-intentioned but over-aggressive support of Zionism. The big newspapers did not often consider anti-Zionist views or expressions of opinion newsworthy.

It is an incontrovertible fact that the overwhelming majority of Americans with diplomatic, educational, missionary or business experience in the Middle East were convinced that support of political Zionism was contrary to our national interests and to all that the United States has stood for. Opponents may argue that they are wrong, but not that they should not be heard.

One result of the lack of full debate has been that our Palestine policy was considered in many quarters entirely without reference to its surroundings, the Middle East. To most Americans it was a purely humanitarian issue, a way in which we could help the suffering Jews. To others, it must be admitted to our shame, it was a political football, a vote catcher in our domestic elections. To a few, some of them loyal public servants charged with responsibility for our policy, it appeared in its other aspects.

This created a tug of war in our own government. The White House, a good part of Congress, and most of our leading politicos, looked at Palestine without seeing the Middle East. State and Defense officials, on the other hand, could not help seeing the Middle East every time they looked at Palestine. (Every now and then they made someone else see it too, and then—for a period—our policy would be changed.)

It could be said that they (and the British) had nightmares about two vacuums. One was the possible political vacuum in the Middle East which the Russians hoped to fill. The other was the actual vacuum in which our Palestine policy was made. The second seemed terribly likely to create the first. Then both vacuums would be filled; that in the Middle East by Russia, our own by the concrete unpleasantness of the new and enormous Russian threat.

It may seem that I have dwelt on Palestine at disproportionate length. The fact is that now and for some time to come Palestine must be the point on which the Middle East centers. Just as analysis of Russian support of partition offers the handiest and most revealing guide to Soviet intentions in the area, so examination of our own Palestine policy and the effects it has had throws light upon the strengths and weaknesses of our position there.

Because of Palestine, we have no coherent national policy for the Middle East. The need for one has been recognized by State Department officials, who have even sought to give expression, in public statements and official messages, to such a policy. That is the best that can be done, but it is meaningless; for the only policy we have been expressing in action has been a Palestine policy which has made any policy we might have for other parts of the Middle East an academic irrelevancy.

Worse than that, it has gravely weakened all our friends in the area: the progressive, Western-minded Arabs who were the best hope of their countries and the best allies of ours; the moderate Zionists, the Ihud of Dr. Magnes, and the other Jews of Palestine whose counsel was for peace and joint development of the country; and the British, whose record is by no means spotless (is ours?) but whose fundamental interests are the same as ours.

There is little point in slinging rocks at a glass house already some distance behind us down the road. We had better use the rocks to shore up our own, still indecently exposed, dwelling. Apart from the broader issues there are a few practical items which need attention.

First, the large-scale displaced-persons problem arising out of the fighting in Palestine. This has a familiar ring to it. We have heard of displaced persons—though not quite so many of them—in connection with Palestine before. Then we bestirred ourselves. Speeches were made; resolutions passed; money was raised and sent; medicine, food, housing and other assistance was given to help DP's settle in new homes. Americans, whose generous response to appeals from the suffering is known over the world, have never distinguished on racial or religious grounds among refugees from disaster. Inevitably we have been wearied by the many demands on our sympathy over the last ten years. Arabs can appeal on grounds of kinship to only a few among us. But their need is acute. For every kind of reason, we must not fail them.

Second, there is the much-debated matter of oil. The extent and world significance of Middle East oil reserves have already been described. In particular, their relations to the economic recovery of western Europe and the conservation of the rapidly dwindling reserves of our own hemisphere should be recalled here. Now the accusation has frequently been made that oil interests have exercised an undesirable influence upon United States policy on the Middle East. On the face of it, that is a ridiculous charge. Whatever influence the oil companies might have sought to exercise—if any—it was, as the events prove, entirely outweighed by the influence behind support of Zionism. If criticism is due, it is because these latter influences paid altogether too little attention to oil and other strategic considerations. The state of our relations with Russia alone should point to the danger of disregarding any factor contributing to our national security.

As it was, Secretary of Defense Forrestal was bitterly criticized because, it was reported, he had drawn the attention of the president to possible threats to American oil concessions. In the opinion of one innocent observer, Mr. Forrestal was doing his plain duty. If he, as the cabinet member chiefly responsible for national security, had entirely ignored the oil, then indeed he would have been properly subject to attack.

That is not to argue that consideration of oil should have been decisive in determining American policy. By no means. It is one among many elements. Overemphasis upon it would be as dangerous as overemphasis on any other of the elements. There is no more excuse for seeing nothing but oil in the Palestine problem than there is for seeing nothing but electoral votes in it; I would not like to guess which crime was the more common in this country.

Aside from the matter of oil, how does the changed military situation in the Middle East affect our interests? While most people underestimated the depth of Arab feeling on Palestine, a few (myself included, though I was cautious in print) overestimated their fighting strength. It remains to be seen what their recuperative powers may be, but the present fact is clear—that the Arabs have suffered a resounding military and political defeat. Should all of us then jump upon the Israeli band-wagon without further thought? In favor of that course some very mate-rialist reasons are advanced. It is suggested, for example, that willy-nilly the Arabs will have to give us their oil, and that the only force worth wooing, militarily speaking, is Israel.

These are debatable questions. Saudi Arabia will not quickly turn to Russia, and the United States might possibly ignore Arab feelings on Palestine entirely without losing its most important oil holdings. It has been demonstrated that for the time being there is no Arab Army which can stand up to that of Israel. But leaving aside possible doubts as to future developments, there is one doubt which occurs immediately. Is our objective in the Middle East to form an alliance with one Middle Eastern country against other Middle Eastern countries? Purely from a security viewpoint, is it worth while to antagonize the many for the few? Even though, in this case, the few seem able to defeat the many, they cannot possibly police them. Clifton Daniel's analysis for *The New York Times* (November 28, 1948) of British views is relevant here. Commenting on the relative weakness of Arab armies, Daniel reported:

> It was always British policy to limit the Arab forces under their influence to a size that would not overburden the slender budgets of the impoverished states or encourage Arab chieftains to make trouble by warring on one another.
>
> What the British wanted in each Arab state was an army capable of maintaining internal order, resisting minor incursions from neighboring territories and providing British forces with a secure base. The British forces themselves would protect the Arab states from danger of invasion by other great powers.
>
> What Britain wanted from the Arabs, in other words, was not fighting men so much as friendly territory—space for army and air bases and a big buffer between the Soviet Union and the British sea and air routes to the East, and British and American oil fields in Arab territory.
>
> Israel has but small counter-attraction to offer in space and resources.

Debate over the strength of Israeli as opposed to Arab armies leads one astray from what is, for Americans, the essential point. It ignores the nature of our real objective, which is the stability and peaceful develop-ment of the Middle East. We are not looking for one ally in a shooting war. We are asking all the peoples to ally with us in a common, preferably peaceful, effort to make a better world. Our policy must be to assist (and insist that) all countries of the region defeat chaos and war by making healthy world citizens of themselves.

The precise details of that policy will have to be filled in, one by one, as the situation develops. They would include a little Marshall Plan—made up of a number of projects such as the Hoover proposal for development of the Tigris-Euphrates basin—to advance loans for agricultural and economic exploitation of existing resources. They would include also American support for the prompt imposition of sanctions against any country violating the borders of another, and a categorical demand that disputes in the area be settled peaceably, through the proper international machinery. We have the strength—political, economic and, still, the moral strength—to make such a program work.

The idea that American technical skills be employed for the development of backward regions has now been officially proposed by President Truman in Point Four of his inaugural address. Point Four could hardly be described as a specific program. It was tossed off as a suggestion well meant but not well studied; and the danger is that it may arouse hopes which cannot, for a long time, be satisfied. But immediately after the speech, State Department and other official planners got to work, and there is every indication that the President's words will be, in the best Washington language, "implemented."

Nor is the way uncharted. American technical advisers have been provided, officially or otherwise, to the governments of many underdeveloped lands, including Iran, Egypt and Afghanistan. Many more have been requested. Lebanon, for instance, asked for expert assistance in harbor development, and in taking a thorough and accurate census. In the past, such requests have received spasmodic support from one part or another of our government. A co-ordinated program of governmental encouragement should be effective, particularly if allied with the investment of private American funds in productive ventures abroad. A number of American companies such as United Fruit and Aramco have already acquired rich experience in this field.

A program of this sort for the Middle East will be fulfilling an old dream of the late President Franklin D. Roosevelt. When he was flying home from Yalta a few weeks before his death, he asked his pilot to go down for a close look at the deserts of Asia Minor and North Africa. An army engineer told him that the water table was only fifty feet or so beneath the sand. "We ought to be able to do something about that," was FDR's comment. The shah of Iran told me that at Teheran the president had said to him that after his term of office had expired, there was nothing he would like better than to go to Iran and direct a large scale reforestation program. And Frances Perkins reports him as saying, "When I get through being President of the United States and this damn war is over, I think Eleanor and I will go to the Near East and see if we can manage to put over an operation like the Tennessee Valley system that will really make something of that country. I would love to do it."

And for a statement of our basic aim, I would not try to improve upon the words that Franklin Roosevelt said to the representatives of the first United Nations Conference (on Food and Agriculture in 1943).

"Our ultimate objective can be simply stated: It is to build for ourselves, for all men, a world in which each individual human being shall have the opportunity to live out his life in peace; to work productively, earning at least enough for his actual needs and those of his family; to associate with the friends of his choice; to think and worship freely; and to die secure in the knowledge that his children, and their children, shall have the same opportunity."

∴ XXIII ∴

A Footnote for Americans

THE Middle East is part of what appears to be a newly developing bloc of countries stretching from the Atlantic coast of Africa to Singapore.

This is still a tentative sort of grand alliance, based upon certain things these peoples think they have in common. For instance:

Tinted skin. They are not color-conscious except as they have been made so by the realization that the "white" races regard them as different—and inferior. This gives them something in common, against the white races.

Religions. Many of them of course are Moslems, but most of those who are not have at least this in common with the Moslems: they are not Christians. Christians regard them as different—and inferior. This gives them another grievance to agree upon, against the Christians who are the white races.

Foreign exploitation. All of these countries have been to a greater or lesser extent under foreign domination within the near past. Some still are. To the other grievances which unite them, they add: exploitation and/or political domination by white Christians. "Down with foreign imperialism!" is the cry. (The fact that the Russians join in the chorus loudly does not escape notice.)

Sense of technological inadequacy. Combined with the feeling that the West has been rooking them is a realization that if they are to hold their own there is much they have to learn from the West. This is, in their eyes, chiefly technological. Their idea is, give us the machines and the knowledge of their use, and we'll be as good or better than the West. Westerners who are not wholly proud of what the Occident has accomplished with its material skills are still not confident that the simple transmission of those skills to the Orient is going to solve anything much.

Finally the Oriental countries have in common a feeling that youth has not been, and must be, served. They also have a problem: their nationalist movements, now about a generation old, have not yet solved the problem of how to replace or supplement old leaders with new. This may be primarily a Middle Eastern difficulty, but there is certainly a striking dearth of young talent rising to the surface in governmental or political work. There was, indeed, a time of promise when the Young Effendis were coming to prominence. But the intensity of antiforeign feeling threatens to eliminate these men, who had mostly studied in foreign schools and been influenced by foreign ideas.

This tentative formation of a "grand alliance" is, next to the Soviet-Western Democratic split, the most significant political development in the world today. It may be difficult for us to understand, in many cases, why the Orient should feel the way it does. What reason, many would ask, is there for regarding the United States as in any sense imperialist? Perhaps what we need is to see, for an instant, how we and our foreign policy look to others.

The Middle East is a good place from which to examine American foreign policy because it really is *foreign*, because it cannot be treated as if it were simply an extension of domestic politics. In England and western Europe, for instance, we find views and situations which roughly correspond to views and situations existing at home. And when we think of foreign policy we think, most usually, of policy toward England and western Europe in relation to Russia and Eastern Europe. This gives us a false picture of the world and the role we can play in it. It encourages our insular belief that everywhere we turn we can find people who think as we do.

American "democracy," like French or Chinese or Syrian "democracy," is the product of a particular climate, culture and history. Its precise social patterns and forms of government are not readily transplantable. What is good for one society may be wholly impossible for another. That does not mean that there are no social and political standards of general relevance. There are certain basic human values of dignity, decency and individual liberty which, *mutatis mutandis,* prevail

over large parts of the world and which, far more than forms of government, divide the humanistic from the totalitarian states. But those values
may be better preserved, in one society, by a monarchy than by a self-
styled "democracy" or a "dictatorship of the proletariat."

And so we must stop thinking foreign policy in terms of clichés
which spring from our own lives and not from the lives of the people
with whom we must reasonably and realistically deal. In the last para-
graph, I drew the lines between humanistic and totalitarian, not between
democratic and totalitarian. "Humanistic" is an approximation, to be
sure, but it is a far closer approximation than "democratic" to describe
the groups whom we can hope to ally with us in a struggle against
totalitarianism. Outside the British commonwealth and western Europe,
there are few people indeed with whom we can talk understandably
about democracy.

When, anywhere outside that area, someone urges you to support the
"democratic" forces, examine him closely. Either he is very sloppy in
his choice of words, or he doesn't know what he's talking about—or he
is trying to fool you. If he is talking about the Middle East, for instance,
you might ask him this: Is it democratic to value a man according
to his race or religion? That is the basic premise upon which the
newest so-called democracy of the area has been founded.

There are groups in all parts of the earth whom, for moral and practical purposes, we should support. But we can neither choose nor support them wisely if we do so under misapprehensions.

We are likely to misapprehend until we re-examine the standards according to which, theoretically at least, we like to conduct our foreign
policy. Do these measuring sticks we have traditionally employed
actually measure anything relevant to our present problem? Persistence
in talking, or rather, boasting, about them has made our policy look, in
many instances, like the product of a split personality.

We are for democracy. We shout it from the rooftops. Yet in Greece
we give arms to uphold a monarchy not noted for its liberal views, and
the King of Arabia is our good friend and ally.

We are against imperialism, and take a dim view of foreign (especially Russian) troops occupying another land. But that, apparently,
does not apply to American troops in certain Pacific islands. Nor have

we insisted that the Dutch evacuate Indonesia or the British the Suez Canal Zone.

We believe in the self-determination of peoples, yet we made no effort to invoke the principle in Trieste, and we acted directly against it in Palestine.

Some of our departures from our revered formulae have been good, others extremely bad. Even when they have been good they have done some harm, as is always the case when you say one thing and do another. The despair which has led many countries to abandon hope of effective American leadership has been in large part due to this contradiction.

A critical examination of these formulae will bring to light some difficult and embarrassing problems which we have so far refused to face. (I am talking of the public and the public press, not of the professionals in the State Department, who could hardly avoid facing them and who might have done a lot more than they have to bring about public awareness of their existence.) To favor democracy and oppose imperialism cannot, for example, entirely do away with the hard fact that empires have existed and, though abbreviated, still do exist. They provided government and administration of their own, and, usually, built up none to take their place. In many cases they filled a vacuum; in most cases, by withdrawing, they leave one. If the world were stable and content, these vacuums might be left to fill themselves. But Communism does not operate on the principle of *laissez faire*. The Soviet Union would rather fill a vacuum itself—in fact it helps create them for that very purpose—than allow it to fill naturally.

Are we to allow that fact to count more heavily with us than adherence to abstract principles? Or can we evolve some course of action which will satisfy both? Is it not possible to fill the vacuum by United Nations action which would assure stability, peace, and the growth of self-governing native institutions? If we cannot say yes to the last question we are in for some very mortifying times. But if the United Nations is to provide the answer, we must face another set of facts.

For centuries, the world has been dominated by the Western, Christian powers. Not all parts of the world have welcomed this domination, nor can we honestly say that all parts of the world have been given reason to welcome it.

Still most of us, as part of the Christian West, accept its ideals and its values. We could not look with equanimity on their destruction, though we recognize that destroyed they may be. We would prefer to look to a world synthesis combining the riches of all but allowing West *and* East to carry on in their distinctive patterns the best and most lasting features of their own historical development.

That can only be done in peace, by agreement and active toleration. It cannot be done by one dominating the other, for domination is not so easy as it once was. It is a truism, a banality, to say that we must give up the spirit and the trappings of domination.

We recognize that. But are we yet aware of the danger that in the East—Middle and Far East—the United Nations may come to be regarded, and distrusted and hated, as the custodian of Western domination, the new trappings for old imperialism?

The danger of Russia versus the United States in the UN is the seen danger, and a grave one it is. Seen, it must in time, by peace or war, be settled.

The danger of Orient versus Occident seems as yet unseen; it could be ruinous; we may succumb to it from not seeing.